Next  To Ness

by
Siân Jeffreys

NextNessPress in association with
TRAFFORD Publishing

© Copyright 2004 Sian Jeffreys. All rights reserved.

No part of this publication may be reproduced, stored in a retrieval system, or transmitted, in any form or by any means, electronic, mechanical, photocopying, recording, or otherwise, without the written prior permission of the author.

Note for Librarians: a cataloguing record for this book that includes Dewey Classification and US Library of Congress numbers is available from the National Library of Canada. The complete cataloguing record can be obtained from the National Library's online database at:
www.nlc-bnc.ca/amicus/index-e.html
ISBN 1-4120-2681-4

TRAFFORD

This book was published on-demand in cooperation with Trafford Publishing. On-demand publishing is a unique process and service of making a book available for retail sale to the public taking advantage of on-demand manufacturing and Internet marketing. On-demand publishing includes promotions, retail sales, manufacturing, order fulfilment, accounting and collecting royalties on behalf of the author.

Suite 6E, 2333 Government St., Victoria, B.C. V8T 4P4, CANADA
Phone 250-383-6864   Toll-free 1-888-232-4444 (Canada & US)
Fax 250-383-6804   E-mail sales@trafford.com   Web site www.trafford.com
TRAFFORD PUBLISHING IS A DIVISION OF TRAFFORD HOLDINGS LTD
Trafford Catalogue #04-0509   www.trafford.com/robots/04-0509.html

13   12   11   10   9   8   7   6   5   4   3   2   1

Next to Ness

Prologue	5
1) Ness	20
2) 94 Elm Park	34
3) Me	56
4) Sam	74
5) Cali	98
6) Pete	120
7) Jamie	134
8) Marcus	152
9) Josef	162
10) Gavin	186
11) Napoleon	203
12) Sean	225
13) Tinsel	248
14) Ness	272
Epilogue	290

*(For Cali, Sean, Jamie and Pete,
my comrades in adversity)*

Prologue

Back in the late 1980s I developed a really bad habit. Not as bad as stealing from the people I lived with or shooting up illegal substances or even throwing up food after meal which was something of a vogue at the time....no, this was a bad habit of an altogether different nature.

Living where I did at the time, I had become a little consumed, obsessed even, with *how normal people lived*. My friends and I did not live normally, indeed we generally took a perverse pride in living as abnormally as possible but there were occasions – especially when we received yet another eviction letter from Lambeth Council or when the electricity meter needed fudging again and someone had to go down into the haunted cellar to do the dirty with the meter – there were occasions when I did dream of decadence beyond my present estate. Looking back, it seems incredible that grown adults of no mean intelligence and ability should choose to live without hot water, with damp dripping from the walls, with a front door hanging from one hinge, with a kitchen wall so suffering from subsidence that if you hunkered down on your heels you could actually see people walking past the side of the house in the outside world. Dear old house. Rotten old house. Festering, syphilitic, demonic and cursed old house. Is it any wonder I sometimes dreamt of a little bit more?

It began with a vague daydreaming and if it had stayed as such, who knows where I might have ended up? Still there, squatting in Brixton, or dead perhaps or singing in some dreadful band and which was worse? But I didn't stick with daydreaming, I put my dreams into action and everything changed.

I knew quite well what a nice house was. I grew up in what I believe is rather optimistically called Leafy Suburbia. Lots of leaves, yes, lots of leaves and lots of stiflingly boring people with very dull lives. Whatever the boredom levels in London's suburbia, there are very few houses with walls you can peer through and watch the people passing by. Instead, there are houses with neat front lawns and double garages. The houses in Wallington and Reigate and St Albans and Pinner have central heating and bathroom tiles which match the lino, they have fitted kitchens with floors that don't slope into raw mud in the corners. They have switches which make amazing things happen – curtains move and alarms turn on with quiet ferocity, water obediently boils itself in dark discreet immersions and garden sheds hide ugly sharp tools away from the gentle lines of the Amdega conservatories. I know these houses well because I grew up in one. I understood very early on that twentieth century technology had won me the God-given right to be warm and to have carpet beneath my feet and to be entertained from a black box in the corner. We didn't have the TV remote control back then but suburban life was still smug.

In Brixton 1989 however, the everyday living of life was pretty grim. We were young and we were resilient, we were living proof that anarchism worked and more importantly, we were living rent-free. But I still wondered how Thatcher's Golden Boys and Girls lived.

Don't misunderstand me, I despised them, I shouted half-hearted and poorly rhyming slogans at them every Stop The City demo but still I was curious as to the state of their bathrooms and kitchens. This was Thatcher boom time, this was the period just before the Great Crash when property prices took a beating, this was the glorious era of wanton *Me! Me! Me!* And before I reveled in its just and proper thrashing, I just wanted to see how the other half lived.

I started by hanging round estate agents. It's easy, you can pretend you're waiting for a bus, you can even make a political statement by looking the property details up and down with a suitably socialist sneer on your face as if on some research project for Class War Magazine. A scornful shake of the head, a deeply felt sigh as if for the deluded foolishness of these young moths beating themselves to death against the capitalist flame. I'm ashamed to say that I did all this, I acted out my little mime and I doubt very much anyone even noticed or if they did, had the heart to be convinced. All the while I was drinking it in. *Aga with cast iron hood.* I hadn't had the right upbringing to fully visualize such a thing but I got a brief whiff of Country Living and Little House on the Prairie. *En suite shower room, master bedroom with single pane outlook across the river. Fully fitted kitchen in Scandinavian pine, split level dining area with view across the Park.* It was fun at first, it was a diversion from my real life but very soon it wasn't enough. I could dimly sense the interiors of these modern day winter palaces but I saw through a glass darkly and I wanted to touch. So the next step was to go in.

The first time was excruciating, a lesson in self-awareness. I had simply forgotten how far from Normal I had traveled. My friends all looked as I did, we only socialized with others like ourselves, few of us worked and even if we did, we only condescended to accept employment on our terms and did nothing to compromise our appearance. Looking back now, it all seems a little tame. Now we have the grand-daughter of the Queen with a stud through her tongue, we have teeny idols with pierced eyebrows and half of my Year 10 girls have their belly buttons pierced which is something I never dared try. But in 1989, I looked decidedly non-conformist, I looked dirty, I looked rough, I looked poorly educated and obnoxious but most importantly, as far as the twenty-four carat estate agent was concerned, I looked damned broke.

Three and a half minutes and I was back on the street but I wasn't deterred. A week later, I dared the doors of another, this time in Clapham, and had the better sense to take out the nose stud. Long black skirt and big woolly jumper wasn't exactly Harvey Nicholls but I could have passed for a busy mother of three with hubby at the office selling shares all day. The hair had been a problem, dreadlocks couldn't be just combed through, not without vodka to ease the pain, but an ex-girlfriend of Al's (Roedean, horses, trying out hippies to annoy her parents) had left behind a strange sort of floppy velvet hat which covered them all up. I looked strange. I looked thirty-five. I looked as if I really had three children, I could almost visualize the stretch marks. I began to think up names for them; Oliver, Joshua and…and Emily. And that's where it all began really, with Oliver, Josh and Em. I kept them with me even as I moved from agent to agent. Oliver developed a cute little lisp whilst Josh had just developed a fascination for the goldfish bowl with disastrous but terribly amusing results. Em was her daddy's girl, all honey curls and Clara Bow lips. I overdid the gentle criticism just enough to let my maternal pride shine through.

Five sets of details later, I was ready to go in. My first was a five bedroom detached in Hampstead. A little under kept perhaps but that was reflected in the asking price the gushing agent explained. I had my own persona well under control by now, I was Victoria Gillick. I was middle class and frightfully conservative and godly and nowhere near as old as the things I made myself say. I called myself Sarah, Sarah Lees-Jardine after someone I had seen in a copy of Tatler. I wondered if calling my husband Rupert might let the cat out of the bag but to my delight none of the agents were really much interested in my other half. He was clearly just the provider, the Wallet. The decision-maker was me and women like me. I was a mother. And surprised at how much I liked the glow.

House number five was a close shave. Clapham again, this time overlooking the Common. One of those glorious three storey Victorian houses with the original sash windows and stained glass in the doors. But as I came out, promising to ring the agent just as soon as I had talked it over with Rupert, I walked straight into the path of Claire. Claire's surname was a mystery to me which sounds strange as I had been living with her for at least a year at this point but the lives we led didn't really include surnames. People were identified in a variety of ways. Sean was either Gummidge because he came from a little town called Cheddington which as far as we were concerned was in the deepest countryside or he was Big Sean given his physique. Mickey was Mickey Penguin because he ran a tape company from his bedroom called Penguin Music. Giles was Giles with the Taxi. Neil was Jeffreys Road Neil. Simon was Simon Snuff because of his band. Martin was Protag because in the dark old days of his more naïve anarchism he had changed his name to Protagonist. Stephen was Nogbad because he much admired the bad guy in the Noggin the Nog children's cartoon. I knew a Mave, a Tinsel and one really weird guy who insisted on being called The Elusive Stranger because it was his favourite Toyah Willcox song. Surnames simply weren't needed. We had reverted to a quasi-medieval system of identification by either appearance or occupation or inclination. It seems so contrived now and people in my new life cannot believe that these people really were called by these names but they were. I could never have called Nogbad, Stephen. He was Nogbad and that was that.

    Claire would like to have been known as Claire Space Cadet or Space Cadet Claire. She would tell us all the time what a space cadet she was, how crazy she was, how simply *off the planet*. I suppose she hoped that if we heard the phrase enough and associated it with her rather than with any of the other rather strange people that flitted in and out of the house, then she might finally win. It never worked. Nicknames rarely stick because the owner has chosen them.

Claire called herself Space Cadet but to us she was simply Claire. Sometimes 'Claire who deals drugs from her room' or 'Claire who knows Jamie' but usually just Claire.

'Oh. Hi, Claire.' I had trodden on her foot so I could hardly ignore her. The agent looked a little askance. Claire had a penchant for stripy woolen jumpers and unwashed tights, her skin was a mass of piercings long before it was fashionable or even hygienic and she had just that morning cut her fringe into a peculiar inch-high ridge across her forehead. Claire being Claire gave a screech and hugged me. We had seen each other for lunchtime Neighbours which was when most of us got up but I still clearly needed a hug.

'Didn't recognize you, mate!' Claire always called people Mate but she didn't really have any. I cannot remember to this day how she ended up moving in but when she proved to be reasonably unproblematic she stayed anyway. I got rid of her as quickly as I could, explaining then to the agent how I used to do charity work at Centrepoint but I'm not sure she believed me. I could feel little Oliver fading away into make-believe and I suddenly realized how much I would miss him. I was hooked. The houses were more than just houses, they were the key to a whole new fantasy world where I could be just the person I despised in reality, the sort of person I would happily see Up Against The Wall Come The Revolution. But I had to be more organised.

My sister was the answer. My sister is a wonderful human being but she is easy to envy. I couldn't really have described her back then but it's easy now. Princess Diana just after she met Dodi and Carol Smillie circa the second series of Changing Rooms. And she's nice too, beautiful and nice. Her only vice is a craving for expensive clothes which she throws out every six months to whoever is waiting with eager arms. Up until this point I had disdained to accept anything not black but now I made the long trek back to Wallington and availed myself of a couple of very nice pseudo-Chanel suits. I took the plunge then and grabbed some heels. I hadn't worn heels since the age of thirteen. It's quite impossible to leap around to Chumbawamba if you have anything higher than DMs on your feet, high heels were the universal symbol of sexual oppression embraced willingly by duped women. But what a thrill it was to totter around the room, bottom wiggling in a tight calf-length skirt. I was a geisha girl reveling in every blood soaked bandage.

A new woman graced the next estate agent. Still Sarah Lees-Jardine but after a six month spell learning how to be a glamour puss trophy wife. The hair was still a problem, I doubted whether the real Sarah Lees-Jardine would have worn a hat but there was nothing for it. A quick trawl around the Oxfams of Knightsbridge found me a bizarre silk creation, not quite wedding or Ascot but still a vision of sweeping rim and delicate papier maché flowers. Gone was Victoria Gillick, now I was Eva Peron. Fortunately, Oliver, Josh and Em tagged along.

Docklands. My first flat as the new me was in Docklands. Canary Wharf had only just been developed, most people thought it would be a huge white elephant in those days, too far from the centre of things, too poorly connected to the Tube. The Docklands Light Railway was only a distant election promise and nobody believed in the

Jubilee extension. But the agent was insistent; these apartments just had to be seen to be believed, they were the latest word in Third Millennium luxury. So I went. I had no intention of making an offer, I had no funds or husband with which to make an offer but I went for where was the harm? Another flat, another house, another lovely bathroom, another Bell double oven with matching extractor fan. I was giving them marks out of ten with the intention of sharing my judgments with the imaginary Rupert. This one I felt might well be a nine.

I was right. It was a nine, it was damned well near enough a perfect ten but there hasn't been a day since when I haven't looked back and wished I had not gone.

'I must show you the view first! It simply sells the apartment all by itself!' The agent was a man this time, twenty-two maybe, twenty-three. He wore a suit so fashionably cut and coloured he looked like a cardboard cut-out. I was not so cut off from decent society that I hadn't heard of Armani but I was still naïve enough to wonder why something so famous and so expensive could still look so naff on the person who didn't have a clue how to wear it. And he smelt of Paco Rabanne.

He was right though, the view was spectacular. I'm not one of those people with a real heartstrings passion for London. I enjoyed living there but it wasn't home. I didn't yet know at that time where home was but it wasn't London, great as it was for the moment. But as I stood before the enormous sheet of glass and looked over the Thames as the summer sun set towards my right and lit up the dirty brown water with gold, I felt something stir deep down. There was an immense majesty somehow in the sheer mass of population and concrete, modern as they might be, still the towers bore the phantom hint of another London and a London before that. Ragged Celts had come to this very river and had stopped to build simple homes of reed and mud and wood. Romans had built villas and granaries and drinking houses and Boudicca had burnt them down again. Thomas More had scurried from narrow street to the river concourse as had a million million others and for a moment I could sense them all.

'It's lovely!' For once Sarah Lees-Jardine and I were in agreement. The geeky lad sensed a commission. He'd already heard about Rupert's recent promotion to Baring's (how ironic that seemed later) and my little windfall from poor old Aunt Elspeth. We dutifully toured the two bedrooms and walk-in wardrobes, both bigger than the room I had once occupied in Brixton which in all fairness to Brixton was actually an old toilet. The carpets were so deep and clean I instinctively tried to tip-toe but had not yet mastered the heels quite well enough. Eva Peron would not have minced, she would have allowed every pound of her eight stones sink with unthinking carelessness into each fifty-five quid a square metre strip. The hallways were stripped wood, not pine but something dark and shiny. The apartment was brand new so presumably the 'I've just been reclaimed from a Victorian house and polished up by experts' look had been created in a factory but it was damned convincing. I could just imagine how well Josh's little toy cars and trains would slide upon the slippery surface. I began to worry if the children might slip and hurt their heads.

The bathroom was huge. Roman Empire meets IKEA with pseudo marble columns holding trailing ivy, a sunken bath that could take a small horse and matching fittings in that dull bronze metal that looks so much classier than gold. It was getting late. Sean's band, Wat Tyler, were playing the George Robey and I would really have to be home by seven in order to change and get the Tube back up north of the river. I looked at my watch and then realized my mistake. The boy in the Armani had a watch too, a gleaming thing with lots of dials and digits presumably telling you the time, temperature and rate of exchange in Geneva. He hadn't looked at it – he was far too well-mannered – but he had loosened the chunky chrome strap enough to let it dangle like some sad seventies bracelet. I didn't have a watch like that. I had a cheap round face which had been free with Readers' Digest strapped onto my wrist with a cheerful plait of friendship ribbons in ANC colours. It was a great watch, it had funk, it had soul, it had compassion for the Blacks of South Africa and the soon-to-be-released Mandela. But Eva Peron would not have worn my watch. The designer creep took one look and sussed me out.

"Well, if that is all, Mrs Lees-Jardine?' He knew I was a fraud but there was a million to one chance that I wasn't so he kept his options and commission open by being condescendingly polite. I was cross, cross and embarrassed and so I took it out on him, him and that obnoxious flat.

'It all seems a little…lacking in character. Hard to imagine a family living here, even just part-time. I would worry terribly about that glass.'

'It's fully reinforced. And a family creates its own atmosphere, don't you think? You could paint the walls bright colours – reds and greens and yellows perhaps. Primaries are going to be very nineties apparently.'

I hated him. He was a schoolboy in his uncle's suit. He was a parasite sucking the blood from a great city as house prices rose and people like me were forced to squat in abandoned council buildings with gaps in the kitchen walls. I could do nothing to touch him (the recession would do that for me) but I wasn't going to make it easy for him to get rid of me.

"Could I see the kitchen again? Kitchens are so important, they're the very heart of a family home. I bet there's no woman living here, only a man would leave a kitchen so clinical and empty.'

I was right in this anyway. It was as if no one lived in this flat at all. The slab of black marble that posed as a work surface gleamed as if no human fingers had ever dared to sully its shine. There were no crumbs, no stains, no used tea bags sitting dejected by the sink. And the smell was a faint hint of household cleaner; no garlic, no herbs, no tomato puree with sticky crud squeezing out from the tube. This was a man's apartment, a man who spent most of his time at the office and in expensive bars and who only came back here to impress women he wanted to have sex with. I knew I wouldn't like this man, I could almost see him in the shine of the extractor fan. Impeccably dressed, gelled back hair, smooth chin stinking of after shave. I hated smooth chins and after shave. I thought fondly of my friends, the lads from Brixton who endured the depravities of the squat with cheerful acceptance and dirty hair. They smelled of patchouli oil and dreadlocks, unwashed woolen jumpers and wet dogs.

The agent was getting impatient. 'Perhaps you're right. It is very much a bachelor apartment. A man lives here at the moment although he's away on business. Very neat, isn't it? But not right for a family.'

'No,' I admitted defeat, 'and the bathroom facilities are inadequate. For a family. One bathroom is quite unusual nowadays, especially in a new development. Simply everyone insists on at least two. You might have a terrible time selling this place.'

A pretty display of emotions flashed across his lack of stubble. The desire to get rid of me vied against the need to win. This was the eighties, he had no choice.

'Oh but there *is* a second bathroom, en suite to the master. I assumed you went in as I was checking the guarantee on the boiler.'

I was momentarily flummoxed. How could I have missed an entire bathroom? Was hygiene really so alien to me now that I failed to recognize an en suite when I passed one by? He was sweeping ahead towards the finishing line and gave a little *ahem* of amused pity.

'The door matches the chrome of the wardrobes. Perhaps you thought…'

Yes, OK, yes, I had thought it was another poxy wardrobe, how the hell was I supposed to know different, it

was like walking around R2D2's innards. I didn't bother to reply, turning on my heels and heading in the direction of the master bedroom which by now was looking more anally repressed than ever. Who but an emotional dead battery would choose grey and chrome as his colour scheme? What kind of person could
live in an apartment without one single photograph of family or friends, without one picture or ornament, without clothes liberally decorating the floor and peering around wardrobe doors which simply would not shut? *Emotional dead battery!* I accused him, stomping towards what I had assumed was a third wardrobe door and wrenching it open. No surprise here. The grey of the tiles was a shade lighter but the chrome was the same and the mirrors just made the whole room even more surgical. Futuristic toilet made wholly of metal, ridiculously low and wide sink, a gleaming shower cubicle which looked as if it had not even been unwrapped from the showroom plastic. *Anally retentive retard!* I screamed silently at the owner, hoping that the rim of the toilet bowl was as cold as it looked.

     I was just turning to leave when it caught my eye. So out of place, it screamed. A photograph stuck neatly to the rim of the shaving mirror. A photograph in an apartment with no photographs. A touch of sentiment in a place with no friends, family or emotion. A colour photograph, roughly taken by the amateur hand in a rush. It was a photograph which would have been seen every single morning by whoever lived here. It had been put there, sellotaped to the mirror where he shaved so assiduously for that very purpose. The man who owned this flat wanted to be reminded of this photograph at the start and at the end of every single day. It was the only thing that spoke of humanity, of empathy. It was a touch of the outside world in a place of chrome and mirrors. It was a photograph. A photograph of a dog.

    My dog.

Chapter 1 – Ness

Ness was a Battersea dog. Half Alsatian, half collie, she was great big bundle of black fur and bent ears and grey withers. I adored her, I cannot say how much I adored her. She was my first real, proper, clean and uncomplicated love. The relationships I had with men were pretty much disastrous for various dull, obvious reasons I am embarrassed now to recall. But Ness I loved simply and sincerely. I loved her as much the day she died as the day she jumped up from behind the metal grill and licked at my outstretched fingers. She was my first baby, the first creature on this planet dependent upon me and loving me before all others. I should never have bought her that summer day in 1986 but I never once regretted it, not even at the end.

At the time I was living with a boyfriend called Richard. I can define my relationships in one of two ways; the blokes were either decent, hard working and adored me or they were useless, narcissist gits with alcohol, drug or emotional problems. Richard belonged to the former category which meant that I stayed with him because my common sense told me I was on to a good thing. It also meant that I was bored, depressed and uninterested in sex. Being a nice guy, he said he didn't mind which naturally made it worse. In a vain attempt to cement our faltering relationship, we decided to get a dog together. The fact that he worked and I was a full-time student didn't deter us in the least, we were both intelligent semi-adults but we were frighteningly (or wilfully) ignorant of even the most basic requirements of adult living. Dogs looked after themselves, didn't they? I mean, as long as you took them out for ten minutes in the morning and were back sometime in the evening, they slept on hearthrugs and chewed plastic bones. They were like babies, they could be left alone for hours on end and didn't change your life in any significant way at all.

      Battersea has changed a lot since then. From what I can see from the TV the pens are all inside but in 1986 most of them were just covered kennels with a concrete run. I had a romantic notion that I would know the minute I saw my canine soul mate just as I would know instinctively the human love of my life. With men this tended to backfire as the miscreants who caused my heart to leap invariably turned out to be the worst kind of losers but that day in south London I happened to be right. I knew her. The minute I saw her so forlorn and matted, I knew she was the one. Richard wasn't so sure. He thought she looked a bit vicious, as if she might turn at any moment. His days were already numbered but this appalling lack of judgment brought the end very much closer. The great mass of black hair jumped up and licked at me. Our futures were sealed together by the touch of warm saliva upon my skin. A momentary stab of utter panic as I looked for the card on the outside of the pen. If it had gone, then someone else was interested, someone else had beaten me to it and would be taking her home that day. It was there. It was the 26th of August, 1986 and if I had been one day later or one day earlier then I would have lost her forever. Richard had a car and we took her home. She stayed, he did not.

Three years later I left the penthouse flat with its chrome and its fine view across the Thames and I took the two buses and three Tube lines and the long walk up Brixton Hill because I couldn't be bothered to wait with the other thousands of commuters heading for Streatham at the bus stops. Brixton was pretty much run down in those days; lots of litter, lots of boarded up houses, lots of people like me looking for something to do with the next five years. It had a decent sports centre but even that only got built because the locals had rioted. It says something for Thatcherite politics that young people have to riot and burn down buildings in order to get a swimming pool and a set of weights. Brixton proper was the half mile or so around the Tube. The market with its reggae blaring out, the grimy pubs selling weed, the hairdressers turning away white women, the stalls with yams and okra and brightly coloured cottons. I walked through this part of Brixton every day but I didn't know one person who lived there. There was no animosity between the Brixton black community and the white hippy squatters, there was just a mute acceptance that we didn't mix. No suspicion, no name calling, no funny looks, we just didn't really see each other.

Brixton Hill had council flats on the right and enormous Victorian three storeys on the left. It was a huge thoroughfare, always busy, usually safe, although it was around that time that two IRA prisoners escaped from the prison up on the left with a gun smuggled in to them via a pair of trainers and then used it to hijack a car minding its own business coming down the Hill. That was the most exciting thing that had happened in Brixton since the riots. It had a reputation but really Brixton was a sleeping tiger most of the time.

You could jump on and off the 1950s open-back buses whenever you chose (as I knew to my cost having fallen off a couple of them whilst drunk) but that evening I wanted to walk. I had a queer feeling in the very pit of my stomach. Eva Peron was gone, the hat was in a plastic Tesco's bag with the Chanel jacket, and the slip beneath had short enough sleeves to reveal my tattoo so I was safely Me should I meet anyone I knew. But my mind was elsewhere.

So many rational explanations. He was clearly some freelance photographer with fond memories of the first picture he'd ever taken. Or he had wanted to be a freelance photographer but turned out so bad that he kept one of his worst attempts to remind himself every single bloody morning exactly why it was he worked in the City. Perhaps he just liked dogs. Or in particular, perhaps he just liked the look of Ness. She was truly drop dead gorgeous even if she wasn't quite pedigree or even one breed as opposed to any other. My feet hurt so I stopped every five minutes, sitting on uneven walls and trying to rationalise. The git in the suit had tried to usher me out, he had other appointments, I was not going to contribute towards his early retirement playing polo and we both knew it but I wasn't going anywhere. I just stared. In that surgically soulless bathroom-cum-operating theatre, I stood surrounded by steel and gleam and inhumanity and I stared in mute incomprehension at my beloved Ness.

'Nice dog. Time's moving on though, I do have other appointments.'

Resisting the urge to break his nose, I tried to remember my Eva Peron smile.

'Does she…does it live here? Are pets allowed?'

'Oh no. I'm afraid that's a non-negotiable part of the leasing arrangement. Tropical fish, I think. By prior arrangement, of course.'

'Of course.' *You unspeakably useless plonker.*

'So perhaps this dog comes to visit. Would that be allowed?'

He was not just bored with me now but visibly riled. 'I really don't think that the owner of this particular apartment has much time for animals. As I said, he's very much a City man. High earner, foreign holidays, no children. Not a person to have much time for animals.'

'And yet he seems to like this one. No photographs of his mother or father, no girlfriends, no school chums from Harrow. Just a dog.'

He opened the bathroom door as wide as it could possibly go which wasn't that far given some strange futuristic sculpture which might have been part of the plumbing and which ran splendidly up the wall.

'It's just a photograph of a dog, Mrs Lees-Jardine. Now, as I said before…'

And so I had been ejected from the place contaminated by my presence but try as I might, I could not get it out of my mind.

After trudging up Brixton Hill in three and a half inch heels and into Elm Park road, I was pleased to see Jamie emerging from the chippie. We had a strange superstitious tradition, me and Jamie, that the first person you met coming home would colour the rest of that day. So if you got up, went to the local shop for a pint of milk and then met Gavin, then your whole day was going to be unspeakably bad. But if you met Cali or Al or Pete then it was going to be just great. With Lucy or Claire, it could go either way. Life was just like that and so were the people I lived with.

But it wasn't Claire which would have meant another hug smelling slightly of cheap cider and strongly of weed, it was Jamie which meant a cheery grin and a 'Hallo, darling, you look nice.'

Jamie was one of those people that literally no one disliked. I know we say that liberally about all sorts of half-decent people who don't offend us half as much as everyone else but in Jamie's case it was a rock solid reality. No one disliked him. I suppose people may have tried simply from a perverse sense of having to give it a go but to the extent of my knowledge, no one had ever succeeded. No girl could resist him either, he was so God-damned cute. In fact, strange to say, I was probably the only female ever to have resisted his charms but that was only due to the slightly unfortunate circumstances of our first meeting. I was singing in band called Blyth Power who played a sort of Indie-Folk-punk with lyrics about trains, cricket and John of Gaunt (nothing to do with me, I sang what I was given) and Jamie, aged seventeen, had been a real fan. He once drove from Newbury to Darlington, caught the encore and then drove home again. Anyway, he was kind, he was funny, he had the sweetest little face but on the first two occasions of our acquaintance, I honest-to-God thought he was a girl. I even had conversations with him after gigs and my only excuses are that 1) I was slightly pissed which was likely as we rarely got paid in money back in those days, the landlord assuming that a free pint or two would adequately compensate us for the two hundred or so miles just travelled to play in his flea pit and 2) he was wearing incredibly tight trousers and had plumpish thighs and a nice feminine bum. When I found out he was in fact male, the only course of action was the 'best friend road'. I simply couldn't ever imagine wanting to shag someone I had discussed tampons with. But he was lovely. And I was pleased beyond anything that it was he I met coming home that day from Docklands.

  I wanted to talk to someone, I wanted to rationalise it all through. Some complete yuppy stranger had a picture of my dog on his shaving mirror and I wanted to be able to make sense of this and move on. But lovely as he was, Jamie wasn't the person. He had the occasional tendency to say things like 'Wow, man, that's really freaky. That would totally do my head in if that happened to me' which wasn't the rationalising I needed right then.

  'Is Cal in yet?' I knew she wouldn't be but you never knew with diamond merchants.

  Jamie offered me a chip. 'Don't think so. Just Al and Claire.'

  'And Gavin.'

  He gave a grin. 'Probably. Haven't seen him for two weeks. Do you want another house meeting about him?'

Usually I would have leapt at the chance. Gavin (also known by all and sundry as Satan) was the bane of my life. He had appeared at the front door six months previously claiming that Al had said it would be cool if he stayed a few days. Al had been away, we were all watching EastEnders, none of us saw the five suitcases at his feet and there was an empty attic room with a hole in the roof. He came, he stayed, he made my life a living hell. But today, I didn't want to talk about kicking Gavin out, I wanted Cal, I wanted somebody sane and at Number 94 Elm Park, Cali was really the closest thing we had to sane.

She wasn't really a diamond merchant but what the hell. She worked for Van Moppes which was a diamond merchants in Hatton Garden and quite what she did there I still, after so many years of knowing her and loving her, do not know. She was the only one of us with a proper job, she actually set an alarm in the morning which was something none of us had ever done except when touring Europe and even then we usually fucked it up and were woken by Protag beeping frantically outside the house at three in the morning. When I say that Cali was sane, I mean she was the sanest person in the house, at least until Pete arrived a few weeks later. You could talk to Cali about normal things like education and travelling to places other than India to *sort your head out* (Claire) or Thailand to see *the amazing ethnic carvings* (Al). Cal and I wanted to do things with our lives which didn't just involve setting free battery farmed hens and Stopping The City and going to Wales to live on wind farms. We had to be relatively secretive about the things we talked about but she had a cosy bedroom right at the top of the third landing and we'd lie on her bed with its huge quilt and embroidered cover that her gran had made her and we'd talk about men and make up and how to lose weight and whether it was wise to meet for lunch outside Warehouse because of what had happened last time when we only went in for a little peak and spent three hundred pounds and didn't even have time for a coffee. Cal and I were Ally McBeal girls before Channel 4 had even sniffed a good deal there. It just so happened that we had somehow become trapped into an alternative culture which involved feeling guilty if you wore make up, feeling guilty if you wore a skirt and knowing full well that for all the talk of sharing and communal living, there was still not going to be any bloody milk in the fridge the next morning.

Cali wasn't completely sane. She had my weakness which was a desire for unsuitable men. We did at least now recognise that they were unsuitable which was an improvement on our teenage years but we hadn't really progressed. I always used to say (and it was no lie) that if I was at a gig with five hundred decent, respectable guys all hanging round talking about Suzanne Vega, I'd fall hopelessly in love with the one being sick in the toilets. Cali was the same. We were from the same planet but this was only 1989 and we hadn't yet been told that it was Venus. We helped each other out the best we could.

'I haven't got the energy for Gavin, not tonight. But promise me we'll sort him out soon!'

Jamie had tomato sauce on his stubble, just calling out for some cute little hippy chick to lick it off for him.

'Chill out darling, we'll sort it all out, it'll be cool.'
'Right. Good.'

I looked up the road towards the house. A great diseased elm obscured most of the front windows which curved elegantly outwards like the turrets of a castle. From a distance you couldn't quite see the cracks and graffiti and the fact that the house…wasn't **exactly** straight. It sort of…*leant* a bit. Leant lazily to one side, just as we did most mornings, perhaps it was subsiding in sympathy for its inhabitants and their ever subsiding lives.

Jamie was actually heading across the road to see Fletch who was a proper hippy. We had few delusions at No.94 that we were the real thing although we did try when we could get up in time. Over the road, they were no longer a squat. They had nagged and nagged and nagged a local Housing Association to taken them and hey presto they were legal and they had hot water and someone coming round to sort out the dodgy electrics and all those impossibly wonderful things we could only dream about. They were all older than us, mid-thirties probably, and for them life was set. We were still kids, we were babies who could still go back to college or get normal jobs or go back to Mummy and Daddy in the country but for the guys across the road, it was too late for turnarounds. As a consequence they did things properly. None of them actually worked, don't get me wrong, but they knew exactly which benefits to claim and how to push the system. They ordered organic vegetables from the commune down on Railton Road and had a really smart kitchen filled with jars labelled cumin and ginger and cardamom, things I'd never even heard of.

We tried to be like them but we always failed. We made an organic order with the commune once, we ordered thirty pounds worth of veg and Al even cycled down to place the order and pay the cash but when the order came in, none of us could actually be bothered to go and pick it up. None of us had cars and there was too much stuff to be carried on a bike so it just sat there, paid for and ours but never in reality to grace our vegetable rack. That summed us up very well.

Fletch waved from across the road but it was a cautious sort of 'I don't know you very well, you're a girl but you wear make up and skirts and I'm only really comfortable with lesbians with short hair' sort of wave.

'We're having backgammon tournament later,' he called out shyly and in that long-drawn out drawl that people who've taken far too many drags on the spliff always seem to have. 'If you wanna come over, man?.....'

'Thanks, Fletch! I might see you later then.'

I had no intention of going and if Fletch had thought for one moment that I might actually turn up to any of his gatherings, he would never have invited me in the first place. It was good to know though that we had angrily left the hypocrisy and two faced lies of our fascistic, bourgeois parents to adopt some much more acceptable hypocrisy and two faced lies of our own. Fletch was a really nice man but I was his worst nightmare and he, in many ways, was mine. Who needs sensitive caring men who can cook with cardamoms and have books directing them towards the g-spot when you can pick up some useless shitpot with cheekbones to die for and who'll dump you three months later for your mate with bigger breasts?

I turned in away from how hippies could and should live to the house that was, for the moment, home.

I once heard 94 Elm Park called the most famous squat in London. I don't know who said it or why but it always stuck in my mind because it made me proud. Clearly the person who had said it had never actually lived there. Perhaps they were one of the many, many people who stayed the night or the week, the hundreds of northerners and Dutch punks and German freaks who descended upon us occasionally. There is actually a place in East London called Elm Park on the Tube somewhere horribly remote and many a poor traveller ended up there before being redirected all the way back across London to Brixton. We had lots of Dutch visitors as the Dutch music scene was very much like ours at the time. Blyth Power always played Holland at least twice a year and they loved bands like Chumbawamba who were huge here too. The Dutch lived like the hippies across the road at No.91. They had labelled condiments jars and took turns to do the washing up and had rotas that people actually took notice of. They also had deep meaningful conversations all the damned time and had no sense of humour whatsoever. I really didn't like the Dutch, I felt that they were an alien species, not as bad as the Germans obviously (and I had toured Germany more than any other country which was the irony of being in a British indie band) but certainly not people you wanted in your house for more than a week.

This particular week we didn't have any visitors. This was unusual. Normally we always had at least one friend up from Somerset or Newbury, some sad European trying to understand Fawlty Towers. We very rarely had any Americans which was a huge shame as they were seen as the elite. Bands from Seattle and San Francisco were only just starting to make an impact on the indie scene in 1989 and when they came they tended to stay with people who ran record labels and not grubby little squatters like us.

Green Day? Soulside? REM? Oh no, not at 94 Elm Park, you don't. You can stay with the men who run Rough Trade and FireFly and proper grown up labels. They'll have kettles that don't kill you and spare rooms without pigeons crapping on you as you sleep from the corner of the ceiling where there's a bloody great hole. They won't ask you to answer the door to the man from the leccy and pretend to be Spanish so he won't come in. They won't ask you to help unblock the sewerage system or lend you fifty quid until your dole's sorted out. No, Mr American grunge rock star, you don't want to stay at Elm Park.

So, no visitors then. Just me, Jamie, Cali, Al, Claire, Lucy and Gavin. Sean Gummidge had just moved out to live with Ben (who was the love of my life but old, dull news now) and Emma (who had been my best friend until I found her sleeping with Ben, the love of my life and old, dull news now) had just moved out to live with Nat and Stan. Seven was the normal kind of number at Number 94 Elm Park, although I had known four and I had known eleven.

A condemned house with subsidence, rot, seeping sewage from the cellars, huge holes in the roof, pigeons on the landing, a toilet that had fallen through into the room below because of damp floor boards rotting through, seven people, one dog (mine) and one baby on the way (Lucy's).

We thought we knew how to live. We thought were doing OK. We weren't paying any rent so we thought we were doing OK. Jesus Christ. I look back every day and I can't believe it was real.

Chapter 2 – 94 Elm Park

The door was hanging half open as usual. It had been like that ever since I had tried to lock Gavin out in the vain hope that he might go back to Hades but he had simply kicked it in and none of us had actually got round to fixing it yet. Al had pretensions to carpentry but he meant things like fancy oak cabinets with Celtic carvings so putting on two new hinges was clearly beneath him. I gently swung the door open in the safest possible way, avoiding the tendency it had to swing round on the one hinge and hint at imminent collapse. I had already passed the splendid wreck of Giles' taxi engine in the front yard. Strange, we had all protested when he dumped it there a year ago (just to repair it because he had no space and Black Cabs were going to be a real investment for the future and had the best turning circle you could get on the road etc etc etc) but now we just didn't see it or even think about it. Just like Giles, I suppose. He certainly hadn't been round to tinker at it in a while.

The hallway stank as usual. Bungle was the house cat, he had lived at Number 94 longer than any of us and there was no way he was going to use a litter tray, not when there were so many little nooks and crannies. He was unneutered (of course) because 1) no one actually owned him and could be held responsible and 2) the guys at the house felt that it was unfair to deny him his natural instincts. His natural instincts stank but we got used to them after a while, especially when they were competing against the damp, the rotting 1950s wallpaper and the burst sewage pipe in the downstairs toilet which we had nailed up rather than deal with. You see, that was the contradiction of us all. We would rather go to the effort of finding long pieces of wood in a skip and nailing them across the toilet door so we could pretend the disaster hadn't happened, than actually go down to B&Q and get some sealant.

My bedroom was on the first floor and it was the best. 94 Elm Park was a Victorian house on the end of a long terrace of three storey Victorian houses and for some reason the outer walls curved, just like the turret of a castle. This meant that two of the bedrooms – the ones at the front and on the first and second storeys – also curved. They were the biggest bedrooms, they had the most light and the least smell but boy, did you have to serve your time to win them.

I had begun life at Elm Park on the floor of Gummidge's bedroom (which ironically a year later would be mine). I had split up from Ben and was in my *crying every day, contemplating suicide, not going in to college and generally fucking up my finals revision* phase so I guess he took pity on me. Bless him. I knew I wanted to live there. From the description you have just read this might sound hard to believe but think about it. Brixton was a great place to live but rent was impossible. Sure, I had a grant but it was minimal and there was no way I was living in Uni halls with a load of geeky students. Secondly, my friends all lived here. Thirdly, I just didn't notice things like shit on the stairs and peeling wallpaper and mice droppings the way I would now. And fourthly, it was free. A couple of pounds every quarter to pay a fictitious electricity bill but apart from that, completely free.

I had to stay. I had to find a way of living there but how? At this point in time, 1988, No.94 was chocka. Gummidge, Sue and Stuart, a couple of lesbians called Jill and Fee, Alan the Roadie, Jamie, Emma and some others I can't even remember. One day, in desperation, I wandered around the house just looking for somewhere I could bed down a mattress, just a space which would give me a foothold, a place in the queue. And I found it. Next to Alan the Roadie's room was a disused toilet (not the one which later fell through but the one above it). For some reason there was no actual toilet, it was just an empty room maybe five feet six by four with the blocked off refuse pipe on the far wall. I had passed close by it a million times, it was on the little landing on the way from the first storey down to the living room and the kitchen. It was full of junk. Old curtains, mouldy clothes, pieces of wood, paint pots. Within three hours I had it cleared, a lick of paint across the walls, a thick piece of velvet stuffed in and around the pipe and four hooks hammered into the walls. Who needs an IKEA wardrobe when you can have four hooks nailed to your wall? A spare mattress in the cellar was a little large but the fact that it sloped gently up the walls added to the cosiness. Ness always slept on my legs anyway so she didn't mind. I was in.

For four months I lived in a toilet, for four months I heard the rush of filthy water flow past my head as I lay with my pillow against the blocked up pipe, for four months I cried myself to sleep not because I was sleeping in a toilet but because I had lost my man. Then one fine day, Alan upset one too many people with one too many drugs and he was out and I was in. A bedroom. At last.

Within a year, such was the turnover of people, I had graduated to the premier suite. And I surrounded myself with green plants and African carvings and wall hangings. A proper hippy would have stripped and stained the floorboards and restored the Victorian fireplace but Changing Rooms had not been thought of yet and I was happy enough with my silverfish carpet and my butterfly mobiles.

There was a note from Cali stuck to my door.
Have to take a client out for a drink, see you after the gig.
Shit. Shit, shit, shit. There was a crazy yuppy with a picture of my dog on his shaving mirror and I needed to fathom it all out so that I could forget about it. I knew instinctively that the habit had gone. No more estate agents' details, no more viewings, no more Oliver, Josh and Emily. I was cured of all that now but I needed a rational explanation before putting it all to bed. I needed to make sense of what seemed senseless.

The door was nosed open and there she was.

We lay on the bed, cuddled up all soft and warm as I rubbed her belly and sank my face into her neck. She smelt wet and very doggy, Gummidge must have taken her to Brockwell Park, he was crazy about dogs. He'd had two of his own but had had to let both go, unable to cope with the commitment but it had broken his heart. Ness was tired, I could sense that all she wanted to do was sleep. I could stay here with her but Cal wouldn't be back until past twelve or I could go up to the George Robey and watch the gig. The house seemed very quiet and dark. Sometimes it had an atmosphere one couldn't quite describe. Emma had said to me just before she left; *There's something wrong with this damned house, nothing ever moves on here, nothing ever happens, we all just get stuck in ruts and it doesn't let us go. It'll never let* ***you*** *go.*

Ness was asleep and gently snoring through damp nostrils. I gave her one last cuddle and got up to get changed.

The George Robey is one of the first pubs you come to when you leave Finsbury Park Tube station. At least, it used to be. It could well be demolished now for all I know or care, it might be a Chinese restaurant or a snooker hall. I had seen it undergo many incarnations in my eight years or so on the London punk / indie scene. I first went there at the tender age of fifteen when I was lead singer in a punk band called the Lost Cherrees. We were as absolutely dreadful as our name suggested but we did have one distinct advantage. There were loads of shit punk groups gigging around London in 1982 but hardly any were fronted by girls. So anyway we had a gig at the infamous George Robey and there we were, further north than any of us southern suburbia kids had ever been. It was a nice pub then, all mirrors with pretty etchings around the edges and plush sofa-style seats in red velvet. The gig hall was grim but then what else did you need but a reasonably sized hall and a stage? Since then the Robey had gone through a Goth phase when everything had been covered in black webbing and camouflage from Thursday to Sunday and then went back to normal Sunday to Wednesday and then for some reason some git had completely gutted it. All the mirrors went, so did the velvet seats and in came cheap plastic and artex on the walls. It was usually pretty crowded, mostly because the beer was cheap and the door policy unwisely tolerant. I can't remember which bands were on with Wat Tyler that night. Probably The Astronauts who were shit but who had been around for so long that no one could imagine a London gig without them. The lead singer, Pete Astronaut, had been unemployed at this time for fourteen years without a break and was Officially Unemployable which we all found rather impressive. He actually had it stamped across his UB40 and on all his records or so they said. I can't remember who else played that night, certainly it wasn't Snuff, they were far too big by then but there was always the forlorn hope in the back of my sad little mind that the cold but lovely Simon Snuff might just be there.

If I walk into a pub now (and Christ knows that isn't more than three times in a year), the first thing I notice is the smoke. I can't stand it, it makes me feel as though I'm actually breathing in tiny globules of lymphoma, I have to take tiny sharp breaths and then wash my hair as soon as I get home which is usually less than two hours later. Back in 1989 at the tender age of twenty-two, even as a non-smoker, I didn't notice a thing. The place was half full, dingy, smelling not just of fags but of joints, sweat, hair spray and the Gents'. Twenty or so people at the bar, a few sitting on the sweaty plastic, fifteen or so just around the corner to my right watching The Astronauts who were making a horrible racket.

I was on the guest list as I usually was. This sounds really cocky, I know, a sad precursor of that tragic nobhead in the Fast Show who used to be in Crème Brulée and couldn't move on with anything else. With me though it was simply a consequence of being around the same music scene so damned long. Just about every band I went to see, I knew personally as friends, most of them I bloody well lived with. Sean Gummidge was in Wat Tyler, Jamie was now lead guitarist in Blyth Power, Al was in some other band with Jamie, Alan used to roadie for the UK Subs and now roadied for Thatcher on Acid which was Ben's band, Pete was in Chunk. Now, Chunk is a great name for a band. All band names are intrinsically foolish so if you can choose the most obviously foolish of all which also has the convenience of summing up your sound, then you get a certain amount of admiration from the cognoscenti before you've even played a gig. Wat Tyler were obviously named after the great 14th century rebel but Sean and the lads actually knew nothing about him at all. I think it was Gummidge's brother Bro who suggested it and said it was anarchic and they might get some gigs with Crass or Chumbawamba on the strength of it. I knew all these people, they had been my friends since….oh, since before it was legal to get into any of the venues we were actually playing in twice a week. I more or less lived with Julie from DAN because she was Jamie's girlfriend, I was close-ish friends with Ruth from Hagar the Womb, I was an ex-girlfriend of Colin Conflict, an ex-girlfriend of Gigs from The Joyce McKinney Experience, an ex-girlfriend of Ben of Thatcher on Acid and an ex-girlfriend of Simon Snuff from – obviously – Snuff. As you will probably have guessed by now, I was addicted to going out with blokes who were in bands. I would have been termed a terminal and incurable groupie but narrowly escaped that worst of all insults by actually being in bands myself. Not very good bands admittedly but then there weren't a whole lot of them around.

'Hallo, darling, what you drinking?'

It was Mickey Penguin; sweet, too young to be let out on his own, still living with Mum and Dad and running a tape company from his bedroom. He bore a slight resemblance to Ian Beale which was unfortunate because Mickey was a lovely guy so I accepted a cider and black but after making polite conversation about what I was doing nowadays (*'Oh you know, setting something up, an all-girl band probably, starting my PhD next year, might go to America for a while etc etc'*, anything rather than admit I was lost in limbo without a clue where to go), I wandered away. Mickey was with Boring Steve who was actually very nice but nicknames don't stick by accident. I heard later that Mickey nearly died a few months after that very night. He was just running for a train one morning and *crash!* That was him, unconscious on the platform concrete. A brain haemorrhage apparently. As far as I know he made a full recovery but for a long time I assumed he had died. And I thought right up until recently that a brain haemorrhage was the same as a brain tumour and therefore likely to come back, I didn't realise my mistake until years later but I do regret never being able to visit him in hospital, he must have thought me such a cow. That evening however, Mickey was with Boring Steve so I took my pint and moved on.

The great thing about being in a band from an early age, especially if you were there at the beginning of some sort of movement which I had been, was that you could walk into a gig and be sure that you would know at least ten people there. And even more gratifying although I'm not sure whether this was on a conscious level (I hope not), at least another twenty would know you. They would have your records in their carefully ordered collection at home, they would have interviews with you in fanzines that took up more space in their bedroom than the bed, they might even have pictures of you stuck on the wall. It was quite a nice feeling, it bolstered up the fragile ego but it was a bugger when you felt it slipping away. You see, I wasn't actually in a band at that particular period in my life and although there was always the very real possibility that I would be at some future, undetermined point, I wasn't actually then. So I was on edge, nervous. Would I have to stand on my own for any more than ten seconds? Would I have to go to the loo and pretend to fix my make up and hair rather than look like a loner? It was an indescribable nightmare to me, going to gigs on my own. It always felt as though everyone was staring at the unpopular slapper all by herself making a show and pretending she used to be someone. I think this all went back to my early teenage years when my eyesight deteriorated in a matter of six months from twenty-twenty to blind-as-a-bat myopic. I would have to meet my school friends in cafes and department store restaurants and I would stand helpless and hopeless, waiting for someone to call out my name and give me a clue as to their general direction. Contact lenses are a wonderful thing and all that was behind me now because I could see again but the lingering fear of *'are they there and I don't know?'* remained.

This evening I was in luck, a choice of two. Standing by the speakers was Raymond making a half-hearted (and generous given the racket) attempt to dance. Jamie was with him which was good but then so was Nick Evans and I had just come out of a very short-lived relationship with him and although it was all very civilised and amicable, it is hard to make small talk with someone you've only stopped sleeping with four weeks before. My second choice looked much more appealing. The lovely great bulk of Sean Gummidge roaring with laughter at something whilst spilling Smithy's drink and laughing some more. The Wat Tyler clan always sat together, Gummidge was the only social animal of the three, in fact he was the most sociable animal in London. Smithy (guitar) was an animal psychologist from Reading University (hence the classic track on their first album, *Heavy Metal Vivisecter*) and Tuck worked for London Underground although no one knew exactly what he did. Smithy looked like a leprechaun, tiny with all-consuming beard and long frizzy hair. Years later hundreds of Smithy clones would be trying to chat up Philippa Forrester in Robot Wars but this was before their time. They were all school friends and it is amazing what the consequences can be of growing up in a place like Cheddington where the very dullness in the air acts as glue for unlikely bedfellows.

I loved the Wat Tyler boys. They didn't gig that often, they had to fit themselves around London Underground leave and experiments with mice but they were funny and they were clever and you could actually feel with them that you weren't completely wasting your entire life. Just for a moment at least.

I dragged over a stool and got the usual 'Hallo darling!' (Smithy), 'Alright gorgeous?' (Gummidge). Tucker didn't talk to girls. God knows what we talked about, that evening was one of literally two hundred or so a year exactly alike. The Astronauts screeched on, people duly clapped whenever they realised that one song had actually ended, people shouted to be heard and leaned in close with beery breath. It was a night like every other night I had had in six years or more. Some others joined us, it doesn't matter who. Jamie probably and Raymond (who at sixty-five could only dance for so long). Julie might have been there, gazing across the table at Jamie desperate to get him home and all to herself. Perhaps Emma was there but I doubt it. Em and I were not yet at the point where we could comfortably share a table, in fact we never would be again. Ben was not there that night which was good and lightened my spirits a little. We had split up a good year or so before but you know what that first gut-wrenching love does to your entire infrastructure. It's like a slipped disc; everyone's sympathetic for the first few weeks but the pain goes on and on and after a while you don't bother to mention it anymore because it's boring. You just limp a bit.

The conversation had turned to recording studios and I sat back. I was one of those lead singers who did themselves no favours whatsoever. I sang. I danced around a bit. I looked pretty enough in a mini-skirt and big boots but that was it. I played no instrument, I knew no chords, I wrote no songs. I didn't realise how precarious my position was, I should have realised that I was soon to be overtaken, eclipsed, by enterprising young women who actually took up guitars and learned to play them. I was foolishly content to have a group of young men around me to write the songs, arrange the recordings and then hand me the lyrics so that I could then take the accolades. I didn't care about mixing desks and how many tracks they had. I vaguely knew that a twenty four track studio was better than a sixteen and that the Lost Cherrees' first single had been done on a four track which was apparently laughable but that was about it. Girl power? No, as long as they knew my face when I walked into a bar, that was enough.

I started thinking about Ness.

The Docklands apartment had been so utterly devoid of humanity, that was what was niggling at me so very much, that was what would not allow me to let it lie. I sat in the grottiest pub in London and I was surrounded by humanity, absolutely overwhelmed by it, it spilt awash onto the filthy floors and rose up like miasma from a sewer. These people were a little grimy and they were wasting all sorts of natural gifts they had, underachieving because they couldn't get up before eleven in the morning but they were *alive* and they laughed and they loved their friends and covered their peeling, damp-sodden walls with pictures of bands and friends showing their arses to policemen and dogs and dogs and yet more dogs. You walked into any of these people's bedrooms (or toilet-cum-bedrooms) and you knew the essence of their humanity pretty well. I had never been to Pete Astronaut's squat in Hackney but I knew full well that no one had seen the floor in years, that there would record sleeves and clothes and mouldy pieces of food and incense sticks burning vainly in the darkness of a single bare bulb.

And Gummidge's room told me more about his life than any conversation you could ever have with him. Spotless and tidy, the entire space from ceiling to floor from wall to wall filled to capacity with neatly stacked records, all in alphabetical order. Then beneath the records, the boxes of fanzines and newspapers – every copy of Sounds since 1980, every copy of Viz since the very first issue and all in plastic folders. A single mattress with a grimy duvet and an ancient motheaten teddy bear sitting on the pillow. I knew the teddy was the one link he allowed himself with his mother who had died of breast cancer when he was just thirteen or so. Jamie's room was comfortable and full of warm coloured rugs. Al's had too many pretentious carvings and prints of obscure Mexican artists, Lucy's hung with wind chimes and dreamcatchers, Claire's stank of cannabis and there were far too many little plastic bags on the floor.

  We were none of us perfect, we had between us so many faults and insecurities that the future of Britain resting upon our shoulders looked pretty bleak. But it didn't, it rested upon the Armani clad shoulders of estate agents and men who owned surgically clean apartments with no photographs or hangings or pictures at all. A sudden surge of hope. Perhaps he wasn't like that at all. Perhaps he was so close to his family, his friends, his fiancé that when he went away, as he had, he took all his photographs with him. A little sad maybe but sad was better than brutally inhuman. I thought about this for a while as an inane conversation about the intelligence of mice raged around me. It didn't fit. The man who owned that flat was an anally retentive bastard and that was that. No one who chose grey and chrome as their bedroom colour scheme then packed up photographs of his gran so he could remember her from his beachside chalet in Mauritius.

'I am NOT a vivisecter!' Smithy was getting heated but he knew he was being wound up so it was still funny. 'I just design the mazes and the little experiments they have to do, I don't cut them up, I don't put stuff in their eyes…'

'Do you or do you not have a licence…' Gummidge was in full baiting mood. Everyone around the table had heard this argument twenty times before but it was always funny.

'Yes! Yes, you fat fucker, you know I do but that doesn't mean that I actually…'

'Do you have a license, an official licence, which gives you …YOU, Smithy of Wat Tyler, the official right to vivisect any animal…'

'You fat retarded lump of lard, I do NOT vivisect animals. I construct mazes and feeding trays operated by them moving their snouts up and down to see if they're intelligent enough to remember…'

Gummidge was on his feet now, spilling Ribena over Tuck who looked a little unhappy because he was wearing a white shirt.

'Are you or ARE YOU NOT, an official…an OFFICIAL vivisecter? Do you have a little piece of laminated paper which you pin to your white Nazi overalls which says you're a vivisecter? Answer the question, you bloody dwarf!'

Everyone was halfway to being pissed and loving this. Gummidge always put on a good show when he was tormenting either Smithy or Tuck. I laughed along with everyone else but my heart wasn't really in it. I wanted the evening to end so I could go home and talk to Cali.

Smithy was on his feet now, all five foot four of him. 'I'll have you, mate! I'll have you outside!'

'Vivisecter!' Gummidge was laughing so much the Ribena was dripping down his chin. Smithy took a deep breath.

'I have the licence but that's only because….listen, you bastards, it's only because I have the right to anaesthetise them. I don't ever do it but I can if I have to.'

'Mouse murderer.'

'Oh piss off, you fat git. At least I can play my bloody instrument. I could train one of my bloody mice to play drums better than you.'

It went on for a bit, alternatively getting funnier and then losing steam. Fortunately it was time for them to go on so the argument was put back into its box for later and they went to do all the sorts of things that musicians do before actually playing a gig, tuning up, I suppose, and setting levels and all the sorts of things I never had to worry about because I was always in the dressing room checking my hair.

A few people began to wander in from the bar. Wat Tyler had good nights and they had piss poor night and you never had any inkling which it might be. If they were in bad moods they let it show, there was none of this *'we're the band and people have paid to see us so let's smile and do our best'* rubbish. If they were in bad moods, they would grunt at each other, do the shortest set which still allowed them to get paid and then slope off. Fortunately for us, tonight was pretty good.

Most bands have a cohesive sound. What I mean by that is the different influences of the members tend to blend on each track so that all the songs have a similar feel. Blyth Power songs all sound pretty much the same because they're all written by the same person on the same instrument. Snuff songs have a common feel because the lads write together and have exactly the same influences. Wat Tyler songs however could originate on different planets.

Smithy writes heavy metal songs about Lord of the Rings and the art of the Absurd. For example, *Daughters of Albion, Father Abraham and the Little People, The Resurrected Little People Fight Back, The Resurrected Little People Kick Arse*. Great songs if you like long guitar solos. Tucker however likes football and pubs. He likes simple songs with strong bass lines and doesn't much care if there's any guitar or drums at all, witness *Hops and Barley, Bring Me the Head of Gus Caesar* and *Terry Fenwick's Leg Takes a Crack.* Gummidge however loves pop. He likes songs about relationships and being unhappy and taking the piss out of other people because it makes you feel slightly less unhappy. That night they began with their heavy metal version of the Rainbow theme tune followed by Smithy's impression of a perverted Father Abraham using the Smurfs to corrupt small children. People were laughing and calling out, the band were insulting each other's inability to play their instruments, Raymond began to dance to *There's a Guy Works down the Chip Shop Swears He's Satan.*

I was starting to loosen up a little. The nagging worry stemming from the photograph began to lessen. Someone bought me another pint of cider, they forgot the blackcurrant but I drank it anyway. Nick Evans managed a civilised five minutes of 'How are you? What have you been up to?' which was laboured but reasonably painless. Ten minutes went by without me thinking about Docklands and whether or not some crazy freak was going to try to kidnap my baby. Then a half-drunk insult called out from the back dragged me back down to my usual paranoid and self-obsessed self. I didn't need to turn round, I knew damned well who it was, but I turned anyway. Simon Wells, AKA Simon Snuff, AKA guitarist of the biggest band on the scene and *Band Most Likely To Actually Make A Living From It Award*.

 My heart did a sad, pathetic little flip, more out of habit than passion. It was long over between us but I was never very good at letting go. He was my Ben substitute, everybody knew it apart from Simon himself and this was because his ego was so incredibly large and impervious to anything requiring perception. I had first seen Snuff perhaps six months before that summer. Gummidge had burst into my bedroom telling me about this band that I simply had to see. Gummidge didn't often get excited about bands, he'd seen so many that jaded was simply too kind a word for how he felt towards most of them. But that night he was positively trembling. And he was right. Sean Gummidge is never wrong about music, he knows what works and he knows what stinks and he was right about Snuff.

 It was at the George Robey, funnily enough. Twenty or so people with Snuff on second. And they blew the shitty little crap-hole away. I had never heard a band so brimming over with energy and passion and anger, a band so loud and raucous and yet touching the heartstrings in a way which even now defies proper description. They had tunes and they sang about themselves and their girlfriends and their scooters. They sang backing vocals in tune and beat the shit out of *I think we're alone now* in a way that made you feel you had loved Tiffany's version all along. I was transfixed. By the music, by the harmonies, by the lyrics (which didn't mention nuclear war, Thatcher or Apartheid once) and by the guitarist. Oh yes, by the guitarist.

An early review in NME described Snuff as three pale, skinny North London lads who hadn't seen sun or a decent meal in years and it was true. Simon had a shaven head and cheek bones you could sharpen pencils on. White skin so unhealthy his eyes looked black and pointed ears like a goblin. He was thin and he was cocky and he didn't care what anyone thought. Neither Simon, Duncan or Andy had heard of Chumbawamba, they didn't give a shit about South Africa, they thought Thatcher was doing a good job and they couldn't understand why anyone should want to eat vegetables when the world was full of cows. We had never seen anything like them.

The icing on the cake for me was that in a dark room with your eyes squinted up, Simon did, in a way, look a little bit like Ben. Ben was taller and darker skinned but they both played guitar and I was desperate so that was that. I think they call it transference, when you offload all your emotions towards one person lock, stock and two smoking barrels onto a second. It didn't take long. Three songs and I was obsessed, and I always got what I wanted, always. I didn't ever get to hang on to it for very long but that was a lesson I was only just learning. Within a month I was his girlfriend and a regular in the Snuff minibus as they began to conquer the world; dingy clubs, then bigger pubs, then converted cinemas, then Europe. Of course he had dumped me before the American tour, my life was never going to get that good. It ended in tears for various dull, predicable reasons but I still harboured a tiny hope that we might still get back together. We had nothing in common, the sex had been dire and we had completely different ideas about life, the universe and everything but the bottom line was that I really didn't want to be on my own.

That night Simon was with Duncan his drummer who gave me a cheery wave and a 'Hallo, Auntie Siân.' Simon gave me a cheeky grin and I made sure I turned away before he did. Cheap shot but you have to score points when you're down. My mood had altered, I was depressed again. My life seemed pretty well disastrous and going nowhere. I was half a stone heavier than I wanted to be, my hair was ten shades darker than it should have been, I had a degree but no career, friends but no one to talk to and pretty soon it would be Sunday. The worst day of the week when I would lie all day in bed and panic that I had nothing to do and no one to do it with. I began to dread Sunday as early as Wednesday. Wat Tyler went into a really bad version of *Slaughter of the Little People* and I decided to go home.

The light was on under Cali's door. She was in bed but still reading so I sat on the edge. At that point in my life, Cali was the only genuine female friend I had ever had. All the other young women I called friends, I somehow envied in one way or another. Emma because she was skinny and blond, Julie because everyone thought she was perfect, Nat because she was so confident and aggressive she was downright scary. But I didn't envy Cali at all. And it wasn't one of those sad girlie relationships where one of the pair is so fat and ugly that the more attractive one feels safe through association. Cali is lovely. She's tall and slim with great bones and very short, sleek hair which always looks under control. At that time she had a good job in Hatton Garden and later she went on to do even greater things but none of this came between us. We had everything in common and we just liked each other. Simple. If it works, don't take it apart because it won't fit back together again or so Billy Bragg used to say.

I moaned a little about my night, she moaned about her Japanese client who had clearly wanted to sleep with her. Then I took a deep breath and told her about Docklands. She knew about my house-hunting, she was the only one who did and she'd have come with me if she hadn't had a real life to get on with. Then I told her about the bathroom and the photograph. My anxiety took me a little by surprise. I so wanted her to feel the same way about this, I couldn't bear it if she just shrugged it aside as a coincidence not worthy of my consideration. But she was Cali and she never let me down.

'My God, that's so strange. And it was definitely Ness?'

'Absolutely. I could see part of her lead, the tartan one, and I'm pretty sure you can just about see my leggings almost out of shot.'

'Which ones?'

This took me aback for a second as utterly irrelevant but then I caught on. 'They were these tight black ones I got from my sister, Marks and Sparks. I was into jogging, this was ages ago.'

'When?'

I thought hard. The problem with my lifestyle at that time was that I had had so many homes. Lancaster Gate with Ally and Vanessa, Uni halls, Forest Gate with Sam, East Ham with Richard... 'It was when I was living in Tennyson Avenue, East Ham. With Richard the motorbike courier. That's when I first got Ness from Battersea.'

'How long ago?'

'Err....three years, almost three years. August, 1986.'

We sat looking at each other. This strange shadowy man had had a photograph of my dog (and knee) in his possession and maybe on his shaving mirror for three years. Cal made a face.

'Very strange. And you don't remember meeting anyone when you were jogging, anyone who really liked Ness and made a fuss of her? Anyone she bit?'

This was so absurd we both laughed.

'No,' I shook my head in defeat, 'I only did it for a few weeks, maybe a month. You know what I'm like with exercise.'

She nodded in complete understanding, she was exactly the same.

'So what other explanations are there? It can't be that he fancied you because you're not really in it.'

'Apart from my knee.'

'Apart from your knee, which although cute...'

'Isn't that cute. Oh, I don't know. I keep telling myself to forget about it, that it doesn't mean anything. I keep trying to persuade myself that it wasn't Ness at all.'

But it was?'

'Oh yes, I'd know her anywhere, any bit of her. I could pick her tail out of a line up of a thousand, all wagging at the same time.'

'You're a freak. Well, then,' Cali yawned and pulled the quilt up to her chin, 'There's only one thing for it. You'll have to go back and ask him.'

I stared at her. 'Ask him? Ask him what?'

'Why he's got a picture of your dog on his mirror of course. You can be funny about it, you could even take her along with you to break the ice.'

I thought this over. 'I suppose I could…and if I had her with me, I should be safe enough. I know she's as soft as shite but no one else does and she does look pretty mean.'

'Exactly. And you never know, this bloke might be really good looking and rich and he'll take one look at you both and carry you away to his mansion in the countryside.'

'Well, you never know!' But I remembered the cold grey and chrome of the bedrooms, the lack of fuss and mess, the sterile air and I knew that whoever had taken that photograph was not the sort to whisk anyone off anywhere.

Chapter 3 – Me

The next day was Sunday which was a bad thing. I don't know if there's a technical term for a morbid fear of Sundays – Dimanchophobia or something – but it had crept up on me over the three or four preceding years. It's hard to understand now. When you work a full week and you spend your Saturdays washing school uniforms and shopping and doing the whole 'keeping the house and kids together' stuff, empty Sundays are a blessing. To actually lie in until half past eight, to potter about in dressing gowns, to have sandwiches in front of the EastEnders omnibus, to walk the dogs and gather up the remains of some last minute homeworks which should already have been done Friday night – Sundays are good. Sundays are for treats like going to the cinema or Pizza Hut, roast dinner if someone can be bothered to make it. The day stretches out long and fine even if it's raining and it's never long enough because Monday has such a long shadow her fingers reach backwards before she has even begun. But Sundays back in 1989, Sundays at Elm Park, they were different.

For a start, everyone else seemed to have something to do or else was perfectly content to lie in bed and do nothing. I would have loved to have just lain in bed until the next morning if I could have but I simply couldn't. If I slept much past midday then I got a headache and spent the day lethargic and miserable. And of course as soon as you accept that all you want to do is sleep, all the brain can do is wake early and start buzzing with unimportant crap which just won't go away. Jamie was like a cat and could sleep all day, his conscience clear. Claire was usually insensible on Sundays, due to the excesses of her night before, and only woke to roll another joint. Cali got up extra early and got the train to see her mother in some picturesque village outside of Banbury where the cottages were all made of mellow-yellow Cotswold stone and where the ancient church had seen Cal christened, would see her married and had a little plot all ready for her mortal remains under the yews.

     I could go home. I had a home, just like normal people. I could get the Tube down to Morden and the 154 bus to Sutton or to Wallington which is where my mother moved to after she and my father bowed to the inevitable and finally split up. I could take my dirty washing and my brave smile of 'everything's great and the job at the library's great and the PhD's going great' and then I could eat too much and sit around watching the EastEnders omnibus. My sister would say hallo and I would say hallo back and wish I was as slim and as tall and that would be the general limit of our conversation given the light years between us. My brother would never be there. His social life was a blur we never bothered to keep track of, months went by without us speaking one word, never through animosity – no one in my family argues – but simply through having very little in common save that complex whirl of DNA that bound us ever looser.

     That Sunday I decided not to go home. Which of course then gave me the same old depressing choices. There was Camden Market, terribly exciting when you're seventeen and new to the city but a monotonous blur of garishly coloured strangers if like me you had allowed yourself to become jaded. Camden Market always left me feeling emotionally lower than when I'd left the house. At the back of my mind were always the sad impossible hopes – firstly, that I'd meet a new man who would love me forever and whom I would be able to love back despite the unattractive fact that he loved me, secondly, that I'd bump into Simon Snuff who would instantly regret dumping me and beg me to come back (this one was totally interchangeable with me meeting Ben but as the break up with Ben was over a year ago now and extremely old news, Simon seemed marginally less unlikely). Thirdly, I could find some amazing size 10 outfit which despite me being a size 12 slash 14 would fit me and transform me into either a) Debbie Harry, b) Beatrice Dalle or c) Emma.

The reality of Camden Market on a Sunday was always the same. The long boring Northern Line followed by two hours of aimless wandering, desperately trying to find someone I knew, followed by the guilty wolfing down of lukewarm curry followed by a maple syrup pancake and then the last minute acquisition of a tiny, wispy piece of cloth masquerading as a skirt or top which I hadn't tried on first, would never subsequently wear and would never dare then take back.

I couldn't bear the weekly self-crucifixion that was Camden Market, not that Sunday. My other choices were limited. Proper hippies slept in late and then spent all afternoon preparing gargantuan delights from tofu and lentils. Or they paid well-timed visits to other hippy households doing the same, always confident in the alternative culture certainty that a lentil bake can be stretched to satisfy as many scrounging stomachs as are demanding it. I didn't dare go over the road to Number 91 because I didn't know them well enough even though the smells were usually both tantalising and terribly grown-up. The closest thing I had to hippy friends were the Jeffreys Road squatters. They were, now I look back with the advantage of retrospect, a very nice bunch. Four or five lads and one girl whose name I could never remember but whose main claim to fame was that the car doors of her Mini were held on to the main frame by virtue of rope. I knew them all but never comfortably so. They were Ben's friends. I knew them all through Ben and only through Ben, they were terribly right-on and sincere and vegan and politically correct and all the things I really wasn't very good at being. They made feel such a fraud, just walking in through the door put me on edge and I would either clam up and look superior and sulky or I would blurt out something brash and put my foot in it even before I'd reached the shiny-tiled kitchen. I had only ever eaten at Jeffreys Road whilst with Ben and had only ever been since when well protected by Gummidge and Jamie who couldn't for the life of them see what I was getting at.

'Jeffreys Road are really cool people.'
'Yes, I know.'
'So why won't you come to dinner, they won't mind.'
'They haven't invited me.'
'They haven't invited us either! We're scrounging 'cos there's nothing in the fucking fridge!'
'Yes but they like you.'

'They like you!'

'No, they don't. They think I'm a stuck up cow.'

Silence. *'Well, you could come anyway.'*

And so they would go and I would stay and hammer another nail into my own personal coffin of inter-squat relations.

I could have gone over to Nat and Stan's flat. Nat had a tongue like razor blades but she could be warm hearted and generous when the mood suited. Stan wasn't really a Stan, he was something dull like John or Mick or Dave but he was anointed Stan after turning up at some inter-house footie tournament wearing Stanley Matthews style shorts. Stan had what was officially acknowledged as The Best Job In The World. He worked for Greenpeace, earning good money and saving the planet in the process. It was everyone's dream to work for Greenpeace. None of us actually cared enough to offer up our considerable free time to do voluntary work of course but we all liked the idea of being paid lots to do it.

In the miserable aftermath of my break-up with Ben, I had tried to make amends with the cosmic Karma ruining my life by doing voluntary work for Lynx. Lynx was the anti-fur trade group responsible for some really good cinema ads in the 1980s (catwalk models spraying the audience with blood and guts etc). I spent three Saturday afternoons in their Covent Garden shop packing t-shirts into boxes and sticking labels on baseball caps. I was never allowed on the shop floor and appeasing my cosmic Karma was always going to run second place to trying to impress Ben who didn't even care and so I'm ashamed but not surprised to say that on my fourth Saturday I found something better to do. (Lynx collapsed a couple of years later after losing a libel court case which I've always thought was a huge shame because they had some excellent hooded sweatshirts which you could never then get anywhere else.)

Going to Nat and Stan's was out anyway because Nat was the sort of hostess who was only happy to see you if she'd invited you first. The main reason though was that Emma had recently moved in and she and I were not yet on speaking terms. Finding out that she had been sleeping with Ben was up until that point the single most traumatic event of my short life. I'd like to say that the horrible events of that summer to come completely blotted Emma and Ben from my mind forever as something utterly inconsequential and petty but…well, fifteen years later, some sad residue still clings on somewhere.

So, that particular Sunday I was my own worst enemy. I took Ness for a rather perfunctory walk in Brockwell Park, watched EastEnders, tried to ignore the sounds of Claire shagging someone in the room next door and made pathetic attempts to write. Gavin in the room above me then woke and decided to do some sawing. God knows what he was cutting into small pieces - animal, vegetable or mineral, it wasn't leaving his room alive – but it had the desired effect of really pissing me off and stifling the creative juices to the point where they refused even to seep.

As far as the rest of the world was concerned I was a part-time PhD student beavering away on my thesis *Social Conditions in Sixth Century France.* In reality though, the PhD had long been abandoned and I was writing a book, a great rollercoastering trilogy of kings and golden rings and tormented pagan druids being seduced by witch-queens. It was the story of the House of Merovech, sixth century kings of Gaul, and it was a cracking good plot with huge potential. The trouble was I could never get down to writing more than a side or so a week. Paupers dying of tuberculosis in garret attics at least have an incentive to finish the magnum opus before it finishes them but I was too complacent in my life, too comfortable to feel the sharp edge of angst driving me on. Desperate circumstances produce great works, you only need to look at the first and second Tracey Chapman albums. The first, written in times of poverty, abuse and discrimination, is a tortured scream of utter anguish, every miserable chord sneaking into your heart with the brilliance of someone who is not fucking around. One of the most incredible pieces of music ever, immune even to disastrous Boyzone covers later on, it swept the world and touched us all. She sold a million trillion, she became rich beyond her wildest imaginings, ergo she didn't have anything to bloody write about for the second album which is crap. Such is life. Despair at least has the compensation of genius, complacency breeds only a few dull lines forced from an unenthused pen on a Sunday afternoon.

That particular Sunday dragged on and on. By five o'clock I had written up some notes on hypocausts and Merovingian trading patterns which I hoped would give the book that touch of well-researched realism. Ness understood Sundays far better than me and was sleeping. Jamie was at Sean and Ben's in North Clapham, Cali was at her mum's, Claire was probably dead, Gavin had not yet emerged from the haunted pit that was his attic but had at least stopped the sawing. I had watched some crap Sunday evening telly, usually involving nurses or firemen or the 1950s in some combination or other. The phone had rung eight times but never for me. Such days I would have happily erased from my allotted seven a week. If it meant shortening my life by an entire seventh I would joyfully have done it just to lose that feeling of utter hopelessness that the bastards always gave me.

The next day I actually went to work. I had been working at the UCL library for four months now and had moved on from Phase One to Phase Two. Phase One is where you start a new job and you absolutely love it. You look forward to going in every morning, you're as high as a kite Sunday night, you know full well that this is the one job you'll stick at and which will develop and grow and expand until you can actually start using that magical word 'career'. I'd felt Phase One at HMV Oxford Circus and at Lynx, at King Henry's Feasting House and at UCL Library. But Phase Two is never far away. Phase Two lurks smugly just out of range so that your pathetic optimism can never quite reach far enough to blow it out of the water. Phase Two attacks and smothers you when you're sleeping, it gets you when you're simply not ready or prepared so you wake up one morning and you simply can't be arsed to go in.

UCL Library had me well into Phase Two.

It had sounded like my dream job on the surface. No, that's not entirely true, my dream job would be selling t-shirts on the Snuff tour of Japan whilst simultaneously losing a stone and being paid in sex with the guitarist. Whilst this option now seemed rather unlikely, it still held sway in some distant part of my sad imagination. Meanwhile, money had to be earned unless one was happy to survive on the pittance handed out by the Social and so when I came across a job going at my very own uni, the few drips of optimism left in my heart rose up to triumph as ever over reality and experience.

It was a job so dull, so incredibly dull that the days and hours slunk by leaving trails of slime. I had thought that being so close to students all day would be fun but I had forgotten how much I had hated them all whilst actually being one and now that I was year or two older, the chasm between us was intolerably wide.

Students are very easy to despise but they are also very easy to fear. Both of these reactions are based on the fundamental misconception that 1) students actually like themselves and 2) students actually believe the crap they come out with. From outside the group, a bunch of nineteen-year-old undergraduates is as impregnable, as unassailable as some US Navy Aircraft carrier. They are all gorgeous, they are all bright, they all have posh homes and horseshoe drives and younger brothers called Barnaby. They lie in dissolute splendour across sofas in bars and at parties spewing forth great gems of knowledge and perception about Thatcher's economics and the future of privatised industries. They snort and sniff and smoke various illegal substances with a tired languor, they have noisy but passionless sex in other people's bedrooms on top of other people's coats and they never clear up the beer they spill because that's what God made other people for.

Students fooled me for years. I went to some of their parties whilst pretending to be an average undergrad but the experience always turned me inside out with self-loathing. Why was I the only one above a size 10? Why did I not read a quality newspaper? Why did I not read any newspaper, even Socialist Worker? Why didn't my parents own shares? Why could I never pull any of these tanned, yawning gods? I never knew I was lower middle class until I mingled with students, I never cared I was lower middle class until one smooth cheeked, smug-as-shit git told me I should.

I have a searing memory – one of many – which still rears its mocking head, so many years later. My tutor at uni – a very nice man called Dr D'Avray who was the only person before Pete to encourage my writing – had invited all his undergraduates to a dinner party at his house in Islington. I had never been to a dinner party before, my friends did not have dining rooms or tables at which to be seated at. I arrived dressed like Cyndi Lauper and clutching a bottle of Pomagne because none of my friends drank wine either and I thought that Pomagne was wine because of the shape of the bottle. My tutor was incredibly kind, he was a true gentleman in every sense of the word. He took my coat, commented politely on my garish attire and nose rings, looked the Pomagne label up and down as if it was some undiscovered Chateau Neuf du Pape and said, even more kindly, that he had never tried it before but he was very much looking forward to doing so. I had absolutely no idea at that time that in fact Pomagne was a social gaffe. I didn't realise it until years and years later, long after I had fled London to the anonymity of the wild and I was watching an episode of *The Royle Family*. Denise was pregnant or getting married to Dave or something and Jim suggested that they pushed the boat out and sent Anthony off to buy a bottle of Pomagne. The BBC audience roared with laughter and the cold splash of sudden reality-check sent me back a decade into that Islington hallway and that kind man who only then did I realise was just being kind.

Back then students had me fooled. I thought they oozed confidence because of their accents and their beauty and their effortless conversation about things I could not reach. It is only when you look back with the perspective of ten years or more that you realise. I stood at parties wondering why I was the only one with problems, the only one who did not know who I was, the only one who would go home that night and cry a little. A decade on, you can watch them from that beautifully comfortable distance of another generation and you know with warm certainty that every person at every party you ever went to felt exactly the same as you.

UCL Library had me smothered by students all day long and it was horrible. Young pretty students, bored postgraduates, rugby playing medics who farted in the queue – every day whilst safe in Phase One, I woke up thinking 'This is it! Today some gorgeous bloke is going to walk in right up to the desk and take one look at me and that'll be it!' But it never happened.

UCL Library was like all libraries in the world; staffed by incompetent, browbreaten academic men and one witch at the top. Our particular witch was called Pauline and she didn't like me at all. She knew I was not there for the long haul, she knew the moment I walked in that I would up and leave for bluer skies, she knew it even before I slipped into Phase Two and knew it too. Perhaps she could have warned me not to waste my time but I think she enjoyed watching me become slowly more disillusioned as the cancer drew itself out.

That day I was even more useless than usual. Pauline shouted at me for bending the spine of a book the wrong way, accusing me of having no sense or respect. I ignored her and made up my mind to nick five quid out of the fines box later for my lunch. I got numerous ISBNs wrong and was taken off ordering to go and sit at the relatively harmless post of front desk where idiot postgrads wiped their hayfevered noses. That was the day, the very day that I slipped effortlessly and without a care into Phase Three and knew it was time to go.

Ness hated the Tube. She was brave enough on the platform and an angel on the actual train but she hated escalators, probably because I had to carry her and she was such a heavy, unwieldy thing that I always made a real mess of it. She suffered in loving silence and I still wonder how much I used to hurt her as I heaved her up onto my knee and then to my chest, her pathetic paws stuck upwards towards the harsh lights, devoid of all dignity, my living, breathing taxiderm doll.

Cali had suggested this, what I was about to do, this was her idea and now I was following it through but my resolution seeped away with every stop. It was summer time and a lovely evening when I finally coaxed Ness off the bus that had followed the Tube and walked the five hundred yards or so to the flat down by the river. I had left work early at three, claiming headache, and now it was gone six but still very warm. The apartment was on the seventh floor of a monolithic building, new just the year before. Nowadays, it no doubt has a security guard and special reception desk but back in 1989 wealth was admired and no one disturbed G8 summits by rudely reminding them about the poor.

Ness was hungry. We'd shared an Aero but that was half an hour ago. I looked up, trying to work out which of the enormous plates of glass was the window to the lounge I had admired just a few days before. I could work it out by counting the floors but the spreading sun glared across them all, orange and fire. Suddenly I felt both foolish and scared but also full of hope. There had to be a reason, a rational reason for this man having Ness on his mirror. Once he explained, perhaps then I could move on, go back to my friends, quit my job, sort myself out. I'm not sure why this had become something of a Rubicon for me, such a defining moment. We took the stairs because Ness didn't like lifts.

The apartments weren't numbered, this much I still remember because it was such an amusing conceit. The occupants simply called their flats 'First Floor' or 'The Seventh' or even 'Penthouse' which I suppose implied the entire floor of this monstrous monument to Thatcher and her children. I learned later that the architect had devised the levels so that the eighth floor was only two or three feet higher than the seventh and so on. Even more amazing, apparently the lifts were designed to take longer than they really needed between the fake floors so that nobody need know and the occupants could bask in their self-deluded splendour.

My apartment was the Seventh Floor. Its door was metal, chrome maybe, with a tacky geometric design running down the middle which reminded me of *Red Dwarf*. There was no doorbell, no letter box, no knocker, no glass and so we stood, bemused Ness and I, waiting for our presence to be communicated via some kind of cosmic osmosis. Then I remembered. Reaching out rather gingerly, I touched the BBC2 Special Effects Department design reject. *Heat reactive* the estate agent had said proudly like the tosser he had been. Somewhere beyond the door, an orchestral chime rang out, its echo booming gently and Ness pricked up her ears.

I remember feeling panic and excitement, realising suddenly that I hadn't bothered to change from my usual work clothes of sloppy miniskirt and Captain Scarlet t-shirt. The stupidity of the whole situation washed over me until I had no breath and was about to drown when the door opened.

He was not what I had expected. Tall, yes, designer label suit, yes. But he was still not what I'd expected. The man whose presence I had so clearly sensed in that antiseptic mausoleum would have worn such a suit with arrogant possession, he would have fitted its smooth corners as if it had been made for him and no one else. He could have slouched with casual and expensive drunkenness but the suit would still have betrayed his control, his never failing control. This man in front of me now merely inhabited his suit. It did not wear him, he did not own it, he was…he was *uncomfortable*.

This was a surprise. The man in front of me in the Armani was of average build and not especially good looking. His hair was pulled back into the requisite yuppy pony tail but it looked rented, like a tuxedo at a redneck wedding. His skin was reddish and unhappy with the sun we had been getting. He smiled uncertainly, showing oddly perfect teeth. He did not look like the man who could own this flat. But he did look like a man who could fall for a dog. I straightened my back, nudged Ness forward with my knee and prayed to the angels.

'Well, here she is!'

I had rehearsed this in my mind on the long journey east. His response would surely be one of the following; 1) embarrassed amusement that his youthful softheartedness had finally caught up with him and don't tell anyone on the Board because he'd be out on his ear if they thought him a softy etc etc but wasn't she a beautiful dog? 2) Embarrassed awkwardness because it had been me he'd been trying to photograph all along and he had long got over all that falling for weird looking women you don't know phase and could I go please because his fiancé was coming round at any moment? 3) Complete and defensive denial hinting at something dark and disturbing that I was better off not probing. If it turned out to be number 3, I was having someone round to fix our front door the very next day.

'I'm sorry?' He had very fair eyebrows which now creased closer together.

I tried again. 'Here she is! I thought you'd like to see her in the flesh again. You know, instead of in a photo…'

He stared as if I were from another planet or in need of serious help. 'Are you trying to sell something? I'm not interested but if you're collecting for some animal charity…'

Every instinct told me to cut my losses but the lower middle classes find it very, very difficult to walk out on opened conversations. This is why we're such an easy target for unsolicited phone calls selling car insurance.

'No, no, I'm not from a charity. I was here, a few days ago, to look at the flat. It's for sale, isn't it?'

His brow cleared a little. 'Oh. Right. You want another viewing. You're really supposed to arrange them through the estate agent, I shouldn't really show you round. I'm sure there's a no pets policy anyway, I'm afraid.'

I didn't have time for this dancing around.

'You have a picture of my dog on your shaving mirror. I just wanted to know why. I can't understand why you've got her on your mirror, that's all. That's all.'

The eyebrows came back in, this time for the duration. 'On my shaving mirror? I don't think so.'

'You have. I saw it.'

'I think you have the wrong apartment. I think I would know if I had a picture of a dog on my shaving mirror.'

It was hard to argue with this. Presumably he would know. I accepted defeat.

'Sorry. My mistake. Thanks.'

I turned to go, couldn't wait to get down the stairs and out of his sight fast enough. Ness pulled back slightly, she'd smelt something nice from within but I yanked at her with unfair force. We took the stairs two at a time, Ness loving the game, me holding my breath like an underwater swimmer caught beneath coral, desperate for the daylight. We met a couple at the entrance and Ness skidded on the polished marble flooring, her claws unable to grip so that she bumped against the woman's legs.

'Oh for *fuck's* sake!' The bitch looked as if I had held her down and injected her with AIDS. I extricated my baby and we pushed through the glass and bronze to be out, taking great gasps and not knowing whether to take the joke and laugh or succumb to temptation and cry. I sat down on the grass verge that pretended to be the communal gardens. Deep breaths, the sun on my face. It really was a beautiful evening…

'Excuse me…'

He had followed me down. The suit fitted him even worse in real light.

'Look. I'm sorry but it seems I owe you a bit of an apology. You see, it's not my flat, I'm sharing it with an old school friend until I find my own place and I use the main bathroom off the lounge and he's got the en suite. I've never even been in there.'

'Oh, I see.'

He smiled, as awkward as me. 'You were right. There is a picture of a dog. Looks just like this one.'

'It is this one. I could never make a mistake, I'd know her anywhere.'

He hunkered down and ruffled Ness's ears. 'I had a dog a bit like this once, half collie, half setter. Mad as a hatter. But she was my best friend for years.'

I refused to be sidetracked. 'So why does your flatmate have a picture of my dog on his mirror?'

He shrugged, a slight Thames breeze pulling away lank strands from the sad pony tail. I could see that he would have a riotous bald patch right on the crown in five years or less and probably not even know.

'I don't know. But I'll ask him when he gets back. He's in Berlin for a few more days.'

'Oh.'

Another awkward silence and not one of barely controlled attraction straining at the basque of propriety. It was simply awkward because we had nothing else to say.

'I'll come back then shall I? Next week?'

He stood up. 'If you like.'

He looked a little concerned as he took me in properly for the first time, took me in all my unkempt, dreadlocked glory.

'Perhaps if you give me a contact number, I can just let you know what it's all about. It's probably so simple, it's not worth coming back down. Marcus isn't the sort of person you want to bother if it's not important.'

'Right.'

In another world I might have convinced myself that this was an easily seen through ploy to get my phone number but it wasn't. It clearly wasn't. I wrote Elm Park's number on the back of a flier for a Trudy gig that weekend and he put it in his pocket. Another ruffle of Ness's ears and he was gone. Feeling a complete idiot, I promised Ness a portion of chips and vowed to forget the whole damned thing.

Chapter 4 – Sam

I put the antiseptic flat, the strangely wrong man and his school friend's obsession with my dog away in some corner of my mind to be taken out and dusted off when all the other crap had been dealt with. Other crap being handing in my notice officially at UCL (accepted with humiliating alacrity) and generally feeling that life was drifting along without me having much say or input as to where the Hell it was heading. My life at that time utterly revolved around going to gigs, fancying blokes at gigs, going to gigs with blokes, quickly and seamlessly followed by going to gigs to forget about blokes. Some people, I have heard, went to gigs solely for the music but not me.

My pocket diary for that summer didn't have many theatre bookings or art house films or dinner parties.

18th July; Victim's Family at The George Robey

19th July; Wat Tyler and The Trudy at Dingwalls

21st July; Conflict at The Fulham Greyhound or Perfect Daze at The Bull and Gate (Oh shit, a clash! What to do? But Conflict had had their day and there was always the chance that Simon Snuff would be at the Perfect Daze gig)

22nd July; Conflict at the Greyhound again **but….** Snuff at the Kilburn National (no contest)

23rd July; The Trudy at Brockwell Park festival

And so it went on as it had done since I'd first discovered the Indie scene at tender fourteen. How I managed A Levels and a degree is still a complete mystery to me.

Going to smoky pubs and chatting to people about bands and waiting for the bands to come on and then watching the band and going home talking about the next tired old merry-go-round the following night…It was all I had known for nearly ten years. I'd briefly tried a tremulous foray into student life but it hadn't suited and I'd soon scuttled back under the muddy rock that fitted me best.

Sometimes though there were bright spots and highlights.

Chumbawamba gigs were real occasions where every dried up old hippy and idealistic young socialist flocked together in one amorphous unwashed wave to pay homage to the Holy Ones but Chumbawamba gigs were rare in that they actually had real lives or so it was rumoured. They were a mystery to us, were the Chumbas. Intelligent and passionate and frighteningly focussed, they all lived together in a squatted commune in Armley, Leeds. They had stripped pine floor boards and eight foot high homemade beds which doubled as offices where they wrote poetry and pamphlets about Nicaragua. They had rotas for washing up and cooking and shopping and when they did their shopping they went on bikes to local shops which sold local produce made by local people. Chumbawamba pooled all their money into a pot on the mantelpiece and *each took accordingly to his or her need.* They played board games rather than watch telly and only the boys ever wore skirts.

I was absolutely terrified of them.

I was terrified because I was jealous, jealous of the relentless hold they had over the men that I loved. Ben, Jamie, Gummidge, they all swooned whenever Ann or Lou or Duncan or Danbert Nobacon (yes, he of the Prescott incident many years later) entered our lives. They all had very short hair and thin, wiry bodies clad in neutral combats and plain t-shirts. When you actually met them, they were - it pains me to say it – extremely nice and normal. But on stage……few bands can match up to Chumbawamba on stage.

I'd come across them in 1983 when my ragged little band, the Lost Cherrees, did a gig at some squatted factory in Nottingham and they were headlining. We were lacking in all things great, the Lost Cherrees, from imagination to musical ability, from talent to foresight. We played three chord thrash but only knew two chords. Our bass player tuned up the top string and just slid his thumb up and down the neck, after a while he didn't even bother with fitting the other three strings and gained a kind of incredulous notoriety from those who actually bothered to learn how to play their instruments. And anyway, the music wasn't all that important, it was the *lyrics*, the *lyrics* which defined the sort of band you were.

We knew what we had to sing about, there was an unwritten list you simply had to conform to if you were to play on the punk-indie circuit.

Firstly, you had to have at least two songs about nuclear war and the inevitable destruction of the world. It wasn't necessary to actually know anything about nuclear physics and reactors and Mutually Assured Destruction, you simply had to shout out about dying doves and the bleached bones of the billions dead etc etc.

Secondly, you had to have at least four songs about animals, preferably about the horrors of vivisection. No matter that the dye with which we all bleached our hair the night before had no doubt upset the eyes of quite a few unwilling bunnies, that was the fault of **The System** giving you no alternative (of course, there was the alternative of not actually dying your hair but that would have been silly). The Lost Cherrees wrote lots and lots of songs about the tortured animals in laboratories, I even joined Animal Aid and went on demos outside Porton Down Research Lab. We argued passionately that we would never inoculate our own children, we would prefer to see them die in agony than live with the blood of the innocents upon their consciences. We screamed tunelessly down the mike that we despised the good health and immunity our own childhood inoculations had given us, we swore as blind as those poor Draize-tested rabbits that if we were ever seriously ill, then we would surely refuse all treatment that had been perfected as a result of such Nazi torture. We were either sweet, annoying, naïve or bloody infuriating given your position and perspective.

Punk song lyric Number Three was to write about sexism and how women had been exploited by men since the dawn of time and essential Number Four was to write at least two songs about **The System,** fortunately without ever having to actually define it.

The Lost Cherrees actually did quite well given our sheer awfulness. Our second single reached the giddy heights of Number 3 in the Independent Charts which ironically would have meant so much more just five years later when the whole indie thing really took off until it became indistinguishable from mainstream. I still have that newspaper cutting though, putting my band ahead of The Smiths and The Cocteau Twins. We were reviewed a few times in Sounds, once even managing the compliment of having '*the only recognisable tune of the entire evening*' in Blasphemy, a song I wrote about the evils of organised religion. We probably did Blasphemy the night we supported Chumbawamba in Nottingham, screeching out our nonsense to a cacophony of badly played chords and out-of-time drums. The audience knew what to expect with us and bands like us, we were nothing new, nothing old, we'd go a little way, we'd run out of steam and decompose in our own shit. But Chumbawamba were different, the Chumbas could play, the Chumbas used recorders and flutes and trumpets, the Chumbas read out poetry and pieces from Marx and Bentham, they dressed up and hung a washing line across the stage with strange yet prophetic messages hanging from clothes pegs. That night, Danbert stripped down to his underpants whilst Ann wrote something no doubt hugely profound in lipstick on his chest. We thought they were pretentious crap. Time would prove us horrifically wrong.

      That summer though there were no Chumbawamba extravaganzas, not even many Snuff gigs which were the nearest you could get for energy and a sense of occasion. August loomed and August was the Sunday of the year, no bands played in August, they went away with their mums and dads. I hated August.

A week or so after my visit to Docklands, there was a Wat Tyler gig at Dingwalls. Dingwalls was in the heart of Camden Market and bands we knew didn't get to play there very often because it was quite clean and the manager liked it kept that way. There was an unofficial list of bands who simply never got asked because they weren't worth the trouble of clearing up afterwards but somehow Wat Tyler had managed to tag onto the end of a Trudy gig. The Trudy were very Dingwalls, very Camden Market. They dressed up like Thunderbirds and did a five minute version of the theme tune to Captain Scarlet and were quite fun but a bit dull after they'd finished the Captain Scarlet bit which was their only decent song. I went along that night with Emma and Jamie which of course meant an *atmosphere* all the way there.

Jamie had loved Emma but had not loved her enough. Jamie had moved to London to be free of Emma but to show her love, Emma had followed. Jamie had fallen, briefly, in love with me. I did not fall in love with Jamie back because I thought he was a girl. Emma became best friends with me because it was the easiest way to get close to Jamie. Jamie ergo resented Emma, Emma ergo resented me, I actually liked both of them until I discovered Emma in bed with Ben. Ergo I hated Emma. Unfortunately up until a few months before, we had all been living together under the same roof which had been an informative period in all our lives. That Tube ride to Camden was probably quite quiet. I can't remember.

Wat Tyler were crap that night. They'd had a row during the sound check and were splitting up after the gig (they did this quite often) and the crowd which had come to see The Trudy were mostly students with their heads up their own backsides and simply could not appreciate Tyler's football terrace humour. Faced with an unappreciative crowd, Wat Tyler never did the decent thing and braved up to their duty and obligations, putting on a good show and all that. No, they simply retreated into their own little spaces, ignored each other and ignored the wankers who had paid good money to see them. Me, Jamie and Emma didn't mind. We'd been there before and we knew Gummidge would still love us in the morning.

'Fancy a drink?' Jamie was usually skint but he'd got some backdated dole the day before and we had been on the guest list so I nodded.

'Cider and black, please.'

Emma had left us to go and talk to someone more interesting and less likely to either punch her or make her cry. I looked around as there was nothing worse than standing on my own, even if it was only for the five minutes or so it might take Jamie to get me a drink. The trouble with places like Dingwalls was that lots of people I knew didn't bother going because they knew they couldn't blag their way in at the door. Dingwalls was a proper venue run by grown ups who didn't fuck around, you couldn't just lean over some poor seventeen year old sitting at a table with some rubber stamp in his hand and a Tupperware box full of change and tell him you'd be back with his £1.50 in a minute. Dingwalls had bouncers behind grills and it was more likely to be three quid which in those days was bloody extortionate.

    I knew the guitarist of The Trudy who was standing a few feet away but not well enough to have a conversation I could be bothered to sustain above the row of Wat Tyler murdering *Sweet Child O Mine* so I smiled but not over-invitingly so. Raymond was over at the bar chatting to Jamie but Raymond, although adorable, could be exhausting. He was sixty-five at least by this time, a tiny man always in black with his trademark black beret that he only ever removed when wiping the sweat from his pate as he danced. The little I knew about his background (shamefully scarce considering I had known him since I was fifteen) was that he had been a Benedictine monk in Rumania but had been forced to leave by the Communists in the 1950s. He had fled as a refugee to London where he worked as a sewing machinist in the East End. Now he was retired and spent his time going to punk gigs which for some unfathomable reason he adored.

    Ray and I had met back in1983 when the Lost Cherrees were starting out on the gig circuit. I had had scarlet hair back then and wore a silver ankh around my neck because I had had a thing about Toyah Willcox. Raymond was her biggest fan so he started following us around. He was one of the most generous people I had ever met. He always bought drinks, he paid for scrounging punks with tenners in their back pockets to get into gigs, he came round to squats on Sunday mornings with food hampers, he let anyone and everyone stay at his flat and had consequently had his stuff ripped off so many times, he had nothing left to steal. Rumour had it that one sixteen year old pretty boy who had stayed at Raymond's flat at about this time then went on to front a mega huge boy band but enough of such libellous talk…..

Raymond had come to us at Elm Park for Christmas that year, he'd arrived with a big Tesco's box full of food in his arms. He sat on the sofa, very small and old and after a while he had cried a little. He'd cried about his country which none of us could even find on a map, he'd cried about his mother who had died without him ever seeing her again. He wished he could go home, he wished that his country were free, he wished the bastard Ceaucescus would die and leave his beloved Rumania the way it had been….We really didn't have a clue. We made comforting noises whilst wondering whether the oven needed turning up, we nodded and gave him the occasional hug and told him everything was going to be alright. We didn't know anything about Ceaucescu, we didn't understand what was happening in any country but our own, we didn't know why Raymond wanted some dictator and his wife strung up from a lamppost. And so as soon as we could, we turned the conversation around to food and EastEnders and up-and-coming gigs and Raymond had sat back into the sagging sofa and had got drunk. I remembered Ray the Christmas following, I thought of him as I sat in some cheap bedsit far away from London watching a flickering TV showing me a dictator and his wife strung up from a lamppost. We were so ignorant and self-obsessed back then, we saw so little of anything that wasn't our own reflection and sometimes I wish I could go back in time and give myself a really good slap.

Too late. Raymond had seen me and was doing his little arms in the air like a Scottish reel jig. His catch phrase was *'We love you, we luuurve you!'* whether it be to genuine friends or uncaring bands making a racket on stage and this is what I could hear floating in my direction across the heads of oblivious students. When 'Toyah!' was added I knew I would be the biggest bitch in the world if I ignored him so over I went.

'Hallo darling!' You had to hug and kiss Raymond whenever you saw him, it was that sort of hug you gave an aunt. 'How are you?'

Raymond shrugged painfully, momentarily stopping the jig. 'The bastards. They stop my rent. I tell them I am pensioner but they stop my rent.'

He spoke English pretty well but the Mittel European accent was still thick. Raymond usually had problems with either Social Services or with his health and as we rarely had problems with either, we gave his complaints scant attention beyond the sympathetic noises required.

'Bastards.' I agreed, 'Have you been to see them?'

'I wait three hours. They tell me nothing, nothing. They are bastards.'

'Don't worry, Ray, they'll sort it out. You have to keep going in, make a nuisance of yourself.'

He smiled gratefully as if I had offered him the contents of my bank account. Wat Tyler finished their deliberate slaughtering of Guns 'n' Roses and Raymond turned to cheer and jig anew. 'We love you! We lurrve you!' But the band were too deep in their own self-pity to notice an elderly refugee with Social Security problems and did not look up from the instruments they were taking it out on. A really fast version of the usually jolly *Hops and Barley* growled across the venue towards the bar. Raymond pulled at my arm.

'I send Sean! I send Sean Gummidge and the boys, they sort out the bastards!'

Jamie and I gave over-the-top laughs. 'You do that. You'll get all your rent back-dated ten times over!'

'What?'

That was the trouble with Raymond. You could have a pretty good conversation with him outside a gig hall or in the garden of a pub but once you were inside and the band was on, you never knew which bit of the conversation he wouldn't catch and would want repeating.

I shook my head. 'Doesn't matter, Ray.'

He smiled kindly as if at some poor benighted orphan and then his pale, lined face lit up with another joke.

'I send Toyah, my lovely Toyah. She will tell the bastards to give me my bastard money.'

'There you go, Siân,' Jamie grinned passing me my pint. 'Tomorrow morning first thing.'

I raised my eyes in mock appreciation, it was too noisy to explain to Jamie that Raymond had probably meant the real Toyah. He knew her from the late seventies apparently although I never managed to fathom whether they were casual nodding acquaintances or 'Come round my house and have a cup of tea' pals. I hope, I really sincerely hope, that it had been the latter. Raymond's life had been full of so much grey, so much drudgery.... he lived in a council flat in an anonymous block in North London somewhere and when there weren't any gigs I think he sat on some damp-soaked sofa and got drunk whilst *Ieya* crackled out from cheap second hand speakers. I like to think that he had known someone like Toyah Willcox and that she had given him time and a little bit of wild, golden attention to brighten up the grey days.

'We love you, Raymond!' said some spotty oik passing by. Raymond waved, always available, never in a mood, always ready to put someone else first. I took advantage of the distraction and moved next to Jamie.

'Alright, darling?'

He gave me a little hug and kiss on the cheek which smelt of lager and patchouli. There was not a whiff of *eros* about it now, we had sailed safely into the dull but more comfortable harbour of *philos* and about time too.

'Fine, fine.'

He leaned closer. 'I think you've pulled.'

Even lightning and instinctive reactions are complex things. Whenever anybody hinted that I might just be the recipient of some poor deluded git's lust, I could never just be happy or sweetly surprised or complacent and smug. There would be a millisecond flash of unbelieving joy, followed by suspicion, followed by a vain attempt to erect a wall of pride, followed by an equally vain attempt to appear vaguely interested and yet not so.

'Oh? Really? Which blind fool is this then? Did they let his guide dog in?' Meanwhile my head was doing a slow *Oh, I really can't be arsed with this moving business* sort of turn (nonchalant, I think they call it but whatever it's called, I couldn't do it) around the room. My heartbeat would have caught me out but fortunately and thanks be to God, heartbeats don't register on faces. Jamie pulled me a little closer. This was nice because Jamie was nice but the selfish cow inside me shouting '*Not too close, you idiot, he might think we're together!*' was definitely alive and well.

'About three people behind you at the bar. Danielle Dax t-shirt.'

Turning round there and then was of course a no-no. Too obvious. It was a case of turning ninety degrees to the bar and then wondering how to turn the other ninety without catching whoever it was's eye.

'I don't know anyone who would wear a Danielle Dax t-shirt.' I spoke discreetly to my cider which in retrospect wasn't really necessary.

'Martin likes Danielle Dax.'

'It's not Martin? Bloody Hell, Jamie.' Martin was Nat's ex and still wore the brand on his upper arm.

Jamie snorted. 'Of course, it's not Martin, you plum. I was merely pointing out that wearing a Danielle Dax t-shirt does not necessarily make you some kind of non-person from another planet, man.'

'I know that.'

I still couldn't turn my head and anyway there was a really big girl next to me ordering three pints of lager and smelling of unwashed armpits. She kept prodding her elbows into my shoulder and ignoring my smiles of *'I'm apologising but we both know it's you, don't we?'*

'What's he look like?'

'Dunno, man. Blondish. Long hair. Not bad looking.'

'Not fat?'

'Not fat.'

'I don't like blond men. I don't think I've ever been out with a blond man.'

'Nope, they're all dark with stupid cheekbones and always leave you and act like bastards.'

'Right. Point taken. Can you still see him?'

Jamie did a quite unnecessary recce as I cringed. At the same second, the giantess next to me moved away with one last prod for good measure and there was a huge space and nothing to fill it between me and a tallish figure I didn't dare look around at.

'He's definitely looking at you,' Jamie was really making no effort to pretend now and to my horror actually raised his glass to whoever it was.

'You complete bastard, James, what the fuck are you…'

'He's coming, see you later. *Don't start talking about Ben.*' And Jamie was gone with one last whiff of girlie smells and woolly jumpers. I took a gulp of cider and in an attempt not to smudge my lipstick accidentally allowed a goodly portion to dribble down my chin.

'Hi. We meet again.'

It was him. The strangely wrong man from the horribly anal apartment. My heart simultaneously fell in disappointment and gently rolled around in relief. Disappointment because this wasn't a potential Mr Forever-and-Ever after all but relief because I'm never as miserable as when I think I've met Mr Forever-and-Ever anyway. This man clearly wasn't a potential Mr Anything so I didn't mind the dribble too much even though it was bright pink.

'Hi. Mr Dog-photo. No suit?'

He looked different without the cardboard Armani. Just jeans and the Danielle Dax t-shirt and his hair still tied back but not looking quite so yuppyish now. More Status Quo than Stockbroker Wanker. He smiled. Again, those nice white teeth.

'Not my dog-photo. My flat-mate's the weirdo obsessive, not me.'

This was worrying. 'He's a weirdo obsessive?'

He looked a little guilty, as if betraying a friendship. 'Not really, I was joking. At least, he is obsessive about some things, you know, the washing up and taking your shoes off before you come in and using coasters, that sort of thing. But not about big hairy dogs, not as far as I know anyway and I know him pretty well.'

'Right,' I was tempted to ask him what a coaster was but wisely resisted the diversion. 'So. This friend of yours, what's his name again? Mark?'

'Marcus.'

'So this Marcus, has he got back from wherever it was yet?'

'Few days ago. Made loads of money sitting on some committee in Berlin helping the commies set up links with London. He works in the City. Clever bastard with numbers.'

I was again momentarily diverted. Firstly I wanted to tell him that I had just got back from Europe and had nearly been to Berlin but the bloody Inter-Rail ticket didn't take you across the Iron Curtain even though Snuff had got bloody visas and had left me behind in Hamburg….but this wasn't the right time or even remotely the right person. Secondly, I wanted to hear him say 'bastard' again because there was something really odd about the way he said it and then the penny dropped….My friends say 'bastard' all the time and it's just a natural part of our everyday language and usually just implies a moderate annoyance. Then there are people who say 'bastard' because they want to look hard and tough but who never quite manage to pull it off and look like idiots. And then there were people who said 'bastard' with a casual, almost arrogant laziness which reeked, absolutely reeked, of public school and privilege. This was definitely a case of the latter.

But Ness was more important than investigating my new friend's social status.

'So, did you ask him about the photo then?'

My new friend raised his eyebrows and tried to look excitingly mysterious. It didn't quite work but I got the idea.

'Come on, just tell me. Is he going to break into my house in the middle of the night and steal her for laboratory experiments or what?'

'Well, it was a bit odd actually. Oh, do you want a drink by the way?'

'Ahmm, yeah, sure, cider with black please.'

He leaned over a little bit and waved a twenty pound note in the air quite casually and the barman came immediately which was really odd because there were at least five people shouting for drinks along the bar. It was like being with a grown-up, one of your Dad's work colleagues who was in his fifties and knew what he wanted and didn't have time to wait nicely at the bar because he had a big Merc outside. When he'd been served and we had waited in awkward silence, we tried again.

'Well, Marcus was in a shitty mood when he got home because his flight had been cancelled and he'd had to get an AeroFlot from Berlin to Paris and apparently they're an unbelievably bad service and he hates that sort of thing. So I didn't ask him until he got home from work the next day and then he denied it anyway.'

'Denied what?'

'Well, firstly that he knew anything about any photo which is strange because Marcus doesn't lie. Well, obviously he lies to clients and to other stockbrokers because that's what they all do but he never lies normally because he can't be bothered and it's beneath him.'

'Nice bloke.'

'Oh, don't get me wrong, he can be, he can be really nice. Anyway, when I went on at him, he admitted it.'

'What?'

The not-quite-yuppy grinned as if revealing some winning card. 'That he'd had a bit of a thing about the dog's owner.'

'Oh.' This was good. In theory, this was very good, that some complete stranger had become so besotted by my charms that he kept a picture of my dog (and knee) on his shaving mirror. But it just didn't ring true. Men didn't feel that way about me, not men like this Marcus anyway. If he'd been very drunk and seen me on stage at one of Blyth Power's better gigs then *perhaps*....but jogging around East Ham Park in my sister's leggings?......It was less than unlikely, it was damned near impossible.

I gave him what I thought might be a modest grin. 'It's very sweet of you to say so but it doesn't seem....well, in keeping, does it?'

'With?'

'Well...' I struggled for the words which wouldn't insult him as well. 'The flat is very...well, yuppy although I don't usually use words like that but you know what I mean. And the décor was… well, a little stark and I'm….well, I'm not.'

He laughed. 'No, no, you're not! You're very colourful!'

He sounded like one of my dad's friends again so I gave him the smile I reserved for my dad's friends who were all about fifty.

'But really….I don't know your name…'

'Sam, Sam Witherspoon.'

'Right.' The automatic inclusion of a surname shook my balance a little as no one I knew ever did that sort of thing but it didn't really matter. I thought perhaps that people in the kind of circles that this man and his friend moved in probably did the exchange of surname thing. Surnames no doubt linked you with Daddy's firm or the elder brother who had been at Rugby before you. The poor sod had probably been known as Witherspoon Junior for the first eighteen years of his life.

'Look, Sam. Your friend seems to me to have very particular tastes. He likes expensive things and labels and is a bit of a minimalist and in my experience people like that don't find punky hippy squatters with dreads and pierced noses interesting.'

He gave a real schoolboy laugh. 'You live in a squat? How excellent!'

Oh beJaysus, I thought, *Where the hell is Jamie?* 'So, Sam, has Marcus never said anything about me before then?'

Sam shook his head. 'Nope. I've known Marcus since we were both eight and he's never got serious about a woman. He goes out with lots of different women, mostly the sisters of people at work, I suppose you'd call him a serial dater...'

*Oh no, that's not **exactly** what I'd call him,* I thought venomously.

'But none of his girlfriends seem to last more than a month. He gets bored very easily.'

'But he hasn't got bored of my picture? Well, Ness's picture. Do you think it's Ness he wants?'

This amused him quite a lot. 'No, no, Marcus doesn't like animals much, at least not unless he's hunting....' Sam checked himself for a second and flushed, seeming to suddenly remember where he was. Before I could open my mouth to demand further details about this pink-clad, murdering, fascist hunter of a flat-mate of his, he went on.

'He was really rather cagey about the whole thing, touchy even. Told me to bloody well mind my own business. Then he calmed down a little and said he used to watch some woman jogging with her dog a few years ago and she was different from all the other girls he'd known and he used to wonder what it might be like to actually meet someone like that.'

'Someone like that? Someone like what?'

'Well, someone like you.'

'And what am I like?' I wasn't cross just curious. He shrugged, awkward and frightened of offending me.

'Well…not bothering about what people think. Not caring about the things that matter like money and a decent future. Living for today and wasting tomorrow. Not dressing like everyone else, not being bothered about getting served in decent restaurants….'

'Oh,' I pondered this for a while as he nervously sipped at his pint, clearly worried that he was going to get the remains of mine all over his trendy student t-shirt. What he said was pretty accurate when all was said and done but I wasn't altogether comfortable with the repetition of 'not being bothered'. We were bothered about all sorts of things, weren't we? We cared about animals and vivisection labs and nuclear warheads being kept on British soil and Apartheid and things. Not bothered enough to actually do much about any of it but we were bothered.

I clearly wasn't going to throw anything at him so Sam relaxed and tried to make amends. 'I think Marcus just wonders what it might be like to be free for a while.'

'Why isn't he free? Isn't wealth supposed to make you free?'

He suddenly looked quite old, thirty at least. 'You'd think so. I grew up surrounded by wealthy people but most of them were bloody miserable most of the time. I don't know about Marcus, he's always seemed OK with the City life but you never know… I would never have put him down as a man who'd have a photo of a dog on his shaving mirror so I'm thinking I don't know him as well as I thought I did.'

'Well, you never ever really know someone.' Things were looking up. It was possible, just faintly possible, that this yuppy anal retentive wasn't really anally retentive at all, he had just been so repressed by family and public school all his life that he had never learned to express himself in any other way. (I had already erased the word 'hunting' from my memory as far too inconvenient to have to accommodate.) This Marcus was trapped, trapped by money and some flashy City job and parental expectations but all he really wanted was to pack an old rucksack and set off around Thailand. I had a truly brilliant capacity for self-deception and it was in full overdrive now.

'So, Sam. What now?'

Sam finished his drink. 'You two should meet. I've been trying to rescue the best of Marcus from the worst of Marcus for twenty years now…'

A shrill female voice echoed out and there was a smattering of cheers and a general movement from the bar towards the stage. The Trudy were coming on in all their 1960s kitsch. Sam sensed my inattention.

'Look, I've still got your number, I'll sort something out and ring you,' He fluttered the well creased copy of the flier I'd given him at Docklands, the flier for this gig. I wondered why he'd bothered coming, he could have rung me. But then there was the Danielle Dax t-shirt which was a little bit alternative so perhaps he'd wanted to come anyway, perhaps here was another stockbroker casualty wanting to be rescued.

'Does he know you've come here tonight?'

Sam pursed up his mouth to one side. 'No. No, he wouldn't have appreciated it. He doesn't like it when he thinks he's being manipulated. I'll think of some way to get you both in the same place without him knowing. Then we'll see if he remembers you.'

'OK, give us a ring then.' It wasn't appropriate to hug or kiss this man I hardly knew and I simply didn't do the shaking hands thing so I smiled and thanked him for the drink, walking away quickly back into the midst of people who didn't make me feel as if I couldn't bend properly. I watched the gig but I didn't dance and when Gummidge stomped past, growling that he was leaving early, I took the opportunity to get the Tube with him. We didn't talk the whole way back from Camden to Stockwell where I left him to get the Victoria Line to Brixton but it was a companionable silence and I got to rest my head on his shoulder.

Chapter 5 – Cali

Well, I had it bad now.

I had it so bad that I found it hard to sleep without an hour at least of imagining just how handsome, just how rich and most importantly, just how *in need of me* this Marcus really was. (I didn't like the name. Marcuses didn't live in my world and even though it was actually a world I was quite keen to exit myself, I still didn't want to emigrate to a world where Marcuses were cool. Perhaps he had a decent middle name, perhaps that could be my first life-changing suggestion for him.) Ness benefited over the next few days from some very long walks around the park where I could daydream in peace. At night I would tell her my thoughts and ask her hers as she licked Dairy Milk from my fingers. It didn't help that I was now out of work. The summer days were just so long and without any discernible point; I got up simply to avoid lying down. Sometimes I wondered why I actually bothered to get dressed at all and the nadir came inevitably when one day I didn't even bother to do that. It was different for the others, they embraced their inactivity as an intrinsic part of their anti-capitalist lives and ironically often had more spirit and energy than I did because they were not fighting guilty consciences. Jamie would have been quite happy to stay in bed all day because he could write songs supine as well as vertical. Claire lay in bed because her dope-ridden system warned her not to do anything else for fear of never coming back down again and Al laid in bed because he liked sleeping. I laid in bed, guilty and conscience stricken that I was wasting my life away, that I was letting down the parents who had passed on some reasonably superior DNA, that I was admitting in some subconscious, clandestine way that I was never going to make it as a writer just as I hadn't made it as a singer.

      That last was the worst. I had begun singing for the Lost Cherrees at fourteen and had for the next seven, nearly eight years been in one band or another. Standing there and saying 'Good evening!' to Leamington Spa or Newcastle or Stoke Newington, even if it was to ten rather bemused and bored punters was better than not being on any stage at all. And there was more to it than grotty gigs in shitty venues. The bands I had sung for actually put out singles and twelve inches and amazingly even albums. Every now and again we did interviews with Sounds and once I even grinned from the illustrious pages of NME which was usually too highbrow to deal with crap. The Lost Cherrees played the Electric Ballroom, Blyth Power played Camden Palace just a few weeks after Madonna. I would go on tour and sit in the back of Protag's van singing with my lads and sharing sweets and taking the piss out of Gummidge who would be moaning before the M1. Sean Gummidge and I were never in a band together but somehow he managed to cadge his way onto every decent tour when we were supporting someone he did like. Amsterdam, Utrecht, Berlin, Prague, Munich; he never lifted one amp or guitar, he didn't help fetch fuzz boxes or leads, he told us we were crap when we were crap and alright when we were good, he moaned about the free food, the sleeping arrangements and the tapes playing in the van but still, every tour, there he was with his filthy sleeping bag and his great big grin.

Looking back now, I did enjoy life but not so much that I wasn't needlessly miserable for most of it. If some sharp cheek boned idiot was paying me some attention, then I was happy, happy and generous and probably quite decent company. But when the chisel featured lad had gone on his inevitable way, then I was paranoid, depressed and self-obsessed and I don't wonder that people then left me well alone. It wasn't that I didn't get asked out by decent men because occasionally I did. Obviously, these decent men didn't know me very well or they wouldn't have bothered but it did occasionally happen and then, of course, I would turn them down for various spurious reasons. And then – inevitably – I would get a dose of Gummidge's *The Si Flowers Lectures, 1984 – 1989* which ran roughly as follows;

Gum : So, you turned down Martin / Ryan / Andy / Stephen / whichever nice bloke (just insert name) ?

Me : Yup, certainly did.

Gum : Even though he's a really good bloke?

Me : Even though. Weird that, isn't it?

Gum : You know what that makes you?

Me : Aaah, let me see now….a fool? Or perhaps even…yes, I've got it!....a *tool!*

Gum : Mock me, Welsh girl but who's crying into her Dairy Milk tonight?

Me : Perhaps I like crying.

Gum : Then you ARE a tool.

Me : Uh oh, here it comes.

Gum : What?

Me : It's coming, it's definitely on its way, nearly up the path, nearly at the door…

Gum : Don't know what you're blathering on about. You know, this is Si Flowers all over again…

Me : And there she blows! It's the *Si Flowers Lecture*!

Gum : Well? You were the biggest fool ever. You so missed out there.

Me : Probably did. Tell me why. Oh, you are.

Gum : He was a good looking bloke.

Me : Yup, no doubting that.

Gum : In a band.

Me : Also no denying that Si Flowers was, indeed, in a band.

Gum : Funny and clever. Loads cleverer than most people we hang round with.

Me : Also undeniable.

Gum : And now gonna be a lawyer. With loads of dosh and women all over him.

Me : Lucky guy.

Gum : And who did you go out with instead of Si Flowers?

Me : We both know perfectly well who I went out with instead of Si Flowers.

Gum : Wasn't it…Dick Dirt? *Dick Dirt?*

Me : Hey, you know what, I really think it might have been. Hey, I'm a fuck-head, I'm a fuck-head, I'm a fuck-head. Lecture over?

Gum : For now. Lecture over, for now.

Cali worked full time so I counted the minutes until she came home at six but sometimes she was entertaining clients and would be late. The phone went occasionally but it would be a constant stream of orders for Claire or the steady stream of vaguely worried parents for the rest of us. Sam did not ring, not for what seemed an age anyway.

'I never expected him to ring,' I fibbed one night a week or so after the Trudy gig, 'For a start, this Marcus bloke took that photo years ago so why on earth should he be interested in seeing me again?'

'Well,' yawned Cal who, unlike me, did have to get up in the morning, 'He would have taken the picture down.'

'Maybe he has these obsessive habits. You know, you get these people who have to wash their hands every time they touch a...a spanner or something and people who have to…'

'A spanner! Why a spanner?'

'You know! People get obsessions with anything. They have to lick envelopes three times or they can't post the letter or they have to take three tugs to pull the curtains closed or else it's bad luck and if it takes three tugs and they're not quite closed, then tough, they have to stay like that all night.'

She gave me a look. 'And you think he might be like that? And you still want to meet him and have his children?'

'It was just an explanation for the photograph. It might have meant something to him once but now it's just something he's held onto for so long he feels bad every time he tries to chuck it out.'

'Like the spanner?'

'Just like the spanner. Cow. Give us another piece.'

The chocolate was duly passed over and we sucked or bit according to how we felt about chocolate in silence for a while. I always bit chocolate because I felt that it was as much the texture and hardness of a bar that made it what it was as the actual taste. I have tried sucking and I admit it lasts longer but I do find that you lose that sense of...*chunk* which makes a bar of chocolate what it is. Cali sucked but then she had a proper job and ideas about her future and didn't need to think quite so much about other things.

'Oh, your mum rang,' I wished I'd mentioned this before when she first came home an hour ago but I hadn't and it was too late now. She looked a little concerned.

'What did she sound like?'

'Bright. Breezy. Cheerful.'

'Shit.'

I gave a pursed up grin of what I hoped was companionable understanding. I was dead lucky in my own personal family break up. My parents had simply decided that they would be happier living on their own and that there were no hard feelings or angry grudges and that Christmasses and birthdays would still be the same and were we all OK with that? And they kept their word and even now, so many years later, they still spend Christmasses together and their grandchildren's birthdays and even the occasional holiday. Cali had however not been so lucky. Suffice to say that when she married Chris the luscious lawyer thirteen years later in 2002, (in the little medieval church with the Cotswold stone where she had been christened and in her mother's wedding dress) it was me who walked her down the aisle and gave her away.

So we talked a little that night about her mother and what she was going to do, especially about the train set which was apparently worth more than the house and most of it wasn't even her dad's anyway but had been given to her brother as birthday presents.

'She'll be fine. She'll find herself a nice new man like she should have done years ago.'

This was the right tack to take. You couldn't say of some middle aged women *'Oh don't worry, she'll retrain and find herself a career and won't need a man ever again anyway'* so you had to say something very politically incorrect instead.

Cal fiddled around with her alarm clock. It was past seven and we were hiding up in her room because there was a house meeting due downstairs at any minute and the longer we could put it off, the more likely it would be that someone would give up waiting and go out and we could postpone it.

I thought I heard the phone and redirected part of my hearing away from Cali who was talking about retraining as an air hostess. But who then would look after her mother? And she couldn't see her next weekend because of gigs and she couldn't come up to London to stay…

This was unequivocally an impossibility. No one's relatives came to stay. We didn't mind living in such squalor ourselves or having our friends living in equitable squalor but parents and siblings were different. They inhabited a different world where things were clean and cleaned, where cupboards held hoovers and cats didn't crap on the stairs.

Parents came round and said annoyingly unnecessary things like *'Let me come round next weekend and fix that leaking tap'* and *'let me get a builder to see if you need an acro-prop in the cellar, this is a supporting wall you've just knocked through, you know dear.'* Friends didn't try to mend what was clearly well beyond mending, they just took the piss or didn't notice or asked if they could move in. We were, after all, living rent free and as such to be envied.

There was a call from Al, two storeys down.

'Shit,' I finished the last piece of chocolate and struggled up. We always had to struggle up from beds because they were all, without exception, right on the floor with no legs. Most squatters had to move from one squat to another on average every six months and bed legs and bases were luxuries too heavy to be worthwhile. 94 Elm Park was as secure a squat as you could possibly get but old habits died hard.

'Coming?'

Downstairs, Al and Jamie were lounging watching telly on the big sofa whilst Claire rolled a spliff on the other by the bay window. It was a nicely proportioned room, our living room, but we had covered the peeling wallpaper with crap posters and had painted the original marble fireplace black and red. There was a rather unattractive two bar electric fire sitting in the grate blasting out illegal heat. It was high summer, nearly August, but what the Hell, it was free and a house with cracks in the outside walls can be nippy, even in July. I noticed Gavin sitting like a spider in the corner by the partition which led to the kitchen and went over to Claire which was the furthest I could get from him. Cali followed and sat on the arm.

'Right,' said Al who always liked to do things properly but was never very good at following up what he'd begun. 'Lucy's still at her mum's and can't come so is that everyone?'

There were grunts and an upbeat 'Yup!' from Jamie who knew from experience exactly how all hippy house meetings by their very nature always ended up but was determined to defy Providence by at least starting each one on a happy note.

'We need to sort out this letter from the Council,' Al went on, waving an official looking piece of paper, 'It's another eviction notice and this time they're threatening...'

There was a chorus of groans except from Gavin who was whittling some pencil into extinction with a knife.

'Al, we get eviction notices every six months, it doesn't mean anything.' This was me by virtue of being one of Elm Park's longest surviving residents.

'Fuck the bastards! Bureaucratic spongers need their letters shoved up their arses.' This was Claire by virtue of being stupid.

'Al, if we leave it nothing happens. They have to send one out but they know it's not worth kicking us out because they haven't got enough money to do this place up for, like, proper people, man, and we'll just move back in anyway.' This was Jamie by virtue of being sane.

'OK, OK,' Al was getting defensive and you just knew he wanted to be put in charge of composing some brilliantly eloquent letter which would at one and the same time expose the Council's immorality and find a loophole in British Common Law allowing us not only to keep the house as our very own but get thousands of pounds in compensation for our troubles.

'NEXT!' Gavin's dull monotone drifted up from the other side of the room and I glared. Looking back, I do admit now that I was slightly unreasonable, paranoid even on the subject of Gavin. I just hated him so much, every little thing he did annoyed me. Last house meeting for example, he and I had spent an hour arguing over whether or not he was allowed to sell heroin from his room. Gavin didn't know any heroin dealers and had probably never even seen heroin but he was an absolute virtuoso at winding me up. This then had degenerated into the perennial 'why couldn't he eat meat in the house?' argument which was now on its eighth or ninth outing. Everyone else was vegetarian, I always pointed out angrily, you're a guest here, you never even asked to move in, you should respect how everyone else lives.

'I'm not hurting anyone,' was always his reply, 'I don't make you eat it, do I?'

'But we have to smell it. And use the same plates. Which you NEVER wash up.'

Gavin always groaned theatrically at this which was an even older quarrel monotonously resurrected. Gavin did not wash up, he simply didn't want to and so he didn't. Everyone else did it at some point, Jamie very little (*'But I do cook and shop a lot'*), Cali and I a lot but Gavin simply refused to do any household chores at all. The one time an entire house meeting had been devoted to trying to get him to leave and he had finally promised to do something around the house, he had taken the washing-up bowl full of dirty plates and had put it on the back step for the rain to clean. To my fury, Jamie and Al had actually thought that this was quite funny but Gavin's smug face when he saw them giggling had made me want to kill him.

He was winding me up again and he'd hardly said anything yet.

'We need to talk about who's moving into the spare room.' This was Claire, slurring the words and sucking in hard, she passed the spliff around but as usual I shook my head. I have never quite worked out why I refused to indulge in drugs when all my friends, even Cali, were regulars. I think it was down to an innate fear of being the same as everybody else. Not wanting to be the same as my school friends is why I had died my hair like Toyah and got into the punk scene in the first place but then when I actually was a part of it, I didn't want to be exactly like my new friends either. My two little rebellions against non-conformist conformity were 1) keeping my education going and 2) never taking drugs, not even dope. It became quite an obsession with me, refusing to succumb even when I was quite obviously the one person on the planet who occasionally needed to get stoned. Perhaps I was more like the guy who had to wash his hand after picking up the spanner after all…

I jumped in, knowing that I just had to win this one. 'Pete is the obvious. Everybody likes him, he doesn't have any bad habits, he's nice and funny, he works so he'll have money to help out…'

'I don't like him,' This was Gavin who hadn't met Pete but everyone ignored him. Al was looking concerned but it wasn't real concern, just a Richard Madeley *Oh dear, this is a serious topic, I'd better look concerned* kind of concern.

'Do we have to have anyone at all? Isn't it better to wait until the perfect person comes along? Or Lucy might want it for the baby.'

There was a communal snort of air down the nostrils at this. We were stubborn and we were getting used to some pretty disgusting things on a daily basis but even we knew that 94 Elm Park was no place for a baby.

Jamie passed the spliff to Gavin who took it greedily and I felt sick at what I saw as some kind of link between them. I felt better when I realised that Jamie was standing up for me.

'Pete's a really nice geezer. I've got no problem with him dossing down with us. It's not right, having an empty room with all these sad fuckers on the streets or living with their parents.'

This was acknowledged as sage wisdom and I believe some of us may even have nodded in communal sympathy for all those poor, sad fuckers having to endure their parents.

'I've got a mate called Sasha,' drawled Claire, beckoning for the spliff to return home to Mama. 'She's such a well cool lady. I met her picking mushrooms on the park and she was a real laugh, really psychedelic.'

If the rest of us agreed on one thing, it was that we didn't want another Claire in the house. There were polite murmurs which Claire failed to properly decipher.

'So I can tell her then, man? Can she come and lay her head with us?'

Jamie was the best person to deal with Claire because he genuinely liked her and always remembered to be patient. 'I think maybe Pete has been on the waiting list longer but we could put Sasha on for the next empty room.'

I couldn't resist. 'When will that be, Gavin?'

He grunted. 'You'll have a long wait. Why are you so boring? You bring up the same old crap every single time you see me, nobody else cares about me living here, it's only you and you go on about it all the time.'

'Because you were never asked to move in!' It was so obviously unfair to me that we couldn't just pick him up and throw him physically out of the door. Simon Snuff could never understand why we didn't do just that. It was so simple to the working class Hendon eye; we hated him, he was uninvited, there were loads of us and only one of him...what was the problem?

Jamie coughed. 'We don't want to go through all this again, not tonight.'

As always I felt bitterly let down by my housemates' apathetic refusal to back me up over the Gavin situation. They didn't like him either, they just didn't hate him as much as I did.

Gavin smirked at me. 'Anyway, I want to propose one of my mates to move in.'

My heart sank. This was my worst nightmare. Gavin moving in and gradually duplicating himself so that I was eventually outnumbered and had to leave Elm Park myself. Al nodded in what he thought was a reasonable *well, let's hear it because we're all friends here* sort of way which made me want to punch him.

'I've got a mate from Stoke Newington who needs somewhere. His name's Napoleon.'

I exhaled in relief as Jamie snorted. 'Napoleon? How the fuck do you know Napoleon?'

Gavin gave some obviously fictitious explanation about meeting him at a gig (Gavin never went to gigs) whilst Cal whispered to me; 'Who's Napoleon?'

'Eat Shit,' I replied, not bothering to whisper back. This wasn't actually as rude as it might have sounded. Eat Shit were truly the worst band in London, in the world probably. They were all Hackney crusties which meant that they didn't wash and had every part of their faces pierced and tattooed with spiders webs and had only one aim in life which was to go to other people's gigs, get tanked up on Special Brew and wreck it for everyone else. I only knew them by sight, my middle class rebellion only having gone so far. Napoleon was Eat Shit's lead singer and had no front teeth. There my personal knowledge of him ended although I had moved out of his path on many occasions.

Here we were all united. There was no way Napoleon of Eat Shit was moving in to 94 Elm Park. We were squatters, true, we were huge disappointments to our parents, even more true, but we had certain standards and welcoming in a Hackney crusty would be lowering each one a good six feet.

'Sorry, Gavin,' shrugged Jamie, trying to pretend he really was, 'He wouldn't really fit in.'

'He's a good bloke, 'protested the Evil One from his place on the floor. 'You lot are so bloody snobbish. You go on about people being prejudiced about bloody blacks but you're just as bad.'

'Go and live in Hackney with Napoleon then,' I suggested hoping against hope that if I wished it hard enough it might actually happen. 'If he's really such a mate of yours and you have such a lot in common….'

'Yeah, yeah, nice try.' He sank back against the wall, his little ruse to wind us all up having succeeded. I doubt he even knew Napoleon.

'Well, Pete it is then,' said Jamie with some relief, 'Siân, you give him a bell later, yeah?'

'No probs,' I returned at once, 'He can move in next weekend, his dad's going to help him.'

'Nice one. Anything else?'

Claire began to talk about us having a party but at that moment the phone rang. Jamie answered it but held it out to me, shifting up on the other sofa so I could squeeze in next to him. Cal sent me a wink as I took the receiver which stank of grass.

'Hi. Siân?' The slightly upper class intonations came across more clearly over the phone than they had at the gig which I suppose wasn't surprising given the absence of three hundred people and a bad punk band in the background coming between us. 'It's Sam, Sam Witherspoon.'

'Hi! How are you?' I wasn't really interested in how he was, whether he had a bit of a summer cold or had slept funny the night before and had a shoulder ache. It was something to say and we're always taken by surprise and a bit cross when someone actually takes the question seriously and starts telling us how they are. We almost resent them for wasting our time. Fortunately Sam didn't.

'Fine, fine. I may have come up with a plan for getting you and Marcus in the same room at least.'

I felt nervous, stupidly nervous and nervously stupid. 'Right. Nice one. When?'

'Friday night's probably best. He's less bad tempered at the weekend, less likely to be an arsehole.'

'Well, I can't wait to hear how his enemies describe him,' I was quite pleased with this. I was genuinely trembling a little with unexpected nerves and yet I had managed something reasonably witty and reeking with calm. Sam, on the other hand, got a bit flustered.

'I didn't mean to say….he's not a complete idiot all of the time, it's just his job and it takes him until half nine on a Friday night to forget that you're not another trader he wants to con into some deal. Look, you'll have to get used to me and Marcus. I've known him since we were kids and if he's being a bit of a bastard, then I'll tell him he's being a bastard but that doesn't mean…you know…'

'That he's a bastard.'

'Precisely. He's not. He can be a really decent bloke. He surrounds himself with tossers but he's not really the same as them, he just knows how to blend in when it suits him. He's a bit of a chameleon, you could take him to a football match and he'd say the right things there as well.'

I shifted against Jamie's bum. The house meeting was debating the pros and cons of having a rave here in the house but I felt on secure ground leaving the *not in a million years* arguments to everyone but Claire.

'So, Sam. When are we going to meet up then? And can I bring a friend?'

This was meant to be tongue in cheek and girlishly funny, perhaps even touching on the *ingénue* if I was a really lucky but then it occurred to me that it was probably a good idea if Cal came along for moral support.

'Fine. I'll be there with my girlfriend and there'll be lots of people from work. It's just a wine bar near the Tube.'

'Which Tube?'

This obviously threw him. To Sam and Marcus and their City friends there was clearly only one Tube station and that was Bank.

'What? Oh sorry, Bank. Do you know the area?'

'Only from Stop The City demos. And they close most of the streets off for that anyway.'

Another brief but eloquent pause. 'Stop The City? Look, it's probably not a good idea to mention to Marcus that you were on Stop The City. He wanted every single one of you locked up for ten years. He actually said he wanted firing squads for the ones who smashed the windows. It does all go a bit too far doesn't it?'

This touched a nerve. Now, I was as pissed off as any wet liberal with the extremists who took over demos and smashed windows and caused riots with the police but I had enough *nous* and loyalty to know that essentially at least they were in the right. They might be over-the-top and impatient and hot-headed but they were on the bottom line the Good Guys as opposed to the capitalist fascist bastards who sat in their offices and played with numbers whilst people in the Third World struggled to pay off impossible debts and choked behind the noose of Apartheid.

I said as much to Sam as Cali gestured frantically from the other sofa for me to shut the fuck up. Sam was clearly not used to having this sort of conversation.

'But people in banks are only doing their jobs. It's not their fault what multinationals do in Africa, is it?'

I gave him some very interesting information about Unilever and the fictitious myth of choice the Western consumer thought he had been given and how companies like Unilever were in fact more powerful than all the governments in the world put together. Times ten.

I had clearly unnerved him. 'But there's no need to take it out on anything that moves. Some friends of mine nearly got hurt by flying glass this time and they were only going out to lunch.'

'People get hurt,' I explained as if to a child, ignoring Cali's desperate requests from the other side of the room that I change the conversation and talk about music instead. 'Lots of my friends got hurt too, only it wasn't by accidental flying glass, it was by policemen with big truncheons deliberately beating the shit out of them.'

This was not strictly true. None of my friends had ever been hurt on any demo ever but it made sense that there were people who had been and it was only an accident of fate that they were strangers and not, after all, my friends.

'Well, I don't agree with a police state,' he conceded and we found ourselves again on common ground as I made a murmur of consent. 'But then I wouldn't want to live in a world without police either.'

I knew he was wrong here, that we could all live in small communities and solve our own social problems by coming together and talking about them. I tried to shift towards the wall so that I could hear him more clearly. The discussion about the party had become a bad-tempered row between Claire and Al over what colour to paint the hallway. Claire wanted luminous orange and pink, Al wanted to try to restore the original Victorian prints and plaster cornicing. I turned away and tried to ignore them. I knew that Sam was wrong and that we didn't really need the police and we only felt that we needed them because **The System** had brainwashed us into always believing that we needed them because **The System** was afraid of people coming together in free communities just like Cromwell had been afraid of the Diggers. I wondered whether to mention the Diggers but it seemed a little philosophical for a first telephone call. I caught Cal's eye and decided to definitely not mention the Diggers.

'So,' said Sam, 'Do you want to meet up and see what he says then?'

My nerves came back in choppy waves. 'OK. And I promise not to mention Stop The City. Not even a little bit.'

'Definitely not. Marcus was on his way to get himself a McDonald's when some hippy put the window through and they had to close up. He was so pissed off, he went on about it for days. I can understand people targeting banks and the Stock Exchange but to break windows in shops that have nothing to do with anything like McDonald's….'

I gasped in audible amazement. '*Nothing to do with anything?!* Do you really not know what McDonald's do? How they pay slave wages and use eggs from battery chickens…'

'Well, so do Wimpy and you left the Wimpy alone.'

'Yes but McDonald's buy up huge chunks of the Amazon and burn the forest down so that they can graze cattle on it. They are utterly immoral, they spread Corporate America everywhere they go, everything has to look the same and taste the same and think the same.'

I was too engrossed in my own self-righteousness to notice Cal waving at me even more desperately and then giving up with eyes rolling to the ceiling. Sam was not quite the pushover I thought.

'How do you know all this anyway?'

I knew it all because I had read it on a leaflet being handed out at a festival at Meanwhile Gardens and also because this sort of stuff, especially about Unilever, was all over the first two Chumbawamba albums and they were far too moral to peddle lies.

'I read it,' It sounded weak, even to me, it sounded weak. He was generous and let me get away with it gently.

'Well, OK, if you read it…'

'Yeah, yeah, I definitely read it. So there.'

He laughed. 'Just don't tell Marcus. He's got shares in Unilever, hundreds of them.'

The conversation now was dragging up far too many unpalatable truths and I wasn't quite ready to assimilate (or ignore or reinterpret to my own comfort) all of them, not quite yet. I was very good at self-deception as I have said and a mistress in the art of social delusion but there was such a thing as overload.

'Anyway, Sam, I have to go. Where and what time?'

'A wine bar called Harvey's on Cornwallis Street. We'll be there from eightish. You could just drop in and pretend it's a coincidence.'

'Do I know you?'

'What? Oh right, yes, I suppose you'd better come up and say hallo or he might not recognise you. You could say you're a friend of mine from Uni, Marcus and I went to different colleges. Pretend we met at Bristol. See how long it takes him to work out who you are.'

'Bristol? I thought you'd have been at Cambridge. I bet you did PPE.' I was quite proud of myself for actually knowing what PPE was, never actually having met anyone doing the course when at Uni myself.

'PPE? What on earth makes you think I'd be doing PPE?'

'Because you work in the City?'

'Oh. Oh well, I suppose but that's not permanent, I don't really like it much, it's just something to do. No, I did Fine Arts at Bristol. Fat lot of good it did me.'

This was good. This was a very good ending to the phone call. Marcus had a friend who had done a Fine Arts degree. It wasn't quite as good as Marcus himself having done a Fine Arts degree but it did at least suggest that Marcus himself had some compassion and sensitivity and soul. PPE or whatever Marcus himself had done had buried the better side of him for the moment but I could resurrect all the good things in him and make them flower again.

'I'll see you on Friday then,'

I liked to end phone calls. It was one of the most important lessons in my *Women Who Need To Love Themselves* books. I put down the phone and sent Cal a wink of triumph. She sent me a thumbs up and went back to her *Training To Be An Air Hostess?* magazine. Al was talking about uncovering the floorboards and sanding them down. Jamie was reminding him that the floorboards were full of live woodworm and let you see down into the cellar which is why we had three layers of carpet over them. I reminded them all sweetly that we had three layers of carpet over our floorboards because we were always finding new carpet in skips and could never be bothered pulling up the old ones. With that sharpish riposte at all we held dear, I said an early goodnight and went upstairs to cuddle my baby.

Chapter 6 – Pete

Ness loved Pete. She thought he was as good a dog-father-figure as Sean Gummidge and she adored Sean. There are people who quite like dogs and who will stroke them happily enough, even ruffling the ears for a while. Cali was like that. She liked dogs but she did not adore them. Sean and Pete were different, they were like me. Why stroke a dog when you can gather them up onto your lap and cover yourself with hairs as you love the living daylights out of them? Why ruffle a dog's ears when you can roll around on the floor having a playfight? There's no greater trust than having an Alsatian's jaws around your arm as you tussle around on the bed, feeling no fear, not even the tiniest doubt that she might hurt you. Ness would never hurt me. This wasn't a hope or an assumption based on blind feeling or some kind of arrogant ownership thing, it was simple knowledge. She couldn't hurt me. It was as if the bond between us had removed her teeth and her claws for anything save gentle teasing, the soft hold the mother dog uses on her pups. Ness had never had pups which was a huge regret of mine but she did have me.

I had subconscious categories in which all the people I knew fell based on how they were with dogs and how they were with Ness in particular. Mum, Cal, Dad, Nia, these were the rufflers but not the rollers. Emma, Claire, Al, they tolerated but basically ignored anything on four legs. Gavin, for all I knew, ate them or offered their still-beating hearts up to his Dark Lord. But Sean, Jamie, Pete and most of the other lads in squats around Brixton and Hackney knew how to love a dog.

Martin had Banshee, a great Scooby Doo of an Alsatian which he fed on vegan muesli and who consequently could hardly walk straight but by God, did he worship that dog. She went everywhere with him, if you had Martin coming round, you had Banshee dribbling over your legs and knocking over tables and trying to get up to your lap. Martin only went out with girls who loved Banshee too and the fakes didn't last; Banshee would dribble on them, they would scream, they would leave, relationship over and good riddance too. Nathan had Gus who was a ratty little terrier-cum-Jack Russell and who would hump anything that caught his eye from chair leg to human leg to kitchen bin but he was terrified of the real thing. Nathe adored Gus so much it had made him utterly defensive, he was always standing up for his baby when people took the piss, taking him out of the room if he felt Gus might get upset when someone shouted *'fuck off away from my food, Gus!'* or *'Get off my leg, you little bastard!'*

Sean was the worst sentimentalist of us all over dogs. He had a thing about black Labrador puppies and had had two, Hassle and Freda. He was very good with them in that he fed them chocolate (OK, we didn't know that it killed them then) and took them for long walks and let them sleep under the duvet with their heads on the pillow. The trouble was that Gummidge was, and for all I know still is, the busiest man in London. He worked at a record shop and distributor in Portobello Road called Rough Trade and every single night he went to gigs. So, the pup was left alone all day and then in the evening was taken on the Tube to some forsaken part of town but found herself being tied up outside because most pubs in London wouldn't let dogs in. So, Freda was given away to some hippy friends with a garden and a few years later the same thing happened with Hassle. But Sean didn't let them go lightly, he really suffered like the teenage mother giving up her mistake-pregnancy baby for adoption. He knew he was doing the right thing and that the pup would be happy but that didn't mean he didn't cry and think about her all day, every day for the next year.

The day after the house meeting (which had been very dull by past standards because no one had ended up in tears), I rang Pete and gave him the good news.

'Oh, that's *excellent* news, man! Oh my God! Are you sure? Oh my God, this is *so* brilliant! You wait 'til I thank the guys. Will you thank the guys for me tonight? This is going to be so cool. Are you sure the guys are cool about this?'

This is just an excerpt. Pete could enthuse for Britain, he was the least cynical, least sceptical, least manipulative person I have ever met. I used to wonder whether he was all there, whether he'd been dropped on his head as a baby and could as a consequence never distinguish between bastards and good guys, sarcasm and straight talk, jokes and truth, honesty and *definitely about to rip you off.* How Pete has become the super-slick, mega successful, millionaire tax exile King of the World that he has without at the same time becoming a bastard, I shall never quite understand.

Cali and I were convinced at this time that Pete was heading for a really big fall. No one could be that open, that naive, that generous without being taken for a ride in a truly big way. He was asking for it with that massive tombstone-teeth smile, those big brown eyes, that mop of deeply unfashionable curly brown hair. Pete worked for a music publishers which made him work incredibly hard for crap money but he never ever asked for a rise. He lived with his mum and his little sister and had a gorgeous girlfriend called Luisa with waves of honey blond hair and a Kylie bottom.

Cali and I both adored Pete but we could never work out why he always managed to find himself really beautiful and devoted girlfriends. Luisa didn't just have a Kylie bottom, she had a Kylie face and Kylie legs too plus an actress mum who had played Louis Collins' wife in some SAS film. Luisa was sixteen but sixteen with an income, sixteen with a childhood full of famous people coming round to dinner and tweaking her little Kylie nose. Luisa presumably mixed with the trust-fund sons of all sorts of stars but she had chosen Pete, our Pete. Cal and I could never see past the 'cute but too much like a brother' thing. And he was far too young for us anyway, only eighteen when he moved into Elm Park and seventeen when I first met him down the front banging his head up and down to Snuff. Pete was the sort of person who collected t-shirts with bands' names and logos on and then saw nothing wrong with then wearing that t-shirt to that band's gig. Nobody else I knew did that. There was *no way* I would ever wear a band t-shirt anyway except to bed because band t-shirts were for the punters who didn't actually know the band but to the *actual gig…?* Pete though didn't care. He had a beautifully simplistic and single minded personality and he actually really didn't care if people thought him cool or a prat. His logic told him that if you liked a band enough to buy their t-shirt, then surely it made sense to wear it and surely the most logical place to wear such a t-shirt would be when jumping up and down at the front of that band's gig? He didn't see how that made him a prat and looking back many years later, I can't quite work it out either.

So, later that week Pete moved in and it was great. OK, my daylight hours were still mediocre at best but at least Pete got home by six on the dot and was never, ever known to be pissed off about anything.
'You know, I'm really a bit pissed off about that,' he'd say with that great grin across his face. Pete had just the biggest mouth and the biggest teeth and it was as if the muscles in his face did not actually allow any movement other than upwards. He couldn't frown. He couldn't sulk and look miserable, he couldn't be nasty about anyone or even suspect them of being nasty about him. If Pete complained of being 'a bit pissed off about that', firstly it was said in the most reasonable, accommodating and unpissed off way imaginable and secondly, it was usually about a TV programme being cancelled or his Chinese takeaway being a little bit on the cool side.
I told Pete about Marcus and Sam and the photograph because I wanted a reaction totally devoid of any reservations or doubts or warnings or common sense and I knew I wouldn't get that from anyone on the planet but him.

'Oh *man!* That's *excellent!* Ness's photo on his mirror for three years? Wow, he must be mad about you, darling, I bet you can't wait to meet him!'

This wasn't strictly true. As Friday grew nearer, I had begun to develop real, physical nerves, an unmistakeable sense of nausea. Usually I swamped such fears with chocolate and self-delusion, clouding my fears with visions of waking up next to some gorgeous (and clean) bloke who wouldn't fart or run off with my thin blond friend. In my mind, Marcus and I had already been dating for a year, split up over a misunderstanding, had emotional scenes at airports, faced a pregnancy scare and a life threatening disease together (sometimes me, sometimes him but always very draining on the emotions and fun) and had finally got married in a Scottish stone circle. Occasionally my concentration would lapse and allow reality to poke her ugly nose in along the lines of ; *What on earth are you doing?? He could be a complete maniac! And what's a yuppy stockbroker going to see in you? Have you looked in the mirror lately? Have you been near a scales?*

The last was a nasty and unnecessary dig from my subconscious because the rest of me knew full well that I hadn't been near a scales since the age of thirteen. What was the point? Why deliberately upset the equilibrium of complacency when you could remain in blissful ignorance? I knew if I'd put weight on because my skirts got a little tighter and as they were all elasticated anyway, it didn't happen, problem solved. The other issue was not so easily dismissed though. Although I am considered, or so I am told, reasonably good looking, we have to include the word *relative* here. All the men I knew found big boots, sloppy torn t-shirts, brightly coloured or bleached or as-black-as-vinyl hair attractive. They also liked tattoos and pierced nostrils. The prevailing fashion amongst ordinary people of padded shoulders, fitted trousers and big hair simply belonged to another world, we just didn't physically see such women, they didn't register with the hippy optic nerve. It was starting to become obvious to me though as Friday loomed nearer that Marcus might need some persuasion before he found dreadlocks and piercings attractive.

'Cali is going to make me look half way respectable,' I confessed to Pete, 'I told her she better start tonight to be anywhere near by Friday.'

He slurped his tea and spilt most of it on the clean duvet his mother had brought round earlier. 'Wow, you must let me see you before you go. I haven't seen an ordinary looking girl in ages! What d'ya reckon Simon Snuff would think?'

Tact was not one of Pete's strong points, he didn't really understand raw nerves not having any himself. The fact that I had recently been dumped by Simon Snuff and was extremely sensitive about the entire episode wouldn't necessarily have occurred to him. Pete stayed friends with all his ex-girlfriends and assumed that everyone did the same. His heart was big and open and full of love for all mankind (*agapae* the Greeks called it) and had never been broken, not even cracked.

'I don't care what Simon Snuff thinks. I just don't want to put this bloke off. He might be really nice.'

Pete's whole face lit up with expectant hope for my future joy. 'I hope so. He sounds like a really cool guy.'

I couldn't quite see how he'd come to this conclusion so fast but then everyone was a really cool guy to Pete. Attila the Hun would have had some redeeming feature in Pete's book, a skill with the snare drum perhaps or excellent dress sense. Pete reached out to turn over the record which unsurprisingly was Snuff's album, newly released and selling nauseatingly well.

'Well, I had a really crap day at work. Lots of people really pissed me off. Did you meet Cali for lunch?'

I nodded. I often met Cal at Hatton Garden for lunch in a little sandwich bar-cum-deli. She would whiz in with a posh suit a little crumpled and reassuringly not quite her and sometimes she would bring me a little packet of uncut diamonds that had dropped on the floor. I'd get really excited and pour them into my palm and look at them, then carefully pour them back in and show them to a few people over the next few days and then I'd drop them on my bedroom carpet and forget to pick them up again.

Pete scratched the record putting his coffee cup down.

'Fuck. Hope that's alright. I've got another one in a different colour sleeve and Duncan gave me a test pressing… anyway, so this Friday then! I've got a good feeling about this, he's definitely the one for you.'

Pete said 'I've got a really good feeling about this' an awful lot and as he always saw the best in every situation, everything did usually turn out for the best anyway so his eternal optimism was always proved right. (I read Voltaire's *Candide* years after this and laughed out loud.)

Pete's enthusiasm was as always infectious. Perhaps it would be the start of something new and not necessarily the disaster I was anticipating.

'Well, I promise to come straight in and tell you all about it, soon as I'm back.'

He looked as though I'd offered him a trip to Disney World.

'Really? Excellent. You sure you don't mind? I'm stuck in on Friday 'cos Luisa's at her Mum's so that'd be really cool, thanks. I'll wait up.'

'No probs, I thought I'd wear your new Tyler t-shirt.'

He laughed uproariously. The latest Wat Tyler offering had a cartoon of Michael Jackson performing oral sex on a monkey and was rather sweetly entitled *I'm forever blowing Bubbles*.

Pete laughed some more. Snuff roared out guitar and bass and drums on a crackling hi-fi and we sat on his bed in companionable silence. Men are good friends when there's no hint of sex. It isn't that common, Billy Crystal was damned right about that, but it does happen occasionally and this was one of those relationships. We talked for a while about band names and which was the best one ever. Pete was keen on 1970s rock so went for Def Leppard as being at the same time impenetrable and possibly deep and yet also stupidly silly. I quite liked DaisyChainsaw, a band I'd seen recently somewhere or other. In my world, band names should have a pop edge to them but an underlying *fuck-off* menace too. In the early eighties all the bands we went to see had the same kind of grim, humourless monikers; The Dispossessed, Discharge, The Exploited, The Parasites, Vice Squad, The Vicious Circles, anti this, anti-that, hate this, hate that. Fortunately this had chilled out a little by 1989. We went to see bands like Mega City Four and The Senseless Things. Pete and I both agreed eventually that Chunk was an inspired name and probably better than the actual band (which was a shame 'cos Pete was the drummer) but that Snuff had to be the best band name ever.

'I used to think it was...you know…about tobacco!' Pete had the good grace to go red and look abashed, shaking his curls in embarrassment. 'I'm such a *complete idiot*. Like a hardcore band are going to name themselves after a type of old man's tobacco! And then I thought it was after those sick films where they really kill you.'

He wasn't alone. Recently, some poor punk in Darlington had won a kind of notoriety by writing to Rough Trade and asking if they had any Snuff videos as the one he had had snapped through overuse. The armed forces of Her Majesty's Constabulary had then paid him an unannounced visit at dawn and he had spent the next eight hours in the cells before the whole hilarious mistake had been untangled. The police had thought the whole thing quite funny, the punter returned to a wrecked flat and wasn't quite so amused, even less so when sent a sarky letter from the detective who'd ordered the raid. Ha ha ha, we all thought, bloody hilarious, fucking *POLICE STATE*! We knew **The System** read all our mail and bugged all our phone calls and had copies made of all our house keys, we'd always known it and here was the proof! Snuff just thought it was good publicity and sent the guy a t-shirt.

Snuff had actually come up with their name whilst very drunk in the pub one night. Names being bandied about had become so ridiculous that Andy the guitarist was in danger of bringing up his lager through hiccups.

'That's enough!' he'd spluttered, 'That's senuff!'

And so there you have it. From such simple circumstance comes genius.

We got back to talking about my predicament.

'He might really have a thing about you.' Pete was very generous in his interest in other people's lives and unlike most people, it was never as an introduction or comparison to his own. 'I mean, why else would he have your picture all this time?'

'Not strictly **my** picture…'

'You reckon he fancies Ness then?'

Ness was lying across the bed between us. Sean had just come round and had taken her to Brockwell Park to chase sticks. He was pissed off about something and usually borrowed someone's dog until it went away. Ness was muddy and a little wet still, Pete's duvet needed his mum again but he didn't care or even notice. Ness was lying heavily as if dead across his knees, breathing noisily as her lips blew up and down exposing her teeth. As I watched, she gave a little shiver, a high pitched whimper and I tickled the sensitive hairs between her pads to make her twitch.

'I just can't imagine why he should remember me.'

'That's not fair. Why shouldn't someone remember you?'

'Because, dearest, I'm not particularly memorable. Not me. What's memorable about me is having stupid hair and tattoos and bits of metal in my nose but underneath all that, I'm pretty ordinary.'

Pete was a gentleman and as such, determined to prove me wrong. He thought a while and then grinned in triumph.

'Hang on, wasn't there that bloke you told me about, that bloke who got really obsessed with you and followed you around everywhere and wrote you letters all the time?'

I couldn't think.

'You know, you went round his house and he had that massive poster…'

'Oh shit! I remember, what the fuck was his name….'

'It was something really weird, not a proper name at all…'

My memory was bad at the best of times but this bloke had been four years ago at least…Aah, now I had it.

'His name was Chris but he called himself The Elusive Stranger after some Toyah song. He used to follow the Lost Cherrees around everywhere. He was totally obsessed with Toyah and was convinced I was some kind of reincarnation because I had the same colour hair and used to wear an ankh. And then I went round his house, I can't even remember why, and there was this massive poster, life size, and I sort of looked at it and assumed it was Toyah and then when I looked at it again….*fucking Hell, that's me!*'

Pete took another sip of cold tea, still smiling wide. 'That must have been *so cool,* to have someone make a poster of you and put it on their wall.'

I wasn't so sure. 'It wasn't actually, it was quite creepy. You know, I was alone in this house with him and I'd never met anyone who had posters of people they actually knew on their walls before – I mean, it was right next to his bed! – and I couldn't work it out at all. Was it a compliment in which case I'm being an ungrateful bitch or was it freaky and perverted in which case I was a stupid cow for going to his house. I didn't know what to say to him but I couldn't wait to get out of there.'

'So, you've had two men so obsessed with you that they have pictures of you on their walls!' Pete thought this was all wonderful and I was wonderful and the squat was wonderful and life its bloody self was wonderful. I knew better.

'It was because I was in a band and he was obsessed with Toyah. He couldn't get anywhere near her and I looked a tiny bit like her so he got hung up on me instead. And I don't know why this other bloke has a photo of Ness. It could be something really boring.'

'Look on the bright side! This could be totally genuine, a real love story! And if he turns out to be dodgy, I'll go round his flat and sort him out! I'll protect you if he gets too mental!'

The thought of Pete protecting me was funnier than him making a joke about it but it occurred to me much later that I shouldn't have laughed, that Pete was the sort of friend who would actually die to protect someone he cared for, he was the sort who would jump in front of buses or dive into freezing rivers to save someone who probably wouldn't do it for him. And he would probably still be smiling when they fished him out.

Chapter 7 – Jamie

That Thursday Cal came home early and did a great job on me. The raw material she had to work with was not too promising, it had to be said. Since splitting up with Nick Evans a few weeks before, I'd let myself go a little and my dreadlocks (which if I'm being totally honest weren't real dreadlocks but girlie cheating dreadlock plaits) had started to stick together in clumps (which was ironically what real dreadlocks were supposed to do anyway). My skin was suffering from a surfeit of chocolate and chips and a complete absence of any sort of cleansing, toning and moisturising routine whatsoever.

So we had a real girls' night in, me, Cali and Pete who could always be counted as an honorary. Pete declined the actual tortuous processes of eyebrow shaping and pore squeezing but watched with a gaping half-moon of amazement across his face as the ladies did their thing. Whilst we sat with stinging face packs (ignoring the *not advisable for sensitive skin* warning) Cali bit the bullet and started to comb out my dreaded plaits. Real dreads of course had to be cut off right down to the skin but I was never quite brave enough to go the whole hog with anything in my life really and so had opted for hair which although painful, could at least be saved. Two hours later she had the worst of it conquered, only having to resort to scissors twice. I was in agony with my scalp feeling as if it had been…well, scalped but it was worth it.

'Right, after it's dry, we'll crimp it to make it straight,'

Cali took a sneaky look at her watch. It was half nine and we'd worked through EastEnders and all sorts of crap TV. She, of course, had to be up at seven as did Pete whereas I could lie in until ten if I wanted. Ten? Who am I kidding? I hadn't been up as early as ten for weeks.

'Don't worry,' I started to feel a bit guilty at the me-me-me-ness of the last few hours, 'I can do it tomorrow.'

'Right,' Cali plugged the hair drier into the wobbly, DIY socket that some helpful squatter had put in years ago with a wish and a prayer but with very little electrical skill. 'What about clothes?'

This was a real problem.

Usually I wore black leggings with brightly coloured miniskirts and tight black tops with long gashes cut out of the shoulders and sleeves. This was great for slobbing around Brixton and standing at the bar at the Robey, even greater at showing off my tattoo without having to bare my upper arms but it probably wouldn't do for Harvey's.

'I've got this top,' I reached up to the carrier bag hanging from one of the many six inch nails which served as my wardrobe. 'I got it from Camden ages ago, never worn it. See what you think.'

It was a tight affair of black shiny stuff with raised stitching running down from the bust to give it a corset look. It was tarty by itself but half covered up might look a little bit *Dangerous Liaisons* if I was really lucky.

'I thought with my red silk skirt, the floaty one…'

'Can you iron it?' Cali was in Mother Mode but that in itself could not persuade me to iron. None of us ironed, we only bought clothes that if truth be told could not actually physically be ironed.

'I could wet it and hang it up to dry, that sort of uncreases it. That's as good as ironing.'

'OK. What about your tattoo?'

I made a face. 'Problem. I don't really want to flaunt it but I don't want to wear a jumper over this top and it'll be too hot anyway.'

'What's wrong with your tattoo?'

Pete was lying full stretched out at the foot of the bed, watching the evening's proceedings with undeserved fascination. Ness had been relegated to the floor and was making occasional disgruntled groans.

This was a good question. I had two tattoos actually, a spider on my shoulder which had been quite sweet seven or eight years before but which, in the intervening years, had spread out a little so that the individual hairs on the wee beastie's legs had now merged together so that it just looked really fat. I had a much more impressive art deco fairy on my arm, all blues and greens and turquoises with the odd splash of yellow on her wings. It was beautifully done and still new enough to see the fine lines between her fingers and toes. The fairy wasn't really the problem. Many women get to a certain age – and I reached it at least a decade early – where they cannot bear the sight of their upper arms. White and pasty with hints of cellulite to come, no, not on show tonight, not on show ever.

'Have you got a jacket?' Cali was now in Mother Superior Mode or she would never have asked me such a question. I simply didn't wear jackets. I had grown out of the leather-jacket-with-the-studs-and-bands'-names phase and had never managed to find a substitute. Leather jackets were simply a no-no around most of my friends anyway. People like Ben and the Jeffreys Road crew had opted for the vegan alternative to leather which meant that I hadn't dared to wear the rather gorgeous maroon suede coat I'd bought from Portobello three months ago. It wasn't as if they'd have actually *said* anything – although a few of us had been known to spray paint onto fur coats in our time – but there would be …an **atmosphere.** A definite atmosphere. Leather shoes however were for some reason more acceptable. I doubt the cow would have appreciated the difference.

'I've got that see-through black shirt from Warehouse,' Cal suggested with her usual generosity because Warehouse was not cheap. 'You won't see the tatt very clearly and you can still see the top.'

'Thanks!'

My spirits genuinely rose. To most people, Warehouse are simply a reasonably priced high street store with some nice enough styles for twenty somethings but to people used to buying from jumble sales and market stalls run by art students, it was the equivalent of designer label. With Warehouse literally on my back, I could hold up my chin a little bit higher and convince myself that I was no different from anyone else. I could of course have worn my sister's clothes but Sarah Lees-Jardine, my unlamented alter-ego, had gone. I didn't mind dressing up straight for a bloke but I wasn't stupid enough to think that I could fabricate an entire new life and get away with it.

Not then I wasn't anyway.

I had originally thought of asking Cali and Pete to come along but at the last minute I changed my mind. This could turn out to be a pretty dire evening and these two deserved more from me than having to waste an entire three hours of their lives simply acting as my back-ups and emotional supports. No, this was a mess I had got myself into (well, me and Sarah Lees-Jardine, the stupid stuck-up cow) and it was a mess I was going to sort out all by myself. If a photo of Ness had come to be where it had no reason to be because I had annoyed someone in some way, I didn't really want my two best friends having to act as sniper cover. And if this bloke really was cute and interested in me, I didn't want him thinking I'd brought my boyfriend and sophisticated diamond merchant best friend with me either, no sirree.

So, in my newly straightened hair and borrowed Warehouse shirt, I went it alone. As I walked down Brixton Hill though, Jamie came skipping along to catch me up. He was going to North Clapham and I was grateful for the company, if only until Stockwell. When I get nervous, it isn't just a mental thing; my legs feel like they won't bear my weight, my heartbeats overload, my fingers twitch, my stomach wants to expel anything digested within the last forty-eight hours – on the very few occasions I wish for my youth back, I remember what it really is to be young and then I don't wish for it back anymore.

'Where you going then, darling?' Jamie looked like a furry lolly pop, all stripes and lickable smells. He was never dull, our James, never in black like the rest of us miserable gits. He was a walking rainbow who smelt of sweet shops and unhousetrained cats.

'Oh, you know, Uni thing.'

He made a pretend freaked out wave with his hands. 'Wow, stuuuu…dents! Watch yourself amongst the unwashed.'

'You can talk, stinky.'

'I perspire pure incense, man, students just sweat pretentious essays they've nicked off their geeky mates in the library.'

'True enough.' We walked along in companionable silence for a bit, past the Roxy cinema which was showing Betty Blue, past the brand new Pizza Hut on the corner, down towards the shabby entrance of the Tube station.

'Jamie, didn't you ever fancy being a student? You've got A Levels, haven't you?'

We slipped through the barrier as usual, no one noticed, no one cared. I don't think I ever paid for a Tube ticket back in the 1980s, none of us did. We had a cloak of invisibility we just took for granted. Jamie flipped fifty pence to the guy with the dog.

'Yeah, I've thought about it. I went to your college for an interview last year - don't you remember? - but the whole thing freaked me out. So many men with beards and in tweed suits! I wasn't doing it for the proper reasons anyway.'

'What do you mean?'

He gave a lopsided grin, utterly charming, utterly irresistible. 'I was in my *wanna be like Siân* phase! Siân was in Blyth Power so I joined Blyth Power, Siân was doing Medieval History at UCL so that's what I wanted to do.'

This took me completely by surprise. No one envied me, no one on the planet wanted my life, what on earth would they do with it?

I pulled his arm. '*There was no phase*! Jamie, there was no phase! What the fuck are you talking about?'

'Doesn't matter. Nope, if I went to Uni it'd be to do summut like Theatre Studies, Drama, you know. Johnny Depp, that's who I'm gonna be, Johnny Depp.'

'Who's Johnny Depp?'

We turned left at the bottom of the escalator and sat down on the platform to wait. Jamie shook his head at my ignorance.

'Edward Scissorhands, you plum. Didn't you come with us to see it at the Roxy?'

'No. That was a Ben / Jeffreys Road thing.'

He put his arm around my shoulders. 'You have gotta get yourself off this groove, man. Ben was a year ago, move on.'

'It's not just that. I don't feel…as if I fit in.'

'They're really cool people.'

'I know, I know. It's me, I'm the one who's all fucked up.'

The train rumbled in, we stood and waited for it to empty and then took seats. I leaned against him because he was warm and furry and beautiful.

'Don't you want anything else, James? Where are you going to be in ten years time?'

He was only twenty, bless him, thirty was a generation away, thirty was never going to happen to Jamie, he would look the same and be the same for ever. He started talking about the band he was getting together with someone I didn't know, leaving Blyth Power and writing his own songs, gigging Europe and putting out albums, maybe getting a Peel Session……I knew then that he would **never** leave this life of ours, that he would still be in bands and living in dodgy houses at forty. And so would Sean, they loved this life too much to want to cash it in for something which might look safer but which wouldn't be them. And I knew then too that they would make it work. Hundreds of hippy squatters would chase the dream and fail and wake up at forty and despair. They would look back at twenty wasted years and curse themselves for hanging on in there for one more gig, one more record deal, one more tour. But Jamie… Jamie would make it work. He would gig and tour and live in horrible houses with strange people and yet he would prosper. Being true to himself, eventually he would prosper and rise above it all without one second of compromise. Jamie was so goddamned talented, so full of energy, so utterly cute, Johnny Depp, whoever he was, couldn't hold candle to this dreadlocked pixie sitting next to me. Maybe not this band, maybe not the next but eventually there would be a band which would take him up and up and there he would stay. Still Jamie, just better off.

'You're not happy, are you honey?'

'You know me, never happy unless I'm miserable.'

The train was gathering up reluctant speed now, disappearing into the black. Jamie nudged my shoulder again and again, like Ness when she wanted a walk.

'Wass the matter? Tell me all about it. Wass the matter? Wass the matter?'

'At this precise moment, it's because I've got a prat dressed like a belisha beacon bugging me on the Tube. But otherwise, honey-bun, I guess I'm just one discontented cow.'

'You need to get out of Elm Park, it's not good for you.'

'Hey I sweated blood and lived in a toilet for four months to get that room.'

It was Jamie's stop. He got up, one hand on the ceiling strap, the other held out for me.

'Why don't you come with me? We're going for a drink, Ben won't be there. He's in Leeds with Chumbas.'

I nearly went. I, oh so nearly went. And what would have happened to me then? How would my life have turned out if I hadn't met Marcus that night, if I had taken the hand of a truly good friend who didn't know what else to do with me? Would I have had the guts and staying power to rise to the top as Jamie would, as Sean would, as Pete would? Or would I watch them climb the ladder ahead and above of me as I sat clinging to the bottom rung? I knew then with absolute clarity that I couldn't stay in this life, I knew that I would suffocate and wither and fail, that I would end up something I despised even more than the me I despised already. So, I gave Jamie a helpless shrug, told him to have a good night and watched him bounce his way cheerfully off the train and away to the Northern Line, a bright flash of multicoloured stripe in a very grey crowd.

     I stood outside Harvey's Wine Bar half an hour later and wondered if I'd be allowed in. Normal people with normal lives never have to experience that five second 'Will we get in?' frisson of fear as they enter a new pub or bar or restaurant. But anyone who's ever had funny coloured hair or facial piercings or even studs on their leather jacket, knows that being turned away from pubs was an integral part of being not quite normal in the 1980s. It is still a part of my psychology today. I am nearly forty and as respectable as anyone could wish to be and yet even now, as I walk into a nice restaurant or meet work colleagues for meetings in the local hotel bar, I still feel that 'shit, he's going to ask me to leave' when the barman catches my eye.

     Through the glass doors I could make out a long bar to the right stretching out away from me with sofas and comfortable chairs to the left and the hint of a garden right at the end. Everything was very light and bright with shiny chrome along the edge of the bar and the furniture and there were also splashes of colour; what looked like Mexican prints on the wall and an illuminated mosaic of glass behind the bar. It wasn't that bad at all though it wasn't really me. I was at that frustrated stage of life where I knew what I didn't like but hadn't the faintest idea what I did.

     Pushing open the doors took courage I didn't know I had and didn't until then know I'd need. There were lots of people, all the seats taken and at least twenty or so standing. Young men in their twenties with their ties loosened, knocking back Budweisers, heads thrown back with casual confidence as they laughed about work or the boss or the dire performance of their team last season. The women were all thin or at least that's what I thought but on closer inspection, they weren't. Some were the terrifying City Perfects I dreaded with their size 10 suits and big gold Sade earrings but some were quite ordinary looking although all more conventionally dressed than me. I couldn't see Sam anywhere although there were lots of pony tails around.

Still drawing on the reserves of courage now rapidly running out, I made my way through towards the end of the bar. There was a lot of shouting and laughter, lots of good humoured joking, some posh accents and expensive suits but apart from that, nothing too alien. I had almost been expecting someone to turn round as I walked by and shout INTRUDER! but everyone just ignored me. The music was something dire, Bon Jovi I think, but then the unmistakable opening to *Like A Prayer* began its sweet slow chorus and that made me feel better. You can be as alternative, as hippy, as punk or indie as you like but that still doesn't mean that you can't like Madonna.

Life is a mystery, everyone must stand alone, the garden was a courtyard with high walls and Mexican style pots filled with tall reedy things. *I hear you call my name*…It was packed with City workers celebrating a summer Friday night and at first I couldn't see how I was ever going to recognise let alone find someone I had only met twice… *And it feels like…..home*. I heard my name being called and there he was by the wall on my left, at the edge of a group of seven or eight people.

'Siân! Hi! It's Sam, Sam Witherspoon!' He broke away from his group and joined me at the door. I tried to look past him to the people he was with but it was too rude not to at least acknowledge him.

'Hi Sam, how are you?'

I tried to look again over his shoulder. A fat bloke with sweaty armpits and red cheeks, that clearly wasn't him. A thin intense looking man nodding his head up and down, up and down like some sort of executive toy bird on a pole. Two men with their backs to me, both with short slicked back hair….

'How's it going?' Sam beckoned over a pretty blond woman with narrow silver rimmed glasses and introduced her as his girlfriend Helena. He didn't introduce me as anything which in the circumstances I suppose was fair enough.

'You look different,' Sam had his arm around Helena's shoulders, 'Marcus won't recognise you!'

'He probably won't anyway, we've probably got it all wrong. And even if he did recognise me, why should that matter now? Isn't one of those girls his girlfriend?'

'No, Marcus is single at the moment. Well, actually Marcus is always single especially when he's dating someone!'

'Don't be bitchy now!' Helena poked him in the ribs and gave me a sweet smile. 'Sam says you know him and Marcus from way back, you must fill me in on all the gory details!'

'Oh. Yeah. Right.' I didn't know quite how to handle this. Clearly, she wasn't a particularly long term girlfriend because Sam had obviously not filled her in on my pathetic little story. Actually, if we were being quite honest here, Sam had told her a pack of lies. She caught sight of someone she knew and left us, Sam came in close.

'How are we going to play this one then? He doesn't know you're here, I've not mentioned the photo since he bit my head off the other night about it. Shall I just introduce you and see what happens?'

'I suppose so. But what if he doesn't recognise me? I can hardly say I've been in his bathroom on false pretences.'

'Well…just say you've seen him somewhere before. Ask him if he ever lived in…where was the photo taken?'

'East Ham Park.'

'Come on then.'

And he led me over to the little group by the wall, positioning me next to a tall man with very dark shiny hair and the most ridiculously high cheekbones….I should have listened to my instincts and gone then and there. Cheekbones have never done me any good, they always suggest such fine things and deliver such crap…This man, this man who turned to look down at me now had the good looks of Alec Baldwin or Clive Owen. The Croatian one from ER. Smooth. Beautifully sculptured eye sockets. And smooth.

He was way out of my league.

I wasn't being falsely modest or insecure, he was simply way out of my league, I don't even think we played the same sport.

'Marcus, this is Siân, a friend of mine from Uni.'

'Oh. Hi.' He raised his pint an inch or so by way of greeting but clearly was none too impressed. An immaculate blond stood at his left, clearly not too happy at Sam interrupting them. She cleared her throat as elegantly as possible but Sam thwarted her again.

'Siân was saying how she's sure she's seen you somewhere before. This is Marcus, by the way.'

'Hi,' I smiled as gorgeously as I could which probably wasn't gorgeously at all because I have a crooked front tooth that I forget about for months on end. 'I'm sure I've seen you somewhere before! Didn't you used to live in East Ham?'

He snorted as if I'd asked him if he used to sleep in horseshit. 'East Ham? I don't think so. Imagine me, Sophie, the sound of Bow Bells. I don't think so.'

'Oh,' I wasn't sure where to go from here. He was absolutely without doubt the best looking person I had ever seen in real life but he was certainly hard work. I decided to stop fucking around. 'I've got a dog, Ness. You might remember her. I always used to walk her round East Ham Park.'

At that point someone jostled me from behind and I had to step forward and so missed the very moment when he recognised me and the penny dropped. I missed the two seconds of unguarded emotion before he pulled himself together and slapped on the mask.

'Oh! Oh, you're the one with the *dog!*' He drawled with quiet amusement, whether at me or himself I wasn't sure. 'You bastard, Witherspoon, have I been set up here? Have you set me up, you snotty nosed little bastard?'

And then it was all laughs and back slappings with me not really knowing what was going on but feeling that it had all gone rather well anyway. The blonde looked cross.

'Am I going to be allowed to know what's so funny?'

Marcus gave her a pretend-drunk nod of the head. 'It's not at all funny, my love. Sam here, Sam the Arch Bastard, has discovered by means of poking his nose into my private en suite – what were you looking for, you perverted little creep? – that I used to have.....*a penchant* for this young lady here. And now he's magicked her up to embarrass me in front of all my friends.'

The blonde looked me up and down as if at some exotic insect she couldn't quite make out. It was as if the zoo keeper had told her that the cage contained some creature really rare and beautiful and yet when she looked inside, all she could see was a shabby brown thing.

'I see.' She clearly didn't but it didn't matter. Sam, Marcus and I were drawn into an exclusive little circle of people who did see and who didn't mind and who were perfectly OK with the whole thing. Sam went to get me a Baileys and Marcus pointedly turned his shoulder away from the blonde and gave me his full attention.

'So. How is that lovely dog of yours?' And I knew then that it **could** work. That despite the suit and the slicked back hair and the yuppy job, here was a man who liked the look of me and loved the look of my dog and could, just could, be Mr Right. So, we talked a little about Ness and about the beagles he had back at his parents' home and then we talked about Tianenmen and the Marchioness disaster because he'd been invited and hadn't gone. Then we shared memories of Berlin because he had just been there and I had been there too. I remembered not to get too drunk and I didn't talk too loudly and I really did rather well, given the nerves making me feel sick. I even remembered to pretend I'd been at Bristol Uni and even more amazingly, had the front to ask him questions about UCL without giving it away that I'd been there myself for what seemed like my whole damned life. And then we talked about Mad Max and Bladerunner and whether Rutger Hauer was the coolest man alive and everything was alright. Amazingly, everything was alright.

When I got home that night, I was still buzzing and broke my promise to Pete, taking Ness round the block and going straight to bed. I was a little drunk and not a little delirious but not so drunk or delirious that I couldn't remember every single moment of that evening. Nothing especially amazing had happened, we hadn't kissed or exchanged phone numbers or knowing looks but we had talked and had found things in common and when I said goodbye, he had reached out to touch my arm, saying 'See you soon.'

One odd thing though. I'd gone to the Ladies with Helena who was very nice and interestingly as intimidated by Marcus as I was. She lent me her lipstick as we tried to flatten our hair gone frizzy in the heat.

'Hey, Siân. You know when you told Marcus that you were the girl with the dog? Did you see his face?'

I tried to remember but could only recall the calm, ever so slightly mocking smile he seemed to have permanently in place. Helena however had been more observant.

'He was totally shocked! You should have seen his face! He looked like he'd seen a ghost, his whole face went up about three inches to his ears.'

'That's the effect I have on men, it's a curse you know!' I had had four Baileys which is the only excuse for such an asinine reply. Later at home though, I could just imagine the shock the poor man had gone through. Here he was with his wealthy, well connected friends drinking to million dollar deals and penthouse apartments, when along comes a face from the past he'd left behind, a face which belonged to another Marcus who might just wish he'd taken another road. I settled back contentedly and made room for Ness's head on the pillow. This might even work. I might even find this long lost Marcus and drag him kicking and screaming back to life. And then we would live happily ever after, all three of us. It was half past one, everyone was asleep. But I was bursting with excitement, I was so full I was going to explode. And so I scampered down to Pete's room and woke the poor bastard up.

After chatting selfishly to an uncomplaining Pete until two, I kissed him goodnight on his nose and pulled one of his extra curly curls before closing the door, the Snuff album still playing. I could have taken Pete and Cali to Harvey's Wine Bar that night, I so nearly did. I was going to use them as shields, as back-me-ups, as human pints of Dutch courage but in the end I decided to go it alone. So Cal and Pete never met Marcus. And he never met them. And as

I look back over time, I have at least that small consolation for which to be very, very thankful.

Chapter 8 – Marcus

Marcus rang me two days later. He actually bothered to get my number from Sam and actually bothered to ring me. This was something I could scarcely have hoped for. We chatted a little about this and that, about what had happened on the news, the rumblings behind the Iron Curtain, what we both thought of *When Harry Met Sally*. No one used the term 'chick flick' back in 1989 but that's clearly what Marcus had thought of it.

'Sentimental crap!' he drawled, not bothering to hide his disdain, 'If you fastforwarded that poor bastard to five years time, he'd be screwing the eighteen year old nanny and drinking a bottle of Jack Daniels a night.'

'He'd be doing that anyway. At least, this way he gets to wake up next to Meg Ryan every now and again.'

'High maintenance. He was right about that. Emotional high maintenance. Even worse than the ones who borrow your credit cards.'

'Well, it's better than waking up at sixty with just a hot water bottle and colostomy bag to keep you warm at night. It's better to have tried than run away.'

'Hmm, maybe. I might have known you'd have liked that film, no woman I've ever met admits that it's crap.'

He was right. I love *When Harry Met Sally* but then I was very much a chick flick fan in that sort of '*Oh! A happy ending! Oh, I wish I could meet and fall in love with a really nice guy, Ooh, I like her hair*' sort of way. When we'd sparred in a friendly manner over that, he then described an art gallery opening he had been to the night before. And so it began. He was describing a life he led *without me in it.* He might have met another woman at an art gallery opening, he might have gone there with someone he really liked, he hadn't gone with me that's for sure so he'd gone with someone, someone who wasn't me….The poor bloke had only met me once and already I was jealous of every one of the twenty five or so years he had existed without me and by implication, every single one of the people he had met in those twenty five years. Massive dollops of familiar – oh! how familiar! – insecurity came rushing down in that same old avalanche, crushing in its path anything remotely balanced and rational.

    Marcus fortunately hadn't much enjoyed the opening.

    'Pretentious rubbish, most of it. Bricks and drainpipes pretending to women's internal organs, you know the sort of thing.'

    I desperately dragged up the long-forgotten memory of a trip Richard and I had taken to the Tate. There had been bricks there too, a whole pile in the middle of the floor and I had embarrassed Richard terribly by taking the piss a bit too loudly. But then Richard had not been my soul mate and Marcus…well, Marcus didn't like bricks pretending to be a uterus so that was a start.

    'They had that brick thing going at the Tate three years ago,' I said confidently and thanking God I was alone in the lounge and could be a bit of a prat. 'I wasn't impressed. The fire extinguisher had more artistic merit and might at least have been some use.'

    'And only a tenner at B & Q.'

I laughed, so relieved. His voice was so damned posh, it strolled along at its own pace down the wire, it wafted down great waves of public school and family money and yet he'd heard of B&Q! And he'd said tenner not pounds or *pie-nds* like the Queen. Things were looking up. I'd married him the night before and given birth to our second child who tragically had a hole in the heart which of course had brought us even closer together but in reality things were looking just as good.

'Sam is in big trouble, sneaking through my en suite, you know. I've threatened him with imminent eviction. What next? My boxer shorts drawer? My collection of novelty socks? What did he say to you about it all?'

I was slightly caught out here, not really wanting the relationship I was planning to have with Marcus to be based on lies but there was little else I could do in the circumstances.

'He recognised Ness, I think. And got my number from a friend of a friend. He recognised me from Uni.'

'Hmmm. Fair enough. Perhaps I'll wait until he empties my bin and steals my toe nail cuttings before I chuck him out. So…where is it you live again?'

It was a deceptively casual question from him but I caught a very real frisson of *this is an important question dressed up to appear casual.* I am many things, most of them not very admirable, but I am sensitive to people's real meanings and thoughts. That's why I always know when a boyfriend is about to cheat on me even if he hasn't got the faintest idea himself. I panicked slightly. In my daydreams, we had gone out for meals by the banks of rivers and shared exotic holidays in Thailand and Bali, coming home to be married and retire to the country but none of these fantasies actually involved him coming here, to Elm Park. I knew instinctively that this could never happen. If he ever caught just a glimpse or God forbid a whiff of this place and its inhabitants, then he would disappear from my life forever and I would have lost him, apparently again.

'Near Clapham,' Which was not a lie. Brixton is most certainly and without a shadow of a doubt near Clapham. Just as the North Peckham Estate is actually more-or-less Dulwich and staying with a mate in Birmingham is actually spending the weekend with chums in Warwickshire. We see what we want to see, we hear what we want to hear. Marcus seemed no different.

'Clapham? Nice one. I've got friends with a horribly drafty old Victorian monstrosity overlooking the Common. They go on about the sash windows and don't seem to notice the Force Nine gale that's coming through the gaps and freezing everyone's bollocks off inside.'

This was quite funny and I laughed but he was not yet off the scent.

'So have I just insulted your pad then? One of those period houses by the Common that antique dealers love?'

I looked around at the crumbling cornices and the fireplace painted black and red, the original bay window with, yes, sash windows but nailed up and an old hippy hanging draped across diagonally in place of a curtain.

'Well, yes, it is Victorian. And yes, we do have the original sash windows so you'd better stop there whilst you're just marginally behind, mate!'

He liked this. Clearly I was what the older boys at Rugby had called *a damned spirited filly ready for a ride!* Or something.

'Well, I apologise. I was brought up in drafty old houses and have an absolute antipathy towards anything built before 1980.'

'I know. You like to live like the cast of Blake's Seven, all chrome and weird plumbing pretending to be avant-garde sculpture.'

'How the bloody Hell did you know that?'

There was an edge to his voice, a stab of suspicion and the casual amity between us had gone. I mentally kicked myself. Obviously Sam hadn't told him that I'd been wandering around his apartment pretending to be a potential buyer (and thank Christ for that). Quite how Sam had explained being in Marcus's en suite was obviously more believable than the truth which was that a bored and frustrated hippy liked pretending to be Eva Peron and duped estate agents into taking her around properties she would never in ten lifetimes be able to afford. Let's face it, anything Sam had told Marcus was likely to sound a more sane explanation than the truth.

I tried to repair the damage. 'Just a guess. You City slickers like everything very simple and modern, don't you? Less is more and all that. One artichoke dressed up like a palm tree, three cherry tomatoes and a green bean in the middle of the plate at twenty five quid and calling itself nouvelle cuisine. Tell me I'm wrong!' *And please tell me you have a sense of humour and aren't going to take offence because you actually do think that food dressed up like crap art is worth stupid sums of money.*

God was smiling.

'Oh, you bitch! Give her a saucer of milk! I'll have you know that some of my best friends own nouvelle cuisine restaurants and I am a frequent and loyal patron.'

'And do you stop for a portion of chips on the way home?'

'A kebab, dear girl, a kebab.'

And so the rift was mended and forgotten but I made a mental note to act surprised and admiring when I was invited to his flat for the first time (and how could there not be a first time?) The call was drawing to a natural, lazy close.

'Well, my dear girl, I must let you get back to doing whatever it is you do. And what is it exactly that you do? Sam didn't say.'

The old lie came easy, half because I had convinced myself that it was the truth many months ago, half because I knew full well I could pull it off.

'I'm a PhD student. And I make ends meet by working in the college library. Although I'm on a sabbatical from work at the moment.'

'A student. How terrible for you. I was a student once but not a very good one. Kept running out of money. I was at UCL. Where are you now? King's I suppose.'

Shit. Another time to panic. I could see the web of lies getting thicker and thicker until one day it tripped me up and choked me. I could hardly tell him I'd just finished working at UCL Library given that two nights before, I'd pretended never to have been to the bloody place. Shit. One more lie and then that would be it. No more.

'Well as you know, I did my degree at Bristol. That's where I met Sam, but I'm doing my PhD through the…Institute of Archaeology. Very dull. What you do is much more interesting. Controversial of course but interesting.'

There was an odd silence, I could almost hear him rerunning my words and peering at them through some mental microscope.

'You were actually at Bristol at the same time as Sam?'

'Yes. Not in the same year though and he was doing Fine Arts. Not History.'

'I know.'

I let a moment pass, then jumped in to end the horrible silence. 'What's the problem? Bristol not good enough?'

Another pause. 'No, of course not. It's just that Sam never mentioned you before. He usually bangs on about everyone he's ever met until you want to shoot him but he never mentioned you. You weren't at his twenty first?'

Shit and double shit! I almost felt like cutting my losses and just putting the phone down. This was getting messy. Why wasn't I at Sam's twenty first?

'I think I was ill that weekend, no, my mum was ill and I had to go and visit her. Or something like that. Anyway, Sam and I weren't in exactly the same… you know, what do you call it?…. social group.'

'So you didn't go out with him then?'

Relief! Floods of lovely relief all over me. He was jealous! Here was me worrying about thin chic women at art gallery openings and he'd been concerned that I'd had a thing with his best friend. The cool City whiz kid. The Gordon Gecko of the pressed suit and horrid pink tie. Wanting to know if I'd had a thing with his best friend!

'Oh no, I hardly knew him really. And he's not really my type. He just took a fancy to my dog and used to walk her sometimes.'

'Hmm. Lucky dog. Seems to be a very popular mutt.' There was clearly still some suspicion there, I could feel it palpably down the line.

'Sam's really nice,' I said quickly, 'but he's not...not very *dynamic*.' I didn't know Sam at all but I had no qualms in trashing his personality if it might get me somewhere. Marcus clearly didn't have much loyalty either.

'He can be as soft as shit. He's a bloody hippy in a suit sometimes. I've spent twenty years trying to toughen him up and he's still like a bloody puppy. You throw the stick as far as you can bloody well throw it and he still brings it back, you beat him with the bloody thing and he wags his tail for more.'

This was quite funny. Sam was a bit like an overgrown puppy now I thought about it, not as much as Pete, but there was that certain *be nasty and I'll still come back* quality about him. I hoped Helena was as nice as she'd seemed.

'Marcus, there's no need to be quite so nasty about Sam, he did risk your wrath by reintroducing us after all.'

'So that came from him did it? Not you?'

This threw me a little. 'Err well, obviously I wanted to see you too, to clear some things up.'

'What things?'

'Well…things.'

'Right. OK, we need to clear some things up then. I agree. I just wasn't expecting…I wasn't expecting to see you again. This is all somewhat odd, out of the blue.'

'I know. It is for me too.'

There was another silence. He was the man, he now clearly had to either suggest a meeting or else say goodbye knowing that in so doing he was rejecting the idea of meeting up forever and ever amen. I was liberated and on the Pill and living in a Brixton squat where we took on the Fascist Council and occasionally Stopped The City but there was no way I was going to make the first move and ask a bloke out.

'So. Siân.'

'Marcus.'

'Would you like to do something this weekend? See a film or go out for a meal or something? No runner beans dressed up as Picasso, I promise. I think we need to be…re-acquainted, work out what's happening here.'

Victory!

'Sure, that'd be nice.' *Nice! Nice?* Since when did I ever use the word 'nice'? But cool would have been worse and excellent just sounded too Bill and Ted.

'OK, a film then. I'll see what's on at Hampstead. I'll get back to you in the week.'

'Fine. I'll see you then.'

He put the phone down first without saying goodbye but I didn't mind. He hadn't asked me what I'd like to see but I didn't mind that either. And he certainly hadn't considered that going to Hampstead was probably the most inconvenient place that someone living near Clapham could choose to venture to but what the Hell? I had a date. I something to do on a Friday night that didn't involve gigs, squatters or spliffs and as shallow as that might sound, that was what mattered.

Chapter 9 – Josef

Going to the cinema can be a very strange and unexpected thing. It can be a mediocre and utterly predictable thing too and none the worse for that, but sometimes, it has the capacity to turn you all over.

I remember a few years ago now, Sam and I took the children to see *Star Wars; the Phantom Menace*. I remember being mildly excited, I had of course been the first generation of eleven year olds to see *Star Wars* when it came out, my dad got us tickets to Leicester Square and still talks about it. This wasn't Leicester Square, this was somewhere a very long way from Leicester Square but it was still pretty much an event. The kids were jumping up and down, so were a hundred other people's kids, there was popcorn on the floor already and Coke spilt on the sleeve of my coat and the lights went down after the adverts and the screen did that funny shimmying in towards the edges thing and there was the dry as dust Film Board Certificate and I settled down comfortably…And then it happened. Completely unexpected. That sudden screen full of black infinite space with a thousand stars and the massive yellow writing appearing slowly from the bottom and the music, the thundering crash which told you more than words where you were and what this was and what you were about to see.

I was thirty something years old and hadn't seen a *Star Wars* film for twenty years and yet my heart turned over with a kind of sick thrill and shiver I remember from those days of being eleven.

Cali's husband Chris had to be dragged inside Peter Jackson's *Fellowship of the Ring*. She and a couple of friends manage to cajole him to the ticket office, get him to the nachos stand, get him past the pre-pubescents standing guard. By the time they pulled him bodily into the actual theatre he was nearly in tears. Sometimes a film isn't just a film, it's a hugely demonic medium that can either gather up your childhood dreams in its hands and enrich and cherish and bring them back to life or it can crush them into hot little embers of something unrecoverable. Chris nearly bolted from his seat during the adverts, he was in real tears by the time the Board of Censors darkened the room.

If Jackson had got it wrong, he said to me a few weeks after when they came up to stay, *you can't just go back to the book and say 'Oh well, no harm done, I just won't go to see the other two.' Something would have been spoilt.*

Cali wasn't quite the Tolkien fiend her husband was but I understood. Sometimes a book encapsulates an entire portion of your life which then becomes embedded in the pages and which releases its scent every time you then open the pages and read. So whenever I read Tolkien I remember, subconsciously mostly, what it was like to be twelve and frustrated with the banalities of the world I inhabited and full of desperate sadness that there was no more to this existence but school and work and grey skies and human beings with comfortable existences but no passion and no glory and no sense of the absolutes worth fighting for. There is a basic appeal to Tolkien that you either get or you don't, you either find an answering cry somewhere in your psyche or you read on deaf. Jackson took a bigger risk than the New Line producers and moneymen realized, he was playing with a million sensibilities, a million people's sense of self and identity. He was daring to put into real form and face the thirsty yearning we frustrated adolescents had pinned upon characters in someone else's world.

I knew the minute I heard the music and saw the first scene with Elrond in battle armour that it was going to be fine, said Chris over chilli and rice as we sat and looked out across the far off mountains. *I just felt this huge wave of relief come over me and my heart rate slowed down and I just opened my eyes properly and just breathed it all in. I didn't even bother to see what they'd done to the story, I did that when I went back the next day, I just breathed in the costumes and the music and the carvings on the walls of Rivendell. If you can breathe in a film and get to its heart, then it must be OK.*

Marcus was meeting me at West Hampstead Tube station. This was a bit of a disappointment because every lad I knew met me at the Tube station or in the pub or at the bar, no one ever said 'I'll call for you at seven', or 'I'll pick you up at half-eight'. It also meant that I had to sit on the Tube all the way from Brixton to West Hampstead which is a bloody long way during which time my stomach would be getting queasy and the palms of my hands sweaty and the only thing to look at would be my own reflection in the glass on the other side.

The London Underground is apparently a marvel of the modern world. The Metropolitan and District Line an engineering colossus to make the grown man weep. But it was designed by men who would rarely ever have to travel down its deep, dark throat, down those cavernous and twisting guts as the grey walls scream past. Or if they did, it was when surrounded by journalists in top hats writing with ink pens upon crossed and tailored knees as the Leviathan trundled along. No one fulminating the wonders of this great British marvel could ever have imagined fifty, sixty to a carriage or that their own classes might have to endure such a come-down. A century after its glorious inception, London has lost its love affair with the subterranean beast, now it lies like some mass of curled coils, some malevolent serpent raising its head now and again to belch out foul smells and nameless noises into the dark. No one actually knows, I'm sure, how the myriad coils link and cross and divide each other; all sense of depth and direction get swallowed away the minute you sink down the escalators.

God, I hated the London Underground.

I remember a few months before that summer of '89, I had gone down the stairs at Brixton to catch the tube to UCL Library. Right at the bottom, in between the two platforms (Brixton is at the end of the line in many, many ways but it still had two platforms and I always chose the one which then left second) stood a rasta in full array. Nothing unusual in that, nothing unusual in him sneering '*BloodClot!!*' at me as I rushed by, nothing strange in that. There was only one train waiting so I jumped in, sat down and waited. And then the rasta began to shout.

'Dis train! Dis iz de det train! Jump on bee-ord me brudders and zistairs, dis iz de det train!'

Well, I ignored him as did everyone else. There were always nutters on the Tube, it was part of the fabric of the place, normal rules did not apply underground, people were not prepared or bothered to judge you in the same way. So, if this helpful gentleman wanted to tell us all that we were alighting upon some long-foretold Train of Death, then so be it. Far be it from me to actually tell him to shut the fuck up because he was scaring people, no, the man had a right to believe in the Death Train if he so wished and anyway, the tosser probably had a knife.

Five minutes passed, then ten. This was usual. It usually happened when you were late for the most important date of your life and whilst stuck in a tunnel full of vegans who thought deodorants caused cancer. All the while, the rasta was ranting on and on, quite politely as it happened, telling all and sundry that we were all going to die. And then of course I thought of Moorgate and the newspaper reports about carriages being crushed into blocks the size of Minis and I wondered then if the rasta was playing a double game, pretending to be mad and therefore harmless with the intention of therefore enticing more people on and thereby maximizing his casualties. I always, always assume the worst can and does invariably happen and that avoidance is by far the most sensible and indeed valorous way to play it. There's little shame in running away from the nastier aspects of life, especially when the maniac who's just put Semtex under the wheels of your London Underground carriage is thoughtful enough to give you a running chance.

So, I got off the Tube, raced up the (as ever) stationary escalator and got the bus to work. An hour late, naturally. And no explosion killing and maiming hundreds on a packed commuter line either. Naturally. But I still think I was right to take the good man at his word.

This Tube that hot summer evening was fortunately not packed. Space doesn't make the system any friendlier, we just have more places to where we can avert our eyes. Apart from the nutters, the worst thing about the London Underground is the sheer boredom of having to actually use it. I used to take the piss out of the Poems on the Underground but to be honest, sometimes they were a bit of a Godsend. I still remember the one above and opposite me that evening as I went on my first date with Marcus.
My name is Ozymandias, King of Kings. Look upon my works, ye mighty, and despair.'
Funny that. How arrogance and self-belief can come to nought. Marcus simply reeked of privilege and self-belief. I had only met him the once but it was a natural scent to him, like a pheromone, an evolutionary aid to help him attract the best and most plentiful mates. Did Marcus ever look back at his mistakes and feel humble? Does he now? I didn't know then that he had ever made any, I had the image in my mind of some semi-god who glided through life on the crest of an upturned lip. I liked to think though, that evening as I sped beneath the earth to meet him, that there was a chink in the polish, some scratch upon the veneer that I could find and make my own to widen. What I was looking for or expecting or fooling myself was there, I'm not quite sure. The same old stereotype of the hardened cynic crumpling at my touch into the wounded boy probably. What we then do with the

wounded boy isn't so clear because, let's face it, the thrill of the daydream is getting shat upon by the hardened cynic. We rescue him, we melt him, we clutch him weeping to our breasts and then we quickly allow the fantasy to end, we bring the curtain triumphantly down. And there's a bloody good reason for that too.

Looking back so many years later, I doubt now that Marcus ever felt the humility of fucking up. Angry at himself, yes, blaming other people, certainly, but kingly acceptance of fault was probably beyond him. I was looking that night for some kind of Ozymandias of my own, some faint hope that a man so glorious might look upon me from his heights and reach out his hand. That to him I wouldn't be just some untidy little student with no sense of purpose, not some scruff who needed a good haircut and a facial. It was time someone saw me, the me my Ness loved, the me I wanted to meet too.

Still on the Victoria Line, the train was filling up. It was Friday night, the middle of July, and the capital's people were ready to go and celebrate being alive. Being cramped and underpaid and unable to afford decent housing but still alive and, more importantly, alive in *London*. I faced three Evening Standards, the staple diet of the Londoner who wants a read. A week before, the Marchioness had capsized in the river, thirty or so bright young things snuffed out of existence, their little flames swamped by the filthy water of the Thames at high tide. One Standard announced some kind of enquiry into the disaster, another had been turned on its spine and I could make out something to do with

Manchester United being sold on the Stock Exchange for 20 million. Football only interested me when it occasioned some kind of communal celebration like a World Cup. Then all the lads from Brixton and Clapham would get together in one house, drink all afternoon, shout at the TV whilst the few girls tolerated sat and pretended to care.

The third Standard was folded over and I could just about make out something to do with Oliver North. I really should have been more interested in the whole Irangate thing but it was all so far away and involved reading broadsheet newspapers which made you look like an idiot. I yawned. Suddenly there was a noticeable frisson, a definite move of heads towards the right as a very short young man got on at Green Park.

Josef.

Before realizing what the idiot was wearing, I smiled and nodded him over. Josef was a very good friend, at least I was his friend in the sense that Josef didn't really have friends in the conventional understanding of the word but I was as close as it got. He was one of the founding members of The Mob, one of most iconic hippy / indie / anarcho / or whatever bands of the mid-eighties. People would hitch from Scotland to see a Mob gig, their split was the most lamented band split London had ever known and their return was still rumoured on a monthly basis even five years on. Josef had formed a new band, Blyth Power, and was singer/drummer/main man. They were moderately successful but the tattered banners of old Mob gigs still clung to their reputation and ensured greater numbers than they probably deserved. Being asked to sing back-up for Blyth

Power had been a great triumph for me, back in 1985. Suddenly I was in a band that toured Europe and had proper rehearsal studios and recorded albums and did NME interviews.

Josef nodded his head, like a wise old monkey, great jaw jutting out as he sat down next to me. A small man, probably not five foot five, slightly built with a prominent chin he was always referring to in his songs. I finally took in what he had on. Oh shit. The rumours were true then, Josef Porter really had joined the Guardian Angels.

'Siân .'

'Hi, Josef. How are you?'

I could feel everyone looking at him (bugger it, looking at us!), some curious, others a little amused, others openly grinning. I knew I couldn't just ignore it; *Guardian Angel! Monstrous Prat! Self-Righteous Arsehole!* screaming all around the carriage. And yet, Josef Porter was neither prat nor arsehole, he was probably the most intelligent person I have ever met, before and since. But there's no denying a Guardian Angels bomber jacket is not the best advert for an elevated IQ.

I can't remember when they first started to patrol the New York Subway, some time in the 1980s, but they were quite a force to be reckoned with over there. Big, usually black men, who stood at the end of a subway carriage, arms folded and looking out for the first sign of trouble. Muggings went down, they said, whenever an Angel was on the subway, rapes and picked pockets too. There were endless debates in serious broadsheets about the true social comment such necessity was making. Was this indicative of the breakdown of law and order and a population's desperation or was it the first step upon the road to community policing by the people for the people?

It was only a matter of time of course before the Guardian Angels flexed their pretty wings over here. The trouble was that a carriage full of people is naturally very quiet and well behaved when there are two twenty stone Afro-Americans from Harlem standing at the end of the aisle with enough gold jewelry on their knuckles to break every tooth in your mouth. Very quiet. But as soon as the Bronx Bouncers handed the beat over to their London counterparts and flew back to Manhattan, that's when the trouble started.

London's Guardian Angels were neither black nor twenty stone. They tended to be very well meaning and could wield a mean 'stare-you-out' stare for thirty seconds before dropping but that was all. Londoners are not New Yorkers. Londoners rarely believe the genuine good in anyone and even when they do, it's a green-light for taking the piss.

'So, Josef…….How's Blyth?' I chickened out at the last minute. A more worthy friend would have thought '*sod the bastards, he's my friend and I'm going to show an interest in his new hobby*' but I was twenty-two and not very mature and even less worthy a friend and what a crowd of Londoners I would never see again thought of me was more important.

Josef spoke to the floor. 'Oh, you know. Getting on. Tour coming up.'

For someone who, I knew, could produce such incredible lyrics, he was hard work sometimes. Josef must have been a nightmare to teach at school. All those brains, all that understanding, all that creativity bursting out, and yet nothing there that an O Level syllabus could harness, nothing at all. He excelled at Medieval History but only when comparing it to cricket. He knew more about Chaucer than anyone I've ever met but could only write about him as a Hackney squatter plying his trade for Special Brew. Josef once dedicated an entire album of songs to the Percys of Northumberland and I honestly believe that of the thousands of anarcho-punks who bought the damned thing or who danced to the tracks live, I was the only person apart from Josef who actually knew who the Percys were.

Nothing there for the O Level syllabus to bring out, to encourage to blossom, to see grow. I can just see him as a schoolboy, daydreaming and getting sent out. Writing essays he was interested in and not the essays he'd been set, bullied by the rugby team for being no good at sport. He left school with nothing I believe, just a guitar and a head full of history. His teachers no doubt felt they'd failed him, that the system had let him slip through the net and to a certain extent, they'd be right. But Josef was no fool. Josef chose his own path, even if it made no sense to anyone else.

'Where are you touring?' I was just being polite really. Blyth Power always, always played the same tours. A few dates in Holland and then too many in West Germany. A couple in Berlin as the highlight and then home.

'Oh you know, Utrecht, Munich, Berlin.'

'Nice. Looking forward to it?"

He shrugged, letting little out as usual. He knew as well as I did that touring Europe with Blyth Power was not actually very nice at all. Seven or eight people cramped together in one big white van, all excited at the off and bored of each other by Zeebrugge. Gigs in bars and dingy clubs with disco-lights beneath the floors, stages eighteen inches high if you were lucky, no stage at all if you weren't. Sleeping on people's floors, eating crap, moaning about the stink in the van, falling out, wishing we could tour America like other bands. Talking about going on tour was great. Reminiscing about going on tour was even better. Showing off because you had been on tour was the best. But as a real-time experience…I don't miss it much.

Josef sat back and folded his arms, the bright red of his jacket like a bloody great beacon. Some young lads were grinning at each other as they swung from the ceiling straps like monkeys ready for a scrap.

'You look…..unusual.' Josef had finally noticed I wasn't quite the same old scruffy female he was used to. I had one of my long tight skirts on with another semi-respectable Warehouse top loaned yet again from Cali and my hair was…well, there was no other word for it…my hair was decidedly *curly.* It was this that was clearly perplexing Josef. No person we knew save Pete had curly hair. People had crimped hair or dreadlocked hair or no hair but they simply did not ever, ever have curly hair.

I was embarrassed and then cross with myself for being embarrassed and then even more conscious of feeling embarrassed.

'Uni thing,' I explained which covered a whole multitude of imaginary sins. He nodded, understanding. Uni-things were part of the other world that I occasionally inhabited, the other world Siân of Elm Park disappeared to every now and again but which meant nothing to anyone else. The Guardian Angels jacket still sat between us, encasing him in its awfulness and making it impossible for me to look at him. It was such an *un-Josef* thing to do. Join a New Model Army re-enactment society, yes, right up his street. Go and live with pseudo-Anglo-Saxons or Vikings in some Welsh commune, sure. But join the *Guardian Angels??* A sudden horror struck me. What if he was going to West Hampstead? What if he was just on patrol and going anywhere and decided to sit with me until my stop and Marcus saw him? How on earth would I explain away *this?*

Josef was humming something to himself, the train stopped with a sharp screech, everyone stared with sudden fascination at the multi-coloured wiring which ran along the tunnel wall.

'Where are you going?' *Please God, don't say 'Oh anywhere really, perhaps even West Hampstead, who knows?'*

'King's Cross. Train thing.'

'Aaaah.'

Josef was a trainspotter, of course he was. And as such often organized Blyth Power tours around the best British Rail depots and holding yards, Jesus, the bloody band was named after a train. I didn't bother to pretend to be interested. Train spotters know their own kind instinctively and don't take kindly to well-meaning intruders who have no intention of staying the course. We sat in semi-awkward silence until the train shuddered up again. The lads swinging on the straps were still sending us confrontational looks but I pretended not to notice. The one thing you could absolutely depend on on the London Tube was that no matter the innocence of the victim, no bugger ever intervened to help any other bugger in trouble.

We exchanged a few more words, mostly monosyllabic. And then he gave another polite and anachronistic nod of the head and was up and gone through the sliding doors. The lads jeered something after him as he passed them by, one of them grabbed at his jacket and made a wanker sign. I turned away and pretended not to see. I can't remember if I saw Josef after that, that might well have been the last time which is a shame. If anyone had been bored enough to listen in to that ten minute conversation, they'd have thought we were two averagely intelligent people with little to say to each other or to anyone else. Which is a shame because Josef and I wrote great letters to each other. I'd tell him about Lothar I of the Merovingians and his dreadful brothers, he'd write to me about Jack Cade and John of Gaunt and of how the Percy and Neville feud of the 15th century was really no more and no less than the spats Conflict and Chumbawamba occasionally had. I still have his letters. A week or so after the Guardian Angel incident, he wrote to me about some awful work he was doing for Hackney Council. He had to help clean and clear out council re-lets, in his words *'supplementing the modest income from my music by scrubbing floors, scraping ghee off encrusted cookers, hoovering up after the underprivileged and generally doing the kind of grim domestic tasks I've spent years avoiding in my own home.'*

Josef had one day that summer been sent to clean out the flat of a tenant who had died.

What had happened was that the former owner of the hair I was picking up in greasy clumps from the floor, had passed away without warning in his armchair whilst listening to Santana on cassette. Neighbours only discovered his demise a week later when the man's two-year-old finally made himself heard and they broke in to find him, by which time the electricity had run out, most of the water in the downstairs toilet had been drunk and the edible contents of the kitchen scattered around the ground floor, much of it around the sepulchral armchair where the baffled child had been trying to induce his recumbent father to eat.

Happily by the time we arrived, the body had been removed – minus the hair and most of the liquid content which had soaked through the armchair and discoloured the carpet. The mother apparently wanted to come and see the flat and I'd been asked to remove the 'more disturbing elements'. The 'more disturbing elements' included the maggots, the child's excrement and the pathetic attempts he had made to emulate his father's domestic routine.

A man who can clear up after such a thing and remain philosophical about it all has no need of my help when faced with thugs on a London Underground Tube. But I still feel I should have said something because if Josef Porter was anything in this world, it certainly wasn't a wanker.

By the time I emerged up into the bright light of a Hampstead summer evening I was in a real state. Hair, make up, teeth, breath, all checked and doubled checked, stomach sucked in, cheekbones sucked in, bottom sucked in, how I managed to take in oxygen too was a mystery. I knew what I was like when this nervous; I said stupid things, I interrupted other people's conversations, I laughed too loudly, I forgot every Golden Rule of How To Get Your Man. And worst of all, we were not on my home ground. Meeting people at The Robey or The Fulham Greyhound, familiar cesspits whose every corner I'd known for a decade, that would have been fine. I'd know where the loos were, I'd be able to say a casual 'hi' to people as they passed by as if to remind my lucky date exactly how popular and important I really was. Marcus at the Fulham Greyhound? Perhaps, perhaps. The saloon side actually wasn't bad at all, perhaps I might suggest it. But not the Robey, dear God, never the Robey.

I didn't know West Hampstead at all well then and know it not at all now. A main high street with lots of wine bars and pizza restaurants, a posh independent cinema up the hill on the left. Lots of well heeled, good looking people with plummy accents or was that just my imagination? A moment's panic. Were we meeting at the Tube or outside the cinema? I sorted through the mess in my head. *Meet you at eight then, outside the ticket office.* Fine, the ticket office. Panic again. Which ticket office? The Tube station had a ticket office and so presumably did the cinema. Or was the cinema's a box office? What did posh people call the place you bought a cinema ticket?

I had a lightning look around. I couldn't picture Marcus' exact features in my head but I knew I'd recognize him if I saw him. No sign. It was five to eight. I could walk up to the cinema, check it out and still get back to the Tube and not be too late, panic, panic, panic. I caught hold of myself. *For Christ's sake, it doesn't matter! Ticket office, box office, cinema, Tube station, it doesn't bloody matter. You'll bump into him somewhere, he asked you out, don't forget, he rang you. He's the one with the bloody picture on his shaving mirror, what the hell have you got to prove?*

All this was undeniable and I felt a little calmer. Right, a relaxed, not-a-care-in-the-world amble up the High Street, a casual look into the windows as if I might just pop back another day and buy a cardigan for eighty-five quid or a pair of boots for two hundred and fifty.

'Hi. Siân, isn't it?' Right at my shoulder, out of thin air. I gulped before able to catch it back, made some desperate attempt to rearrange the *'caught on the hop and looking stupid'* face into the *'vaguely interested in something else more profound'* face I'd been practicing.

'Marcus! Hi!' And then he did something totally unexpected, something no man had ever done to me before. He leant over and he kissed me on the cheek.

People in West Hampstead probably kiss each other on the cheek all the time, they probably do that 'flex your lips into the air approximately two inches away from anyone's actual skin' thing whilst mouthing 'dahling!'. But this was actually a nice, affectionate, very smooth chinned kiss. And he smelt of soap not of aftershave which was also a pleasant surprise. As I backed off like a rabbit caught in headlights, I saw also that he'd done something with his hair. It wasn't quite as gelled down as before, it wasn't spikey exactly but it was certainly…..ruffled. Marcus had ruffled his hair.

The effect was extremely pleasant.

'You look nice.' He caught me on the hop again, that was exactly what I'd just been about to say.

'No, take it back, you look lovely.'

And that made me all self-conscious of course and embarrassed because although I had made a real effort and Cal had done my make up and the Tube journey hadn't quite melted all of it down my chin just yet, I wasn't lovely. I knew my limits. I was good looking enough, yes, but in that way that Emma Thompson is really good looking until you see her next to Keira Knightly.

'Err, thanks. You've ...done something to your hair.' *Jesus! What a cretinous thing to say! He's not your girlfriend, he's not some friend of your mother, you're not going to sit around a couple of cappuccinos and discuss hi-lites. Pull yourself together.*

Fortunately Marcus was several hundred degrees cooler than me and recognized a swimmer struggling in the current.

'Come on, we can talk as we walk. Film starts at eight fifteen.' And he took my hand, *he took my hand.* Not knowing quite what to do (my usual boyfriends didn't hold my hand in public until they'd been fucking me at least a month), I sensibly just went along with the flow. We crossed the road like kids, nearly getting run over by an irate Black Cab and giggling as we jumped the curb.

'They can't hit you anyway, their insurance goes up.' I quipped, slightly drunk at the touch of his fingers around mine. It wasn't in retrospect an incredibly funny remark but he laughed as if I'd made some kind of witticism.

'True, I'd never thought of it like that. I shall wind up cab drivers more often in future. I hope you haven't seen this film before…Jesus wept, why don't people mind where they're fucking going, 'scuse my French…..I've read the Stokes biography of Mishima but I've never made time to see this film. It's supposed to be very good.'

I wasn't keeping up at all. First of all, not only had he ruffled his hair so he didn't look quite so much like a Square Mile Fascist, he had definitely dressed down and I'm sure he'd done something to his voice. He wasn't quite as…well, posh. There were clear signs here of him actually making an effort to make me like him. Someone had actually bothered to make an effort to make me like them. I couldn't recall the last time that had happened. And what on earth was he talking about with his newly proletariat accent? Who the hell was Stokes? Who or what or where was Mishima? I made non-committal comments about having not seen it either (*phew! Wasn't that fortunate*? we both agreed) but that I'd heard interesting things about it. We got to the cinema, a small dark doorway on the curve of a junction and had to race straight in, Marcus flashing a bundle of notes in a leather wallet full of plastic cards (I had one dirty Lloyds cashpoint card which allowed me to take out fifty pounds and no more. Marcus, I saw, had at least one from Barclays which upset me a little but that was something for a later date).

The film.

Now, I've already said how strange an experience the cinema can be, how frightening, how intrinsic to one's cumulative sense of self. Fifteen years or so on, I can't even remember the name of this one. *A Life in Four Phases* or something, I can't remember the plot except every now and again we'd return to black and white reality and watch some Japanese soldier try to incite some kind of army mutiny before committing hara-kiri and having his mate cut his head off. But I remember even now the moment when Marcus reach out and took my hand again. Nothing more, no fingers rubbing fingers, just a cool press of flesh on flesh but it was wonderful. Two hours of wonderful.

The Japanese guy cut his guts open and his friend kindly sliced his head off for him and the film ended and we all spilled out into the summer darkness of Hampstead High Street. Marcus raised his eyebrows in a semi-sardonic question.
'Well? Intellectually stimulating? Or pretentious crap?'
I laughed, so grateful he had allowed the option. But I was sensible enough to hedge my bets nevertheless, I mean, he could have been testing me.
'I liked the way the plays were depicted in so much colour. It made the suicide seem more stark. But it was a little clever for the sake of clever.'
'My view exactly. Which Mishima novels have you read?'
I couldn't wing this one. I decided to chance everything on the, hopefully cute, admission of girly ignorance. We were walking down the hill, hands free, I didn't have the nerve to grab his.

'Look Marcus, I have an admission to make! I'd never heard of Mishima before now! A complete ignoramus! Am I going to be dumped in the middle of Hampstead and told to come back when I've found an oriental bookshop?'

His face looked a little strange in the streetlights, for one moment I thought I'd lost the gamble but then he smiled again, with perfect teeth.

'Who cares? We can see The Terminator next time.'

Relief. And a few minutes of companionable walking. It was a warm, still night. The pavements full of people saying goodbye, hugging hallo, swigging bottles of beer outside pubs. The Bangles blared out from somewhere. London was a good place to be when she was in a good mood. Then I started to panic. The Tube was coming up. Where were we going? I was no sort of modern female to ask myself to anyone's flat and there was no way on this earth that Marcus was coming to Elm Park. And we'd spent the last two hours sitting in silence, we'd hadn't talked about the photo of Ness or what he'd wanted three years ago. Or what he wanted now. Perhaps it didn't need mentioning, perhaps he was embarrassed. And there was no way I was telling him I'd been in his flat pretending to be some married yuppy because my life was so pathetic I needed to borrow other peoples. Best to let him think Sam had seen the photo and recognized Ness because he already knew me. That made more sense than the truth after all. Marcus was hailing a cab, suddenly looking like a real grown up. My friends bought cabs at auctions and tinkered around with their underbellies whilst dumping them in the front yards of squats. Marcus simply clicked his fingers and made them appear.

'Can I give you a lift? I'm way over towards Canary Wharf near Docklands but if he doesn't mind going out of his way…where do you live in Clapham anyway?'

As I've said, I'm pretty sensitive when it comes to nuances and moods. I can usually tell the difference between casual questions and questions pretending to be casual and this was again definitely the latter. My heart did a little victory roll but then slapped itself back to its senses. There was no way I was admitting 94 Elm Park as my address. 1) it was clearly not Clapham and 2) God forbid he might actually turn up one day and come face to face with that bastard Gavin who would probably tell him I was out turning tricks or selling The WatchTower or getting myself checked out at the STD Clinic. Or even worse he'd meet mad Claire and she'd invite him in and sell him drugs and try to give him a henna tattoo.

I desperately wanted him to know I was interested but giving him my address was a simple no-no.

'I'm fine, it'll cost you a fortune to go via Clapham but thanks anyway. I like the Tube and walking up the Hill keeps me fit.'

Too late. *What bloody hill! There's no bloody hill in Clapham, you stupid cow!*

He gave me a funny look and I motioned towards his cab which was blocking the traffic.

'Thanks for the film. I enjoyed it or at least I think I did. Nope, I'm sure I did. My treat next time.'

He opened the door, seemingly not certain what to say next. He suddenly looked ten years younger, vulnerable, nervous, I think I fell for him completely at that point.

'Can we go out next weekend? Go out for a meal? We need to talk properly. In retrospect, perhaps a film wasn't the best idea.'

It was a strange way of phrasing it, *we need to talk properly*, what did that mean? But the cabbie was snorting and cars revving impatiently so I nodded and shouted 'Ring me!' as he pulled away.

It took me an hour and a half to get two Tube trains and a bus to the bottom of my road. My feet ached and my back was twinging in a really ominous way but I didn't care. I had actually joined the real world of grown up men and grown up women where men kiss their dates upon the cheek and hold their hands and take them to see foreign language films in posh parts of London. I had a man who was so good looking it hurt just to look at him but who had bothered to dress down for me and even change his accent and *ruffle his hair* and who was so keen he had had a picture of my dog on his shaving mirror for three damned years. I couldn't wait to see Ness, to take her around the block in the summer night heat and tell her how much I loved her and how good life was going to be.

At home, the door had come off its top hinge and was making a scary noise, Bungle had been sick on the hall carpet and Gavin was playing Nirvana at full volume directly above my bedroom. I didn't care. Not even Satan could bother me this night. Ness came bounding down the stairs and jumped up, paws in my hair, wet nose on mine. In the kitchen, the washing up piled high and rank, the mud on the floor caught the heels of my sister's shoes and Gavin had filled the fridge with sausages. Shit. I refused to rise to the bait, held an old dishcloth between my fingers, picked the sausages up through the cloth and gave them all to Ness.

Chapter 10– Gavin

The incident with the sausages got really out of hand.

My view was that 94 Elm Park was a vegetarian house. It had been squatted twelve years before by vegetarians, had always been lived in by vegetarians and the very few non-veggie people who had moved in since had had the courtesy to realize that 'when in Rome…' etc was just being polite. Other houses were far more draconian than ours. I had been in houses where you had to leave your leather at the door. Where you couldn't eat sweets with gelatine in, where you had to lick your ice creams outside. I've known households where leather sofas have been thrown out into skips and people sat for six months on the floor before finding another, less bloodthirsty, piece of furniture.

We at 94 Elm Park thought we were very laid back about the whole thing. Jamie was a vegan but he accepted that other people weren't so there was cows' milk as well as soya in the fridge. If Al wanted fish and chips he went down to the parade and ate them on the way back. People didn't much like the smell he brought back into the house with him but we didn't make him stand in the garden like other squatters might have. But we did have some rules. Meat was simply the corpse of some unfortunate beast which should have been allowed to live until old age and as such had no place sitting slowly decomposing in our kitchen. When Gavin pointed out that we were quite happy to allow the eviscerated corpses of cows to come in on people's backs and people's feet, we had the answer pat and perfect.

Everyone knows that leather is the by-product of the meat industry, cows aren't killed for their leather, they're killed for their meat. If there was no such thing as the meat industry, there wouldn't be leather either.

I now realize of course that this is pure, self-serving bollocks but giving up leather was such a drag. The waxed jackets that Ben and Chumbawamba all wore, in truth, looked really shit and if you didn't want to wear your bikers boots in plastic, then the choice was pretty poor.

Sausages though, sausages in the fridge were definitely out.

I first heard of Gavin's terrible discovery when he banged on my door at about half eleven the next morning, Ness getting up onto her haunches and barking.

'Where are my fucking sausages? That was my fucking breakfast! Oi! Where are my sausages, you hippy witch!''

I was actually quite frightened of Gavin. He was horribly obnoxious in a very sly, sneaky way. Physically he made my flesh crawl too. Very tall and thin in black, black and black, he had eyelashes and eyebrows which were so pale they were virtually white. His skin was almost colourless, his eyes so pale a blue they were grey. I have nothing against ginger people – Jamie's girlfriend Julie was a redhead and she was absolutely gorgeous - but ginger hair on someone so pale and so mean-spirited and spiteful…..I heard a report on Radio 4's *You And Yours* once which said that serial killers were first, most likely to have tortured small animals when young, second, were likely to be middle children and third, were disproportionately redheaded. I kid you not, it was on Radio 4 so it must be true.

Gavin was undeniably ginger, had an older brother and two younger sisters and as for his personal pet policy….I didn't want to know.

'Get lost, Gavin, I'm trying to sleep,' I lied. 'Go and find another house.'

'Yeah, yeah, yeah, change the fucking record.' And he stomped off upstairs. Ten seconds later, Nirvana came crashing down through the ceiling. Gavin didn't even like Nirvana, he just knew that I didn't either.

The awful thing about sharing a house with someone you can't stand is the fact that you can never relax, never be at ease. Unless I knew that Gavin was out (which was never) or in his room (which was often), I was on edge walking into the lounge or going up to Cali's room or standing in the kitchen. And I resented not being comfortable in my own damned home.

'OK, darling, let's get up.'

Ness agreed, she was used to slothful mornings but things had been getting a little lazy of late. To make it up to her, I gave her toast and jam for breakfast and an hour in Brockwell Park chasing sticks. The summer was at its height and the days long and lazy. I was glad I'd given up my shitty job at the library but it meant signing on again which was a drag although everyone I knew except Cal and Pete did it.

Some had gone one further and signed up for the Young Enterprise Scheme which basically meant that you pretended to come up with some totally bogus idea for a new business and if your business plan (usually a handwritten sheet of A4) was convincing enough or at least not completely hopeless, you were given fifty quid a week for a year. Which is when you then of course declared your business bankrupt and went back on the dole. I knew at least twenty people who ran record companies or published fanzines or printed t-shirts and yet none of them actually seemed to be doing these things at all. Curious, that. But it kept them off the statistics which I suppose was the whole point.

Back at the house, people were stirring. As it was Saturday, even Pete and Cali were around and Pete was making everyone Big Veg for breakfast (this is simply where you throw everything you have into a pot, heat it up for a bit and have it all on toast. It has the added advantage of then gaining in flavour as it sits forgotten on the cooker for the next four or five days. There is a great skill in learning at what point the Big Veg has reached its optimum and at what point it has crossed over into mould).

"Hallo darling!' Pete was as cheery as ever and gave me a hug, curly hair everywhere. 'Where'd you get to last night?'

I thought on this as I helped stir the stew. Quite why I hadn't said anything to anyone about meeting Marcus in Hampstead I'm not sure. Didn't want it jinxed probably. Or more likely was the fact that I didn't want him to meet my friends, not yet anyway. Not until he was…*more like them* and they were…*in another place*.

'Went to the Uni bar. Very dull.'

'You pull, gorgeous?' This was Jamie, looking like he had just camped outside Greenham Common without a change of clothes for six months. One of his dreadlocked plaits was sticking out at right angles to his head and he smelt of warm wool and Bungle.

'I never pull, you know that. Terminal spinster, me.'

'Bollocks. I'd have yer!' And he squeezed my waist, lighting his roll-up on the cooker and strolling barefoot back into the lounge. I could never have walked barefoot in our house. The carpets had never been cleaned and were furry with living things. The floorboards had splinters rising up like Freddy Krueger's steel fingers and the floor not lucky enough to have carpet or floorboards was pure mud. But Jamie was very calm and at one with the whole *'nature isn't all flowers, you know'* thing. He found something positive wherever he looked, from the silverfish in the carpet which were *really amazing* (apparently) to the different shades of shit left by the pigeons on the top landing. Pete and Jamie were very alike in that way although Jamie was so laid back he sometimes couldn't get up from the sofa whereas Pete's boundless joy and enthusiasm for life had him out the door whistling by eight.

Some music show came on and we sat and stared at the black box, I think there was me, Cal, Pete, Jamie and Al who was reading some mountain bike magazine. Squatter lads love mountain bikes. We were all too poor to afford cars and no one but an idiot drives in London anyway so the boys spent all their money on bikes. Lots of them were dispatch riders which in those days often paid cash in hand.

I wondered what to do about money. I had savings from a five grand inheritance I had come into the year before from a long dead grandfather but I was famously stingy when it came to parting with that. I could go back to King Henry's Feasting House where I had worked with Emma; I shuddered at the very thought.

"What's the matter?' Pete was on the arm of the sofa, almost on my lap, nearly spilling stew on my tights.

"Nothing. Just wondering about money. I need to earn some.'

Pete was so predictable, he was like a child sometimes. 'I'll lend you some, no problem. Go on, what do you need? A hundred, two hundred?'

'No, you're OK, sweetie. I'll manage. I was thinking about that bloody Henry VIII restaurant down by the Tower, eighteen quid a night cash in hand. Jamie, does Emma still work there.'

'Think so, dunno.'

'Oh. Shit. Oh, it's crap anyway.'

Pete was all wide-eyed and interested. 'Is that the one where you had to dress up as a serving wench and sing Greensleeves? That sounds well cool!'

'And get my arse pinched by wankers from the City and have gravy spilt down me by Japanese tourists and have all the other girls bitch and moan because they were *'actresses really just waiting for their Equity Card to come through.'*

"Were they!?'

'No, you dickhead, of course they weren't. They just thought if they said it enough times, it might actually happen. Most of them went home with the customers for fifty quid.'

"No?!' Pete's eyes were even wider, bless him. 'Were you ever…you know, were you ever, you know…I'm not saying that you would but were you ever…?'

'Tempted? No, of course I bloody wasn't, you great fool. I'm not that desperate. Oh shit Pete, mind my skirt.'

At that point Gavin stormed in. Jamie nodded and said 'morning' which Gavin ignored, Pete and I blanked him, Al was deep in his magazine and Cal slipped through the door and disappeared back upstairs taking Ness with her.

'I want a fucking house meeting,' said the Ginger Monstrosity, 'SHE's gone and nicked my sausages.'

Jamie curled up in a ball at this and laughed like someone who had got really stoned the night before and hadn't quite pissed it out of his system.

'Fucking Hell, Gavin, nicked your sausages? That must have hurt.'

'It's not funny. They were mine, I paid for them, they cost me two quid, she owes me two quid.'

'Oh come on, man, I'll give you two quid. Come on, let me give you two quid, you silly arse…'

I wasn't having any of this.

'Jamie, he's not supposed to bring meat into the house, he knows that. This is a vegetarian house.'

(At this point, Gavin always made a stupid comment about it being made of bricks and cement so I hurried on before he could interrupt.)

'He wasn't invited to come and live here, (at this point Gavin gave a huge theatrical yawn) 'and he doesn't do anything positive for anyone...'

'What do you do?' came back the Intruder, 'What do you do but put on make up and play crap music and moan about how much chocolate you've eaten?'

This was a little too close to the *actualité* for comfort. 'I live here! This is my home. I was invited to live here nearly two years ago by a vote of all the people here at the time and I cook for everyone and I do the washing up...'

'Oh boring! My bloody parents do washing up, it's what they *do*. It's what they *are*."

'Well, at least I don't bring bloody meat into a house full of vegetarians.'

'So?'

'Well, you wouldn't bring pork if you were staying with Jews, would you?'

'Depends if I wanted to eat it.'

'Christ, you're such a selfish arsehole...'

Jamie uncurled himself and Al put down the bikes. Al was in Mediator Mood, you could see it in his eyes, he sensed a humanitarian mission he could play superhero to.

'Hey guys, chill! Chill!'

When Jamie said 'Chill' it sounded like someone who had taken enough drugs to deserve the right to say such a stupid word and come out of it with his cool intact. Al said it like an actor on EastEnders. The same actor who always has to say '*He's gone to buy* **some stuff**' or '*he's back on* **that stuff**' when actually he means smack.

'We need a house meeting to sort this prick out.' I said, knowing that being so confrontational never went down well with any of my friends who were the least confrontational people in the world.

'I'm not going anywhere,' said Gavin walking into the kitchen, 'and I want my two quid.'

'Tough.'

'Then I want some more sausages.'

'If I buy sausages it'll be to give them to Ness like the last lot.'

He turned around, eyes like very faraway holes. 'Your fucking dog had my sausages?'

I desperately wished I hadn't said that. I had nothing in the world I cared about except Ness and the bastard knew it, everyone knew it.

Jamie got up and stood, not coincidentally, between us, turning over the telly.

'Gavin, just go and chill out. I can't handle arguments this early, man, they're such a downer. Have some of my soya sausages, they're excellent.'

'Soya sausages?' Gavin's wide, fleshy lips turned down so far they almost met underneath. 'I'm not eating that shit, *soya sausages?* What planet are you freaks living on? Sausages are made of meat, that's why they're sausages. If they were supposed to be made from some fucking bean, they wouldn't be called sausages. They're sausages because they're *pork.* Jesus H. Christ, I move out of my bastard parents' house because they won't stop giving me grief and you turds want me to stuff my face full of hippy shit I wouldn't feed that bastard bloody cat with. Sausages are meat, you bastards, there's no such thing as soya sausages, there's just stringy lumps of soya stuck together to look like sausages and tasting of shit.'

He was still cursing as he jerked open the front door and went stomping off down the road to the shop. Jamie and Pete both tried to do the best impression of him, laughing their heads off as they shouted '*Soya??* God damn it man, sausages are PORK! Bloody Hell, Pete, doncha know, sausages are PORK, not BEAN, PORK!!' Al went back to his bikes and I ran upstairs to just check that Ness was OK.

That Saturday we all went to see Snuff at Kilburn National which was too depressing to recall in much detail. When the bloke you used to go out with before he was famous then dumps you and starts to pull five thousand people, it's really bloody stupid to go along and watch but then I was really bloody stupid when it came to being a masochist. And anyway, it didn't hurt so much anymore. I had Marcus to think about, I had a whole new world opening up in front of me which didn't involve satanic housemates and ex-boyfriends with groupies.

Snuff were still a fine thing to see anyway. They had opened up our eyes, these pale-faced Kilburn lads who ate at McDonalds and thought that Nelson Mandela played for Fulham. Every other band we ever saw wrote about race and Thatcher and nuclear bombs, every band except Wat Tyler who played it for laughs anyway. Snuff though, Snuff wrote about the girls who'd dumped them outside the Roxy when they were only fifteen, the time they were jumped by a gang of skinheads on Kilburn High Road, the day their mopeds made it all the way to Clacton. And they told us their ordinary and yet glorious little life stories with such mad passion, with such screaming guitars and thumping bass lines you wanted to cry. None of our bands apart from Chumbawamba had ever really thought about tunes before, not real tunes. But Snuff listened to Northern Soul and Aretha, they loved Small Faces and Rod Stewart and despite the thrash metal guitar, the bittersweet melody of a decade before we were born always came through.

Somehow was Snuff's great anthem, unless you counted the glorious '*Tiff*' of course ('*I think we're alone now, alone no..ow, there doesn't seem to be anyone around, I think we're alone now, alone no.. ow, there doesn't seem to be any sight or sound'*). *Somehow* made me cry because it was about such an ordinary life in such extraordinary chords, a life lived out from day to day in quiet and desperate acceptance that it wasn't going to get any better.

> *From the top of a lager, in a wineless wine bar*
> *I can see the sun set over Blackbird Hill*
> *It's only the cocaine camaraderie*
> *Keeps the punters from going in for the kill*

It played in my head all the way home.

The next day was a Sunday, dreaded Sunday, and Marcus hadn't called (36 hours and the bastard hadn't called). As ever when we want to sleep away a day, we wake at dawn and lie desperate for the brain to stop buzzing full of useless crap, we lie infuriatingly conscious of every buggering bird and car and passerby until finally we admit defeat and get up. But today was different, today I got a phone call.

It wasn't Marcus but Sam. This was a huge disappointment of course especially as it had sounded so much like Marcus for ten seconds, ten seconds when I had sucked in my stomach, lowered my voice pitch and adopted a gamine little smile. All to no avail. It was only Sam.

'I…er…just wondered how everything was going. Marcus said you went out the other night.'

I pulled the phone which was a first floor landing extension into my room so I could sit on the bed. 'Oh fine, fine. Actually I'm glad you rang, Sam. Have you said anything about me being at the flat? I'd rather he didn't know about that, I mean, I wasn't doing anything wrong but it might seem a little…'

'Weird?'

There was a definite *judging* tone to his voice, the toffee-nosed git was judging me.

'Well whatever. What have you told him?'

'Just that we met at Uni. And I recognized Ness from his photo and told you to come to the bar that night.'

'Oh, thank God for that! I was panicking you'd said something about...well, you know…'

'About your weird habit of looking round other people's houses?'

He was definitely not about to let it go and was starting to piss me off a little.

'I don't do that any more. Anyway, what did you want?'

'Uh?'

'You rang. I didn't ring. You rang.'

'Oh yeah, I was wondering if you'd like to meet for coffee. I just need to talk to you about something.'

This was odd. It quite clearly wasn't a *being chatted up* conversation, even I knew that.

'What? What do you want to talk to me about? Can't you tell me on the phone?'

'No. No, I'd rather get out of the flat for a while anyway, it's like a damned greenhouse in here and Marcus is in a foul mood…' He stopped, obviously not having intended that last bit. 'Can you meet for coffee or not?'

Alarm bells were ringing. This, whatever it was, probably was not going to be Good News, it didn't carry any of the helpful little signs that Good News usually announced itself with, like, I dunno, people smiling or saying 'hey, I've got some good news'. But it was a man asking me out for coffee and I was genetically programmed not to say the words 'Not today, mate'. So, although 'Not today, mate' probably would have been a better bet, out came 'OK, I'll meet you at Camden Tube, one o'clock.' I couldn't help it, out it came.

Camden Market has lots of great pubs and really nice outside cafes with curries and chillis and pancakes, places where you can get baked potatoes and sit by the canal in the sun. There is also an underground craphole called the Electric Ballroom which at night serves as a gig hall but which on Sundays doubles as a clothes market and the worst café in the world. It was usually empty and dirty and cold and so we met there.

'I never knew this place existed,' Sam looked around the gloom. It was over eighty degrees outside and the sky was without a single cloud but in the bowels of the Electric Ballroom, you could smell damp and last season's rain.

'We'd never find a seat anywhere else,' was my excuse and it was at least partly true. More true was that I didn't want to bump into anyone I knew but whether this was because I didn't want my hippy-squatter friends to see me with Sam or because I didn't want Sam to see the kind of low-lives that often came running up to me with cans of frothing Special Brew to cadge a quid, I'm not sure.

'So. Sam. How are you?'

I'd seen him three weeks or so before at the Trudy gig, strangely enough here at Camden. He'd seemed relaxed then, quite charming even, and then there'd been the evening at the wine bar in the City when he'd introduced me to Marcus and he'd been OK then. But this afternoon, he was definitely not such a happy bunny. He was biting at his lip in a repetitive gnaw, almost like a twitch, and his shoulders were held low almost as if it were raining.

'Oh, I'm having a shit time at work. Selling shares isn't really me. There's a lot of pressure, lots of guys desperate for this week's big bonus, this week's chance to brown nose the boss. I do enough to get by but they can tell I'm not ambitious. I'm not like Marcus. If he doesn't make the month's top seller at least six times a year he goes crazy.'

'Well. He likes his job. That's good. And you don't. Which is bad. So what do you want to do instead?'

I wasn't really interested in what a burnt out City stockbroker wanted to do instead of whatever it was he did at the moment but fortunately Sam didn't want to talk about it anyway.

'How was Marcus the other night? You went to see a film?'

I smiled. This was more like it, talking about me. 'Fine. We had a really nice time actually. Totally crap film which I didn't get at all but we got on really well.'

'Oh. I only ask because…well, he's been edgy the last few weeks. Snappy. Short tempered. He can be a right bastard when he's like that. I didn't want to think I'd landed you with Marcus in his Pol Pot persona.'

I laughed, taking a swig of Diet Coke which I really wasn't supposed to drink, it being the product of a multinational company pouring cadmium into Third World fields, but I was on a diet and the water here looked really dodgy.

'Sam, don't worry. I know me and Marcus seem like worlds apart but I think we might have more in common than you think. I don't think he's quite as sold on the yuppy-City-penthouse thing as you think. I think inside he's pissed off with it all, I think he wants a change.'

Sam looked decidedly unconvinced.

'I've known Marcus since we were eight, we were both sent to boarding school together. He's always wanted money and cars and power. I don't know what crap he's been feeding you…'

This was getting a bit insulting.

'Maybe he's not feeding me crap, maybe he just likes me. Why else would he have a photo of me on his mirror for three years?'

'Well, it wasn't actually a photo of...'

'And anyway, he took me to see this pretentious Japanese film which is the sort of thing he was supposed to take someone to see but he admitted afterwards he'd preferred to have seen Arnie in The Terminator.'

This puzzled him. 'Marcus does like Terminator films, he likes anything with mindless violence in it…but a Japanese film? What Japanese film?'

I was bored now, wondering if I had enough money to buy a new skirt.

'I don't know, about some bloke who cuts his stomach open and has his head cut off….'

'Mishima? Marcus took you to see the *Mishima* film?'

'Yeah, that's it. Mishima.'

'But Marcus hates Mishima. He thinks he's a pretentious poof, Marcus hates anything evenly remotely homosexual. I'm the one into Mishima, I did a whole part of my degree on his use of Western hagiography, the Saint Sebastian thing..?'

I shrugged, lost.

'Marcus used to take the piss out of me all the time, I had all these posters of *Karakkase Yaro* on my wall, I used to bore everyone solid with bits from *Confessions of a Mask.* Why on earth would Marcus take you to see a film about Mishima?'

'I don't know. Perhaps he didn't check what was on and it's a coincidence.'

'Marcus doesn't do coincidences.'

'This is getting silly. We went to see a film, we might go out for a meal next weekend. Or go and see a band. That's it. Nothing weird.'

He wasn't convinced but there wasn't anything else to say so we made smalltalk for a bit before I made my excuses and left. As I headed for the bright light of the entrance, I heard him call 'look after yourself' and I turned to see him give a half-wave. He still looked confused but managed a 'aren't I a stupid bastard' sort of shrug so I put him out of my mind and went shopping.

Chapter 11 – Napoleon

The next day was memorable for two reasons. Firstly, Marcus rang and asked me out for a meal which was good, obviously, and secondly because Gavin put three McDonald's cartons and half the contents into my bed. It had the ominous ring of something just begun.

'He's a psychopathic, axe-murdering, bastard freak!' I was lying on Cali's bed banging my head against her pillow. Cal was full of sympathy but short of lending me the money to buy a gun to shoot the pale-faced git, there wasn't an awful lot she could do.

'He probably gets a kick out of winding you up,' she said soothingly, 'You're better off ignoring him. He'll get bored and find somewhere else to live eventually.'

'I don't think I can wait for eventually. I don't think I can bear another day let alone *eventually.*'

I could sense sadly that I was starting to bore my friends on the subject of Gavin but I just couldn't rid myself of that hard knot of frustrated anger in the pit of my stomach. Cali wanted to talk about whether to give up the diamonds to train as a florist or whether it was too late for her to have ballet lessons and be a dancer. It had been horse-breaking the week before and nannying the week before that. For a sane and level-headed person, she just wasn't getting herself together over this career thing at all. Fortunately before I had to make an informed comment, the phone rang and it was Marcus for me.

We met on the Wednesday at the Mexican restaurant on Leicester Square, just next to the cinema where they have all the premieres and just opposite the ice cream place where they have the twenty million different flavours. I had spent the entire evening before plaiting my hair, not because I wanted him to see my hair in plaits of course, this was long, long before corn rows got trendy, but because after sleeping in them, I could them take them out and have crinkly, Kate Bush locks which were respectable in a Stevie Nicks sort of way. Pete thought the whole procedure entirely strange; that women should spend ages creating one perfectly nice style only to take it out in favour of another perfectly nice style but I could have gone out in corduroy flares and a Cream t-shirt and he'd have thought I looked cute.

Marcus was a little late but I forgave him without making him earn it. He had come from work but had at least taken off the tie. I hate ties. I once listened to a group of lesbians recite very poor poetry about ties representing the male stranglehold upon the female psyche and how a tie is little more than a tourniquet cutting off the blood supply to the clitoris. It was very dull poetry but they had got ever so red in the face reciting it so I suppose they had felt it strongly enough. I just didn't like ties because they reminded me of proper grown-up people, none of whom would ever let me join their club.

Marcus seemed a little on edge but a couple of margaritas softened the worst of it and we were soon discussing Motherlove which had been on TV in the week. Both of us loved Diana Rigg's demon-mother character and hated the useless pair she spent her life tormenting. Over the fajitas we traded increasingly sadistic ways in which she could dominate her hopeless sap of a son and humiliate the annoyingly feisty daughter-in-law.

'She really needs to give the prat a good seeing to with those finger nails,' was Marcus' contribution to whether the mother really wanted to have sex with her son. 'You can tell he's one of these latent homos who wants to be bullied into submission by some twenty stone jail cell homeboy or curl up under a feather eiderdown with Mummy. Just give him what he wants, I say.'

'But not on BBC1 at 9 o'clock in the evening.'

He helped himself to more margarita. 'Don't agree with watersheds or censorship. Let people turn the damned telly off if they don't like it.'

I beamed. This was a good sign. None of us agreed with censorship either, it was **The System**'s way of controlling what you thought, stifling freedom of self-expression. People should be given the autonomy and dignity of free choice. I said as much. He shrugged.

'Self-expression sounds like hippy bullshit to me. I just don't like censorship 'cos it keeps decent porn off the telly.'

He grinned and winked. *God but he was gorgeous!* I felt I was getting somewhere. I took a mental deep breath and jumped.

'So. Marcus. How did you end up selling other people's labour on the capitalist exchange then?'

'Other people's labour?'

'Sure. Some poor sod in Leeds makes the baked beans or some twelve-year-old in Bangladesh sews the trainers together as he goes blind and you sell shares in what they make to people who are already rich so that they can make even more money and give a cut of it to you for acting as agent. Meanwhile, the kid in Bangladesh gets up and spends another ten hour shift sewing together another set of trainers. Trainers he'll never be able to buy 'cos he's on fifty cents a day. And because he's blind.'

'Is that your own portable pulpit you're preaching from or did they get you one from the kitchen?'

He was clearly a little pissed off which was fair enough but I had had three glasses of margarita and was feeling a bit cocky.

'I'm only asking! You're clearly a very nice bloke but you're doing a very nasty job. I don't understand.'

He put his fork down and seemed to be considering this. 'Why is it a nasty job to sell fractions of companies so that lots of people can be involved and make money from things they buy anyway?'

This threw me slightly. 'Because... because the people actually making the product don't get a share of the profit.'

'No, they get what's called a wage. It kinda goes with the word 'job'. Wage. Job. I can't believe you don't know about this.'

I laughed. He was so damned cute, trying to be angry but not quite managing it. His hair had come ungelled again and was dancing over his eyebrows.

'But shareholders don't do any work. They sit on their backsides whilst people in Third World countries do all the work.'

'If the shareholders didn't invest, your poor little Bangladeshi lad wouldn't even get his fifty cents. He'd be completely buggered.'

'But not blind.'

'No. Buggered but not blind. Capitalism gives him the choice. Do you want to be buggered and dead of malnutrition by the time you're twenty or blind and eating fifty cents worth of crap every day until you're fifty? What do you think he'd say?'

'Well, obviously he'd have to take the fifty cents because the alternative…'

'Being buggered.'

'Being buggered is so goddamned awful. But in a fair world, he'd have a share of the profits of the trainers he was making and some protection so he wouldn't have to work in conditions that make him go blind.'

'So your little Bangladeshi gets a decent wage and doesn't go blind and invests his savings in a little cobbler shop all of his own...'

'Yes.'

'And employs three little five year olds to nail the soles onto his boots because he can pay them thirty cents a day. And they go blind.'

'No but he wouldn't!'

'Marcus laughed. 'Why? Why wouldn't he?'

'Because he'd see how he'd benefited from a cooperative system of economics and he'd want to pass it on to the next generation...'

'Would he?'

'Yes!'

'He wouldn't just think 'Nice one, now I can sit back and exploit some other bugger because I'm the boss'?'

I chased the last of my rice around the plate, desperately trying to remember what it had said on the last Chumbawamba album about Fair Trade and undermining capitalist economics. Damn it, I hadn't really read it, I just like the tunes and the singalong chorus having a go at Cliff Richard.

'I think you're very pessimistic about human nature.'

'No, I'm very realistic. It's dog-eat-dog and that's how it's always been, my dear. My father's family have been in business for eighty years and if they'd turned it into some commie leftie workers cooperative, the light-fingered sheisters who work behind the counters would have done a runner with half the stock years ago.'

'Why? What do your shops sell? If it was something the workers could help create, something useful to the whole community...'

'Diamonds mostly. Diamond jewellery.'

'Oh.' I had to admit this might be a problem for a true workers' cooperative given the nature of temptation but of course in a fair world, there wouldn't be any diamonds hacked out of the rock of South Africa by black children exploited by Apartheid...I wondered whether to talk to him about asking his father to boycott South African diamonds but thought better of it. The conversation had reached an edgy pause. I hated edgy pauses and habitually filled them with something stupid.

'I have a friend who steals diamonds. Well, not exactly steals…no one actually loses out.' I was thinking of Cali and the tiny, uncut, unfaceted little bits she sometimes brought home for me. Marcus looked wary.

'What do you mean?'

'Oh nothing. Anyway, didn't you fancy taking over your dad's shop then?'

'Shops. He's got four.'

'Shops then. I bet he wanted you to follow in his footsteps and all that, fathers always do, don't they?'

This was clearly the wrong road to have travelled down. Marcus was in a worse mood than when I'd brought the blind Bangladeshi boy to the table.

'My father's quite happy for me to be independent. He's the sort that likes his kids to make their own way in the world. Sink or swim. You know the kind. Fifty quid at Christmas if you're lucky. Now, do you want another pitcher of this revolting stuff.'

I nodded, wondering if I dared mention dessert. It was an unwritten rule of sisterhood politics that you really shouldn't display the female's helplessness before chocolate until at least the third date but I wasn't supposed to be living by out-of-date patriarchal fascism, at least not if I could help it. He started talking about university and how all his old friends had turned into wankers obsessed with having children and buying barn conversions in Wiltshire. A barn conversion in Wiltshire sounded like Paradise to me in my present domestic situation but I thought I'd let him just talk for a while. He clearly liked the sound of his own voice. Funny how, even then, I thought he'd make a politician. Margaritas came and were consumed, chocolate mousse did not and was not but I at least got to watch the woman on the next table devour hers in three spoonfuls. Hanging between us all the while was the unspoken, that which dared not speak its name; the photo of my darling dog on his shaving mirror. I wondered whether I should be the one to break the ice. Or was a discussion about how you had held a torch for three years for a strange girl you didn't know best kept as pillow talk? I didn't want to embarrass him. He was clearly the kind of bloke who thought saving face was next to taking in oxygen as one of life's essentials. But I needn't have worried. As we waited for coffees, Marcus broke the ice himself.

'So. Siân.'

'So. Marcus.'

'What are we doing here then? Apart from being overcharged for shit service and cold rice?'

I never noticed service – you ordered food, food came – and the rice had been fine but I could see that having a moan was his way of covering up other emotions.

I made sure I had the lie straight in my head first before opening my big mouth.

'Well, Sam saw the picture of Ness on your shaving mirror and recognised her as mine. So he told me to turn up at Harvey's and there you were.'

'There I was.'

'And now we're here. Waiting for coffees.'

He was tearing up bits of his serviette with vicious little strokes of his perfectly manicured fingers. He was one of those people who didn't make much eye contact unless confronting you. That always made me nervous, I wasn't much good at eye contact myself so for the rest of the conversation I talked to his cowlick and he talked to the decimated remains of his napkin.

'Not sure where we go from now though. What exactly do you want from all this?'

This was jumping the gun a little, I wasn't quite ready to face that sort of question. Trying to make indecision appear coyness, I took another gulp of the green sugary sediment at the bottom of my glass.

'I haven't decided yet. It's early days, isn't it? At the moment we're just…..talking, checking things out, seeing how the land lies.'

I could feel myself falling into cliché after cliché, spouting rubbish after nonsense so I stopped. But I was quite proud of myself. Ordinarily, if a good looking bloke showed an interest in me (not too much interest obviously because there was nothing worse than keen or needy), then I usually jumped straight in without a life jacket and then wondered why I was crying into Ness's fur three months later. But tonight, tonight I was playing it quite cool, I hadn't suggested moving in, I hadn't asked him to stop being friends with his ex, I hadn't asked him any of the hypothetical questions that paranoid girlfriends always ask their new boyfriends. (Examples; *if I was drowning in a river and so was your ex-girlfriend, who would you swim to first? If I asked you to come over but your ex rang and said she'd had a row with her parents, who would you go to? If I had a kidney disease and she had lung cancer and you could only donate one organ, which would you give?* Cali was the worst for hypothetical questions, she usually didn't wait past the fourth date. Men hate them. Men hate them because they simply cannot win. If he chooses the current girlfriend, she accuses him of lying, if he chooses the ex, she accuses him of wanting the cow back and he's probably been sleeping with her anyway and in fact, they've probably never even broken up. Sensible men can sense the onset of hypothetical questions and quickly suggest going out to see a film.)

No, I hadn't even thought of playing the - let's face it suicidal - hypotheticals game. I had merely acknowledged the obvious; that we liked each other and were taking it easy. Marcus still looked a little perplexed.

'So that's it then? Just…talking, going out now and again.'

I was so excited I nearly blew it completely and demanded a set of keys. The poor sod! To have such a fixed and terminally dull life, to hate his job and his friends, to feel out of place but not know where to turn, to have a mad obsession with getting out and getting free, all of it bound up in the hazy memory of a slightly-unhinged hippy girl running her gorgeous dog around East Ham Park…..and now to have the girl in front of him sipping margharita but not know what the hell to do with it all…..

'Marcus, I really like you and I think we might… you know, come to some arrangement.' Shit, that sounded really cold and his eyebrows had come down just like Ness's ears when she walked too close to traffic.

'I mean, get closer. See what happens. Let's just see what happens.'

'Right. OK, we'll leave it like that for now.' He beckoned for the waitress to bring the bill. I sensed very clearly I had upset him and wished I could take it all back and start again without being quite so damned matter of fact, I mean, when was I ever matter of fact about anything? I could do histrionic for Britain, me and Cali could enter the mountains out of molehills triathlon and give the others ten minutes head start.

We walked out of Chiquitas in silence, there was no holding hands this time. He walked me to the Tube, kissed me on the cheek, said 'I'll ring you then' and was off chasing down a Black Cab like some African feline on the hunt. I watched him as he slowly got swallowed up by the theatre crowds, taller than everyone else, straighter than everyone else, pushing to the first taxi past everyone else. Ending up with a squatter anarchist who thought Unilever guilty of worse crimes than Hitler probably wasn't what he was planning every morning as he smoothed on the Armani suit and adjusted his cuffs. Spending his life with a girl who couldn't eat KitKats because of what Nestlé did to Third World mothers and who had spent three months chanting rude slogans at American servicemen whilst camping with lesbians at Greenham Common probably wasn't in his career development plan. Poor sod. No wonder he looked miserable.

A few very dull days later there was a Culture Shock gig on at the Fulham Greyhound. Gavin hadn't done anything since the McDonald's in the bed hilarity, Pete and I had been having a good time going over old Snuff photos from the spring tour, Jamie had said something nice about my Kate Bush hair and I had found twenty quid down by the Tube. I should have, naturally, given it to the poor homeless sod camped out by the entrance with the obligatory dog-on-string accessory but firstly, I was never quite sure whether it really went on food and secondly, I was at that time almost as needy as anyone else. This wasn't perhaps the absolute truth, not perhaps anywhere near the absolute truth if I was honest as I doubted that the lad by the Tube had five grand from his dead grandfather sitting in the Abbey National or two comfortably off middle class parents waiting in Surrey to feed him and wash his clothes. But twenty quid meant that I could go along with Gummidge and Jamie to the Greyhound and stop thinking about whether I'd ruined my chances with my misunderstood stockbroker fascist.

Culture Shock were actually pretty good in a sort of Before Snuff sort of way. This meant that they could play their instruments and had recognisable tunes but not many that you would want to sing on the way home. And of course they sang about **The System** and **The Bastard Government** and **The Bastard System** which was all well and good especially for all the drop-outs jumping up and down at the front who regularly took cheques from the very same **Bastard Fascist System**. I wasn't in the mood for dancing and spent most of it chatting quite happily away to Sean Gummidge.

There was a funny mix at the Greyhound that night. The same old pseudo-anarchist hippies which I suppose included me and my friends and a rank contingent of Hackney crusties who had been refused entrance but were sitting outside drinking Special Brew as the late summer sun glinted on their facial piercings. There was also a small group of Straight Edgers which was interesting as they were a new phenomenon to London at that time. Most of us drank a bit and got stoned occasionally. Lots of people smoked. Some, like Napoleon the Arch-Crusty, drank all the time, smoked all the time and were permanently addicted to some other substances too. Recently however there had been an influx of American bands who had given up drink and drugs and who sang about abstinence and for some reason all wore white trainers with really large tongues and undone laces. Before long, blokes who had previously been quite happy to fund twenty-a-day habits whilst downing thirteen pints before closing time were now preaching to all and sundry about 'the dignity of self-control' and 'the satisfaction of self-mastery'. Most people considered them sanctimonious wankers jumping on a bandwagon going too fast for them to keep up with but they didn't do much harm. It was the trainers that actually annoyed me the most and the big white tongues that they made stand out and up, they reminded me of huge sanitary towels, I couldn't understand for the life of me what they might actually symbolise. Also universally annoying was the Straight Edgers' habit of preaching to anyone in earshot about how much more energy they'd had since giving up fags and lager and getting up at seven to run round the block. I hope they tied their laces up before they went.

Culture Shock came on with their bouncy, pseudo reggae anarcho-punk stuff. I didn't dance. I had danced a lot in my teens but now was more self-conscious about how it looked and what it did to my hair and makeup. The girls the good looking blokes all fancied were always the ones who stood coolly at the edge of the pit, swaying their shoulders sexily whilst sipping at halves of lager. I tried this approach but usually couldn't resist diving into the middle of the heaving mass and ruining what little cool I had managed to acquire. Dancing to bands was, to be honest, actually a lot of fun. It was just annoying that it didn't make you any more attractive.

It was swelteringly hot and Sean had gone outside to fuss some dog on a string. I joined him, wondering how anyone could just tie their pet up and leave them to go inside a bloody gig. Ness was safe on my bed after having been well walked and unwisely overfed with casserole. At least I assumed she was safe……I had been worrying a lot lately about leaving her alone in the house with Gavin.

'My baby, my baby!' Sean was on all fours letting the runty mongrel lick his face. It was quite a sweet little thing but why did all crusty dogs have to be half whippet? It was as if there were some unwritten Hackney Code that prohibited other dogs from breeding. I dutifully gave the poor little thing (like as not to be surviving on a vegan diet looking and smelling like cheap muesli) a stroke but I couldn't summon up Sean's sentimental passion. Real dogs, to me, have to have lots and lots of shaggy fur and long snouts and thick tails that don't look like dead snakes. This poor little thing wasn't scoring points on any scale.

'Got fifty pence?'

There was a tug at my elbow and there was the truly awful sight of Napoleon, spider webs and all. He smelt pretty bad – cheap lager and weed and BO – and his skin shone in the streetlights from the layers of grease and sweat and Special Brew. His dreadlocks had long ago come together as one and hung, defying gravity, at an angle about three inches from his tattooed neck. It usually the best policy to walk past Napoleon as fast as you could – he was never in a state to catch you up – but when you were trapped in time and space, as I was then, it was best to play the craven and give him what he wanted.

'OK, hang on. I think I've got it.' I tried to fish out the fifty pence without having to drag out the ten pound note as well. If he'd have seen it there was absolutely no way I'd have kept it away from him, he was almost primeval like that. If he saw something he wanted, he became very single minded, very animalistic in that he could clearly shut down all other senses and thoughts and reasonings until he had his fingers round that coin or that can or that burger. Napoleon's eyes usually looked lifeless, they reflected you back to yourself and gave you no sense at all that there was much going on in there. But if he'd have seen my ten pound note, there would have been a flash of comprehension, a widening of the pupils, a baring of the blackened teeth and he'd have pounced. You can't reason with an animal, you can't say 'look, it's mine, I earned it' or 'give it back or I'll get my mates to sort you out' or even 'I'll call the police, you stinking, rat-haired git'. None of that would have made any impact on his drug-shrunken brain at all, you might as well tell the tiger leaping for your throat that if he kills you he'll be put down. The tiger isn't listening and if he did listen he wouldn't understand and if he did understand he wouldn't care anyway. He's still going to rip your throat out.

'Here you go,' I fished out the coin and gave it to him, dropping it into his outstretched hand in time to not have to touch him. I turned back to Sean and the dog but sensed that Napoleon hadn't gone away. He stood behind me, just inches from my back, clearly considering very slowly whether I could be persuaded to give a little more. I was actually quite scared of Napoleon and his friends. With most people, even if they're nasty like Gavin, you can actually have a conversation or argument which involves the same concepts. Gavin and I hated each other but we lived in the same world, we used the same words and had the same understanding of the effects of those words and of the consequences of our actions. Napoleon had moved away from the rest of human society to such an extent that normal conventions simply didn't apply to him, he was almost feral.

I was saved by a group of Straight Edgers, one of whom was the guitarist in Pete's band Chunk, coming out of the pub. They were complaining about the smoke inside the gig, boasting about how much greater their lung capacity was now they'd given up fags, how much further they could run, how much more stamina they had in bed. Sean looked up at me from his position on the ground, still half under the dog, and raised his eyes, mouthing what distinctly looked like the word 'wankers' at me. Sean was like me. We didn't drink very much – Sean traditionally had one pint of Guinness with blackcurrant at Christmas and that was it –

we didn't smoke, we didn't touch drugs but we didn't go on about it either. We were vegetarians but we didn't tell other people they had to be, we hated cigarettes but we just turned our heads away when our friends lit up. These Straight Edgers though, they were so bloody sanctimonious in their newfound faith, so full of the Holy Spirit, the inner light within, so sure that the rest of us were all damned to cirrhosis or asthma or cancer or whatever it was that we surely deserved to get. They'd seen Napoleon.

'Jesus Christ, man.' This was the one with bleached hair and the Fugazi t-shirt. 'Is it a bird? Is it a plane?'

'It's fucking nest of fleas!' interrupted the one in Chunk whose name I could never remember but I gave him a quick hallo anyway just so Napoleon would know I had friends. Napoleon muttered something completely unintelligible ending in a distinct 'You fuckers!' The Straight Edgers gathered round him, their trainers flapping against their tracksuit bottoms.

'Jesus, man, what have you done to yourself! You've got no teeth! Cor! Take a whiff of those dreads, rank!'

A braver man than me, he even dared to lift one of the massive lumps of hair and detritus up with his fingers, letting it sink back down with a thud against the crusty's neck. Napoleon was good at terrorising old ladies who thought he'd escaped from an asylum and crap girls like me who knew he should be in one but he was no good against young men filled with testosterone. These young men were especially dangerous because, firstly, they considered themselves on a mission to rid the world of drugged up smackheads like this, secondly, because young men are always trouble when in groups of more than one and thirdly, because they were all so desperate for a fag and a pint of lager that they would quite happily knock seven shades of shit out of Mother Teresa given the slightest provocation.

So mumbling to himself and half raising a grubby little fist to the moon, Napoleon shuffled off away from the pub and down the side road. The Straight Edgers considered pursuing him but couldn't be bothered. Napoleon would clearly be dead within six months anyway and was thus a lost cause. They debated walking the five miles home 'to put some tracks on these sneakers, man!' and wandered off up Fulham Palace Road, rather suspiciously in the direction of the Tube at Hammersmith.

'Christ, what a bunch of prats!' Sean was still on the floor, the dog having taken up comfortable residence on his great belly. 'Oh God, what now? Yuppy alert!'

'Siân?'

I turned round to see Marcus standing by the curb, Marcus in polo shirt and smart jeans. Jeans. I don't think I had ever seen one person I knew in jeans before, my friends all wore combats or multi-coloured leggings or kilts. And here was Marcus outside the Fulham Greyhound in smart, creased jeans and here was me…..Oh shit. Here was me in raggedy-torn black t-shirt, a striped mini-skirt, pink tights and DMs.

'Marcus. Hi. What are you doing here?'

He looked more out of place than anyone I'd ever seen before anywhere. The door opened and a couple of very drunk punks fell out laughing, Culture Shock's encore filled the Fulham Palace Road and I could almost see Marcus wince. Then he saw Sean.

'Alright?' Sean was always polite but people often didn't see past the torn clothes and great belly and shaven head. They thought 'big bloke, shaven head, shit a fascist skinhead!' when in fact what they had was the most gentle bloke in London. The most gentle bloke in London with a crusty dog on a string sitting on his belly.

Introductions are ridiculously English things but we simply can't do without them. I really should have just said; 'Look you guys, you've got nothing in common and you really wouldn't like each other so I'm not going to bother introducing you, OK?' but of course what I actually said was;

'Marcus this is Sean, Sean this is Marcus, my...'

Now, there was absolutely no way I was introducing Marcus as 'my stockbroker friend from the city who deals in Third World commodities and who thinks Stop The City demonstrators should be shot.' So I did what I always did and hid behind my alternative life.

'Marcus is a friend from UCL, we met at uni.'

'Another bloody student!' said Sean amiably. Marcus didn't look particularly happy so I walked with him away from the dirty pub and the giant skinhead on the floor, thinking perhaps if I walked him far enough he might forget.

'So, how did you know I was here?'

'I rang your house, your flatmate told me.'

'Flatmate?' *Please God let it be Cali with the nice middle class voice and with the job in Hatton Garden.*

'Er, Claire, I think she said. Sounded a bit weird.'

'Right. Well, don't worry about her. It's nice to see you!' And it was, very nice. Despite the jeans and the Prince Andrew top, he still looked every inch chiselled cheek boned perfection.

'I was just wondering if you wanted to take your dog for a walk tomorrow on the Common. I could do with taking the car for a spin and it's going to be a good day.'

I nearly grabbed him then and there. He wanted to take Ness for a walk! He was a dog-lover! Well, of course he was a bloody dog-lover, he'd kept her photo for three years, of course he was a bloody dog-lover.

'Brilliant! She'd love that, she's sick of Bro…' I stopped myself just in time. Wasn't I supposed to live in Clapham? So why should Ness be sick of Brockwell Park, you stupid mare? 'She's sick of boring old me, all the time, she'd love some new company. I'll meet you by the children's playground if you want.'

'OK. Twelvish?'

'Fine.' And then three pints of cider and black pushed their way to the front of the stage and I found myself reaching up and kissing him on the mouth. Not the cheek which would have been entirely appropriate, not the nose which would have been cute and gamine, oh no, I had to go and kiss him on the bloody mouth.

To his credit, he dealt with it pretty well. Mild stupefaction, followed by frozen panic followed by a very encouraging movement of those perfectly outlined lips. No stubble. How strange to kiss a man with no stubble. I let him go and gave an apologetic laugh.

'See you tomorrow then.'

He nodded and turned away down the side road, fingers reaching for keys in pockets. On an impulse I followed him, meaning to say something, God knows what, something about lunch being on me but he had broken into a run, shouting out something to a dark shadow hunched over a car parked beneath the streetlights.

'Oi, you! Leave the fucking car alone.'

It was a shiny blue Porsche, even I knew what a Porsche looked like. *Only wankers drive Porsches!* How many times had I heard or said that? The dark shadow slowly separated itself from the metallic shimmer and became Napoleon. Marcus loomed over him like some avenging angel, beautiful and terrible in his fury. I couldn't hear what Napoleon muttered, I doubt Marcus understood it either but it made no difference.

'You've scratched my fucking car, you piece of shit! Have you any idea how much this car cost?'

I heard the unmistakable gurgle of a stoned crusty laugh. And the stupid bastard wouldn't stop, he went on and on, laughing like some lunatic looking up at his monthly moon, completely oblivious to the tall man getting very quiet and very still.

Marcus kicked him first, kicked him so hard in the balls that Napoleon just crumpled to the pavement, giving out a high pitched bird-like scream. Then he kicked him again in the ribs. And again. Napoleon screamed one more time and then groaned and then tried to roll himself up into a tight little ball of filthy rags and matted hair, more hedgehog than human being but still Marcus kicked him. I heard the snap of something breaking deep within and my stomach rose up to my mouth with the bitter taste of bile. Finally, Marcus pushed the rolled up body with the bleeding knuckles still clutching at his knees over into the gutter where it lay still like an animal pretending to be dead until the hunter goes away. Marcus wiped his shoes against a clump of grass by the wall, swearing as he did so and then walked round to the driver's side of the Porsche. I stood very still, hoping he wouldn't look back up the road to see me standing there at the top. He didn't look up. His whole attention was on the paintwork of the car which he checked over like some Sotheby's auctioneer pricing up an Old Master. Then he swung himself gracefully into the seat and roared away, lights taking over the whole of the little London street and leaving behind a sobbing Napoleon and me, very still in the shadows.

Chapter 12 – Sean

I was very quiet all the way home. Sean and Jamie were well used to this and kindly let me be. Neither had seen Napoleon crawl himself out of the gutter and stagger towards the pub, neither had seen him dislodge yet another tooth in a bloody mess of root and crown and even if they had, it would have been nothing new. *Napoleon off his head again, Napoleon tanked up again, Napoleon using again*. Even his fellow crusties would have pushed him around, laughing at the state he was in, not one of them would have listened if he'd even bothered to tell them he'd just been beaten up. There would be no justice for Napoleon. The only witness was certainly not going to push herself forward for someone she hardly considered sharing the same DNA, the only witness was rapidly trying to convince herself that she hadn't seen what she'd seen anyway.

Perhaps he'd had a knife. Crusties did occasionally carry knives, mostly to scratch posh cars with. Of course…Marcus **had** shouted something about his car. Napoleon must have had a knife and Marcus was….defending himself and disarming his attacker. I knew it was bollocks. Even I knew it was bollocks.

It seems very strange that my friends and I lived lives of such material deprivation and occasional angry protest and yet never ever came face-to-face with violence. Violence at demos and Stop The Cities always happened away from where we were, always to someone else we didn't know. We were never the ones taunting the police or throwing bins into windows. And an outsider might have witnessed one of our gigs – Snuff or Bad Religion or NoMeansNo – and might have thought how violent it all was, the shouting from the stage, the swearing through the speakers, the mass of heaving bodies all pushing, elbows into faces, drinks spilt down chests, divebombers launching themselves from the stage to break open the skulls of those below.

But strange to say, it wasn't violent at all. I've been down the front at hundreds of gigs, really wild and heaving gigs, but the most I've ever come out with is sore feet and bruised shoulders. Oh and once, someone's jacket stud caught my hand and I still have the scar but that wasn't his fault or his intention. Violence occurred occasionally at Conflict gigs but usually outside when fascist skinheads came along to try their luck. It was never anything to do with me or my friends, we'd be in the bar having a drink even if there was a bit of a fight going on in some alley way outside. And no one ended up in hospital, no one got stabbed, no one I knew anyway.

I'd never seen someone getting beaten up before. Never. Ignorant observers might think that violence is an intrinsic part of the punk or hippy scene but to be quite honest, it's far more dangerous to be in Sutton High Street at closing time with all the soulboys in their Farrahs than it is to be down the front of a Fugazi gig surrounded by three hundred fifteen stone blokes.

Violence made me feel physically sick. I just didn't have the experience of it to know how to cope or react, it was alien to me, quite alien.

Sean left us at Stockwell, Jamie and Julie snuggled up and then held hands as we walked up Brixton Hill, stopping on the way for chips. Our house was dark, the hall light bulb needed changing and we had to tread carefully across the holes in the rug and the wonky floorboard and the steps that weren't nailed down. I didn't want to talk to anyone, not Cal, not Pete, not no one. I just wanted to go to bed and forget so that I could start again tomorrow with one memory less. My room was dark and I fumbled for the switch, knowing as I did so that something was wrong, that she'd have moved by now, that I'd have heard her getting up off the bed and whining hallo.

She was gone. A deep crease in the duvet where she'd been lying and a plastic rabbit she liked to chew on the floor but Ness was gone. My baby was gone.

Iris Murdoch and other modern day Platonists believe in the Forms. Those perfect origins of all our virtues and failings and sensory experiences. So when we do good we merely share a little in the perfect Form of **Good**. And when we acknowledge an apple to be red, it is simply that subconsciously the true Form of **Red** is calling out to us that here is a pale yet worthy attempt at reaching out to ultimate **Redness**. And so there are times when humans reach out and visualize the Forms, just for a moment, they turn away from the shadows of the cave and see Reality behind them. So, perhaps for one second you may have partaken in true Happiness, that split second you gazed into your newborn's face and felt something descend upon you from *outside of yourself*. Gone a moment later and impossible to summon back because it *didn't come from you* but from another plane where all things wait in their perfect essence.

That moment, that very moment I knew **Fear**. Not fear with a small f, not being scared, not being a bit frightened but knowing subconsciously that it was going to be OK, not the fear we feel when watching a really good horror film, safe in the knowledge that we're in the cinema with popcorn between our fingers. Real Fear flooded through me, turned me upside down and then was gone.

'Ness?'

The room was completely empty. I ran upstairs two flights and opened Cal's door, she was asleep. Pete was at Luisa's and his bed was empty. Jamie and Julie were giggling upstairs in playful lust made loud by alcohol and unselfconscious love. Ness was not with them. Tears and racking sobs started up at the base of my throat and made their way upwards, louder and louder as I took the stairs down again two by two. No one in the lounge, no one in the kitchen. There was her bowl, silver and dirty by the fridge where she had pushed it with her nose just five hours ago when I had last seen her. When I had last seen her. The last time I saw her.

Suddenly I wanted to ring my parents. They would come, they were the sort of parents who would actually get themselves up in the middle of the night and drive twenty miles to deal with some pseudo-emergency that no doubt would have blown over by the time they even arrived. And they'd be sent off home without so much as a cup of tea. I turned to run back into the lounge where the phone was and then I heard it. Whistling. Self-satisfied, smug whistling. And that could only be one person.

They were standing at the broken door, he smiling in triumph at my distress, she confused and pulling at her lead. I resisted the urge to throw myself either at his feet to embrace her or at his eyes to claw them out.

'Give her to me. Please.'

He smirked. 'No problem. I thought you were out all night. Poor dog needed a walk. Brixton Hill's busy tonight though. Lots of *buses*.'

He handed over the lead and I took it carefully, avoiding contact with his hand. I gently ruffled the top of her ears, not wanting the screaming in my head to betray itself and distress her.

Gavin passed me, far too close for comfort, far too close for necessity. I spoke into the darkness much more calmly than I felt.

'If you take her out again I'll kill you. I don't know how or when but if you take my dog out again, I will kill you.'

He laughed all the way up four flights of stairs, right the way past eight bedrooms, right the way up until I couldn't hear him any more. But I could still hear him laughing in my bloody head, all night long I could hear him laughing in my bloody head.

Clapham Common at twelvish we had said. Ness, Marcus and I. A nice stroll around the Common because the weather, as he had predicted, was going to be great all day. Great. All. Day. I got there an hour and a half early because I couldn't bear to be in the house. Fear with a capital F had gone but its pale yet powerful imitation stalked my every breath, my every movement, my every thought. Fear of her not being there when I turned round, fear that I had to go to the toilet and leave her in my room, fear that I would never be able to go out again without her. Without my dog I wouldn't have one thing in the world that looked to me with simple love, not one relationship that didn't judge me and in some way find me wanting. And it had been made so very clear to me the night before how easily I could lose her. Dogs go missing every day, dogs get run over every day, dogs get stolen every day. People mourn, people move on. How could I move on? To what exactly would I move on to?

  I needed to get out of that place. I needed to start again, to reinvent myself into something more comfortable. I needed a life that would push me into being something, not this freedom, not this wonderful autonomy we all raved about which was forcing me to be myself. Let other people be themselves, I couldn't think of a worse person to be.

  Marcus looked good. No grazes on his knuckles, no blood stains on his shiny shoes. Kicking a defenseless and pathetic Hackney crusty senseless must have agreed with him because he kissed my cheek when we met and actually hunkered down to say hi to Ness.

  'I remember this one! She hasn't changed. You have though.'

  I managed a wan smile. Of thanks? Of acceptance? Of embarrassment? I didn't care. Marcus seemed to be waiting for something, some comment on whether he had changed, my rejoinder that would make the little conversation complete. I had never seen Marcus before in my entire life but that probably wouldn't go down too well.

'You look a little different too. From the last time I saw you.'

'Oh yeah? How exactly?'

Oh shit. This was going to be fun. 'I'm not sure. You looked…harassed…..as if you didn't want to be doing what you were doing. As if you were being pushed into something that wasn't really you.'

He licked around his lips, eyes narrow in the sun. 'Is that what you think? That I didn't want to be there?'

It was **exactly** what I wanted to think. How can he have been happy trading stocks and shares all day, selling meaningless pieces of companies, watching prices go up and down but never actually becoming real money? How could he be happy in a suit and tie, how could that dreadful apartment make him feel warm and welcomed after a hard day's work? Why on earth should he have kept the photo all this time, if deep down he was content with what he did? It simply didn't make any sense. The one concrete thing here was that Marcus had hung on to a picture of an imperfect Battersea mutt being run around a park by an imperfect hippy squatter and there must be some reason for that. A self-centred capitalist bastard Son of Thatcher simply would not have had the slightest sentimental attachment to that photo. That was the one fact here I knew to be true.

I took his hand, 'Let's get a coffee. We can sit outside if they don't let dogs in.'

'Changing the subject again?' But he let me lead him over the road towards an Italian café with tables and parasols. I didn't want to ask him about Napoleon. If Gavin taking Ness hadn't happened, maybe, just maybe I'd have challenged him about it but I was desperate that morning, desperate for a way out of the fear that engulfed me. Fear that Marcus might have a violent streak was nothing compared to what I had felt the night before. Marcus might just be my ticket out and I wanted to see how far it could take me.

We drank our coffees over meaningless chit chat. Something about Oliver North, how Marcus thought he should be given a bloody medal, how America encourages its agents to act like James Bond and then slaps them down when they get caught actually doing something. *Bloody cowards, Yank hypocrites*. I didn't think we'd agree on the subject of Oliver North, I couldn't see how selling arms to Third World dictatorships helped the cause of peace and understanding in the world but I did agree with his assessment of America so I was able to smile and nod and say how I agreed. If you only take a fraction of someone's entire conversation, it's amazing how easy it is to find something to agree with. Perhaps that's the answer to world peace, perhaps the UN should have headphones which just cut out occasionally when delegates say things the others might not like.

After coffee we walked around the Common which was packed full of children eating ice cream and sunbathing couples. When he asked me whereabouts I lived I pointed vaguely in some far off direction, hoping against hope that he wouldn't want an invite.

'So do I not get an invite then?'

'Aaah…little bit awkward. My parents are up for the weekend and my sister and all her children.' *Where was it all coming from?*

'And am I not good enough for them?'

'Well, they're a bit much to take in all at once. Mennonite Anabaptists.' *Where the Hell was it all coming from?* And more to the point, where the Hell was it going?

He looked at me, appalled and yet intrigued. I didn't have a clue why I'd said that except it sounded like something which would put a stop to any more enquiries. I was right there at least.

'Bloody Hell, you poor thing. Fancy an ice cream?'

We walked over to the van as I made a mental note of yet another lie to somehow wiggle out of at a later date. Well, it was simple enough. I would just never introduce the man I was going to marry and have children with to any of my family or friends. Easy.

Trying to look attractive whilst licking at a 99 is beyond me so I gave most of it to Ness who ironically made a more graceful job of it than I had. It was extremely hot and I was dying to take off my long sleeved top but displaying fat upper arms and a tattoo at the same time, coupled with the admission that I came from fundamentalist Puritan stock might just have proved too much for him. Marcus looked cool, like a male model in a catalogue. And yet I sensed that he was on edge, nervy. Don't ask me how, I just knew. At last, he came to it.

'I was ….aaah…I was wondering if we might try to sort out what's going on here…what might be going on here. You know, what we both want out of this.'

'I hope you're better with words when you exploit developing countries. You'll never get them to agree to 25% interest rates with that line of patter.'

He gave me a mock punch on the arm that would have been funny and nice if it hadn't reminded me of what his fists had been doing the night before.

'I can't help it if you make me nervous. I don't know any women like you, I haven't had anyone to practice on.'

'Fair enough.'

'So...you don't want to talk about this now then?'

'Sorry, Marcus. I didn't sleep well last night. I'll be in a better mood when…when my sister and her kids have all gone home.' Hey, I knew the little brats would come in useful somehow.

He licked around his lips again, he was going to make them chapped if he didn't watch himself.

'OK, no, problem. Actually, I was wondering if you wanted to go away next weekend. There's a hotel I know in the New Forest, swimming pool, horse riding, all the works. We could relax and get a chance to talk properly.'

I hadn't expected this. Daydreams are one thing but they never ever actually happen, by definition they never ever actually happen. The fact that I hate swimming and can't ride…

'Marcus, that sounds brilliant. Yes, of course I'd love to.'

'Fine. I'll sort it out. Here's the brochure.'

And he reached into his nicely pressed jeans to pull out a folded leaflet. I had a good look as we slowly walked round. Woodcote Manor. Not far from the sea, lots of woodland walks, a massive lake, well, rainfilled quarry anyway, a wildlife sanctuary… Woodcote Manor. All Tudor beams and open fires, not far from Brockenhurst. It was the sort of place I knew I could never get into in my present identity, they would turn me away before I'd even reached Reception but with Marcus on my arm…it would be like going in disguise, a magic cloak of illusion to cover up the real me, the Emperor's New Clothes.

'Oh...one thing, no dogs I'm afraid. One of those hotels that likes being in the countryside but doesn't actually like what belongs in the countryside. I didn't think before I booked, we'll go somewhere else next time.'

It was that phrase *next time* that had me won over. How many women can resist the promise of ***future***? I wouldn't normally have abandoned Ness quite so easily but my mum would have her and it would only be for two nights…..

'That's fine. She'll cope without me.'

Oh, how easily the love of my life was cast aside for a pair of chiseled cheekbones and an accent I couldn't mimic.

'Right, and ..err…there's one other thing….could you not tell Sam? It's just…well, I get the feeling he's not too happy about you and I seeing each other which is odd because it was him who got us together but I get that distinct impression. He's been bloody weird around me lately, I'm hoping he's going to find himself his own place soon. My flat's up for sale anyway, so he's going to have to stand on his own two feet some day.'

'Oh. I see. Well, I doubt I'll be speaking to him anyway, we're not that close. But I won't say anything if it'll make things awkward for you at home.'

'Great! I'll pick you up around fiveish then, I'll get off work early.'

Shit. Shit, here we go again. Which lie this time? House being redecorated? Being temporarily turned into MI5 Headquarters? Salman Rushdie coming to stay? Sudden outbreak of Bubonic plague and everyone quarantined?

'Tell you what, pick me up outside that café we've just had coffee at. My road's a cul-de-sac and there's always so many cars you can never turn round, everyone always has to reverse out and then you get a gridlock and everyone starts beeping and getting pissed off. I'll be sitting at a table at five.'

A two year old would have known I was lying, damn it Ness knew I was lying, there were people walking past me who hadn't even heard what I'd said and yet knew I was lying.

'OK, that's fine.' And Marcus and I walked for another ten minutes or so trying to find a conversation which wouldn't involve his work or western capitalism or politics or families. After stretching out a conversation about Paul Weller for at least ten minutes after it had died a natural death, we agreed to walk in companionable silence. We ended up at his car which was shinily parked where it probably shouldn't have been but no traffic warden had dared to violate its glory with anything as shabby as a ticket.

'Someone tried to scratch her last night.' He said after I had made the appropriate admiring noises, 'Some people can't stand it when someone else makes a success of things. Why take it out on a car? If he'd had a problem, he should have taken it up with me.'

'And what would you have done?'

He gave a self-deprecating laugh. 'Run away probably! I'm the biggest coward going, could never hurt a fly. That's why I'm in the wrong job, not ruthless enough for the big boys.'

'Good. Well, I'll see you Friday then?'

He jumped in and waved through the window, revving up so violently that Ness jumped back away from the curb, exhaust fumes in her eyes. I sent him an angry glare which probably came out as exasperatingly loving which wasn't quite the same thing. People were looking as he streaked away in his own personal little vendetta against the Clean Air Policy. The car would have to go. First the job and then the car. How on earth could we get two dogs and three kids into a Porsche?

Two nights later Sam rang again. My heart sank as soon as I realized who it was, there was no way Sam was ever going to be the bearer of glad tidings, I just knew it. Quite why he was behaving oddly around Marcus I didn't dare think but there was no way I was having him spoil my only chance to get out of my rut. Sam tried his hardest to pretend it was just a social, catching up sort of phone call but we both knew we were waiting for the real point of it. He didn't do badly, poor lamb, managed to string out a really dull story (about someone at work setting off a fire extinguisher all over a Japanese property developer) for nearly ten minutes.

At last he came to it. 'You saw Marcus the other day, didn't you?'

'Just for a walk around the Common, that's all.'

'Oh. How was he? It's just he's been really odd with me lately, hardly talks, gets in late, blanks me at work, won't sit and watch the football.'

'Oh. Well, he was fine. We just had a chat, nothing heavy. No big deal.'

'Oh,' Another one of those silences that during telephone conversations always seem to last twice as long. 'So are you seeing him again?'

This was too much. Sam was clearly jealous, not because of me - I knew my limitations and having two City yuppies fall for me in one month would have been exceeding every single one of them – but because he could sense Marcus finally pulling away. What had Marcus said? That Sam had always needed his protection, like the little brother who was always getting beaten up at school. Sam was scared that his big brother was going to jack it all in and choose another road, a road Sam was too timid to travel down. I decided to end the call.

'Look, Sam, why are you so interested? What does it have to do with you anyway?'

This was a bit abrupt and I could feel that he'd winced. It was like sending a slap down the line, you had absolutely no idea it was coming until...*whack!* There it was.

'I didn't mean to be nosy. I just feel slightly responsible, having got you two together and all that.'

'Well thank you very much but we can take it from here.'

'But you don't know him. He's a very… complex character.'

'We're all complex characters, Sam! Or at least the ones worth bothering with are. I know Marcus is arrogant and narrow minded, I know he probably does some despicable things at work and kids himself it doesn't matter but that doesn't mean he's irredeemable. There's good in him too. You're his oldest friend, you should be saying these things to me.'

Whack! Clearly another blow, this one to the groin. His voice was definitely quieter.

'I know. I'm sorry. It's just when you've known someone that long, you get to see their nasty side as well as their good one. And you can put all the crap they do into context because you've got twenty years worth of good memories to balance it up to.'

'What on earth are you talking about?'

'Look, the Marcus I've been sharing a flat with recently reminds me of the Marcus I used to know at school, the one who did horrible things to caterpillars and spiders…'

This was getting ludicrous now.

'For God's sake, Sam! You're warning me off your best friend because he used to pull the legs off spiders?'

Pete was passing on the stairs and gave me a great big grin and a thumbs up, indicating that pulling the legs off spiders was the best damned thing for the little bastards.

Sam was giving up the ghost. 'I don't know…I just don't like him when he's like this...'

'Sam, I'm going to have to go.'

'One more thing. And don't take this the wrong way.' A pause. 'Marcus has never been violent towards you, has he? He's never hit you or looked as if he might do? I know it seems a stupid question…..No, I'm out of order, forget I said it.'

This would have been quite incredible of course had I not witnessed the demolition of Napoleon. There was no way I was giving Sam the satisfaction of being right in any of this nonsense and anyway, Napoleon was clearly a one-off so I poured as much scorn as I could down the line.

'Sam. We've been out for coffee, a Mexican and a crap film. How exactly has my life become *The Shining*?'

He laughed, a little against his will.

'Sorry. I'm being an idiot. It's just the last time I saw Marcus in this bad a mood was when one of Hartnett's shops got broken into – that's his father's business - and about half a million pounds worth of diamonds got stolen. Marcus was in Tenerife at the time but when he got back he really went for the security guard who'd fallen asleep and mis–set the alarm. Four guys had to drag Marcus off the poor bastard, broken jaw, broken nose, two broken ribs. Mr Hartnett had to pay him a couple of grand not to go to the police.'

'That's hardly the same as giving your girlfriend a black eye for not making strong enough tea.'

'No. No, it isn't. So he hasn't lost his temper then around you?'

'No. No, he hasn't. He's been the perfect gentleman.'

He sighed. 'Well, that he can be. OK, I'm sorry if I've worried you. It's just I didn't know what was up with him recently.'

'I think he's just getting fed up with the whole stockbroker, yuppy, City thing. He's getting frustrated and taking it out on you.'

'Maybe. I'll try to keep out of his way for a bit. Anyway, if you see him…'

'I won't wind him up either.'

'And don't tell him I called? It'd only make him mad.'

Another lie to catalogue somewhere in my already overly mendacious collection. It was getting quite full, my little library of fibs, I was going to have to employ someone to sit in my head and hand out fines when they ran overdue.

'Don't worry. See you later Sam.'

I put the phone down first because that's what strong independent women do. Apparently. Having the phone put down on you subconsciously makes you feel rejected. Apparently. It preys upon your insecurities, it tells you that you deserve to have the phone put down on you because *you're worthless.* At least, that's what my books told me. (When the time came to run away a few weeks later, the books did not come with me and I've not replaced them yet.)

I went back into my room and wondered what to do. Everyone was out at a Senseless Things gig but I didn't want to entrust Ness to anyone, not even Pete who hadn't gone. My best clothes were hanging up on the nails, trying to decrease themselves via gravity in order to look vaguely respectable for Friday. Shit. There was a big tear under the arm of the Warehouse shirt…I reached up awkwardly to pull it down when…..a flash of pure agony and I was falling forwards onto the bed, knowing even as I fell exactly what had happened and what that meant.

My damned back had gone again.

People in general have absolutely no sympathy for their fellow humans with dodgy backs. You can be in the most incapacitated agony ever devised by God and the Devil combined but because there's no blood, no severed limb, no swelling bulge, they think you're making it up. Doctors are just as bad. They really don't know what the hell they're doing when it comes to backs, they just make you stand with your arms outstretched, tell you to move your head to your shoulder, make notes when you can't and then fob you off with Valium.

As I fell, my heart fell with me.

The pain is bad enough – it's like a lower muscle, just above your bottom, ripping from side to side – and the first time it happens you scream a bit and curse and then wait for it to subside which it does, just a little. But the second time it happens you know the truth. You know that the next three weeks of your life are already pre-written. That there is now an unalterable script that you're tied in to following. Predestination. No get-out clause. No loop hole.

As you lie where you fell, the torn muscle screams out a bit and then it calms. But as it calms what is happening is that all the muscles around it are swelling up. Slowly but surely, over the next thirty minutes or so, your entire back from buttocks to shoulders turns into one immobile mass of concrete. And then when you think you've rested enough, you try to move…. No. There aren't the words to describe the joint pain and frustration at not being able to move, not an inch.

When my back first went into spasm about four years before, I had lain on the floor of my parent's bathroom for five hours until someone came home and discovered me. And even when you're discovered, it's not just a case of being helped up and limping to the nearest bed or sofa, no, you lie where you fall and there you stay for two days, maybe three. And so my entire family had to use the tiny toilet downstairs and borrow the neighbours' bath because the useless punk squatter not-so-prodigal daughter had come home and passed out on the bathroom floor. Obviously drugs, they no doubt all thought. Poor family. What a burden to have to carry. And how do you go to the toilet? Well, to be shamelessly pedantic about this, you piss on a towel. You *eat nothing* to forestall what would be an even greater emergency of horrific proportions but you also piss on a towel.

That day in Brixton when my back went for, I think, the third time in my life, it was a long fall down. I could see the next four weeks stretching ahead as if already experienced. The days pissing immobile on the towel, the week dragging myself around on belly and all fours, the week hobbling, back bent and clutching at walls, the week limping and not being able to sit down without it seizing up again.

The mental pain is actually the worst because you know there's no way out. With a cold, you might get better in a day, with an attack of bronchitis it might be a week, it might be a fortnight but it might actually be less. When your back goes, it follows the same boring, dull-as-ditchwater Hell each and every time. And there's no way out, no short cut, no loop-hole.

'*Pete!!*' Thank God, thank God, thank God, there wasn't just Gavin. My heart seemed to freeze up there and then as I imagined what Gavin could do with me in this situation and no one else around. 'Pete!!! Come here!'

It took an astonishing fifteen minutes for Pete to hear me. As (bad) luck would have it, he wasn't listening to any band with nice short songs, oh no, he was listening to Pink Floyd at their most conceptualizing crappiness and it took a quarter of an entire hour for him to hear me. When he did and came running, he was a dear.

'Right, Pete, darling, my back's gone. I need water, some paracetamol, as many towels as you can find…'

'*Are you having a baby!?*'

His face was ashen, his mouth finally finding the right muscles to portray distress.

'No, dickhead, my back's gone. Get me loads of old towels, some water and…oh damn it, lots of chocolate. And could you take Ness with you and see she has a wee?'

And so I lay there. Tomorrow I would ring Marcus and cancel our weekend; not with the truth obviously, he would hardly marry me and father children on me if my DNA was so bloody faulty but some lie, some new lie. He would no doubt think I was blowing him out and never ring me again but the truth was quite out of the question –

bringing grapes and flowers to a sick invalid in a nice Victorian house overlooking Clapham Common is pathetic enough, just trying doing it when you've got to negotiate your way past the leaking sewage, the missing floorboards and the hippy trying to sell you gear. I would just have to hope. Hope that Marcus would understand, hope that Sean would come round and take Ness out and hope, hope, hope, that Pete could find **lots** of towels.

'Conflict or Crass?'

'They're both tosspot bands.'

'Sean, you have to choose. That's why it's called The Great Questions Game. You have to choose.'

'OK, Crass.'

'Smarties or Opal Fruits?'

'Smarties.'

'Gem Stone or Ally Action Pact.'

'I wouldn't shag either of them! They could come round and sit on my knob and I wouldn't shag either of them!'

'Gummidge, you have to choose.'

'Errr, Gem Stone. Why can't I have both of Tallulah Gosh? Or Debbie Harry? Why do I have to have two miserable women? '

'Because they were your choices. Right, OK, Fat Boy, EastEnders or Coronation Street?'

'Neighbours.'

'Oh OK, you can have that one. Chinese Takeaway or Big Veg with baked potato?'

'No contest! BV and BP wins every time!'

'Blind Date or Countdown?'

'Blind Date. I'd shag Cilla.'

'Gum, you'd shag The Voice of Our Graham. Peanuts or cashew nuts?'

'Cashew nuts. Or peanuts if they've got chocolate on them. But not yoghurt, who the fucking hell went and put yoghurt on peanuts?'

'Snuff at the George Robey or Snuff at the Kilburn National?

'Hah! You **so** want me to say the George Robey, just 'cos you didn't have a back stage pass for the National but the National *rocked*.'

'I only didn't have a back stage pass because I was no longer sleeping with the guitarist. You however, Fat Boy, are still clearly sleeping with all three of Snuff, on their own, all at once and sideways.'

'Calling me a bendy boy, Welsh girl?'

'Take it like a man, pillow biter.'

'Two legged pit pony.'

'Sheep shagger.'

'Want some Dairy Milk?'

'Throw it over.'

'Mel Gibson or Christopher Lambert?'

'They're both TOOLS, girl! Both of them, tools! They couldn't wank their way out of a paper bag.'

'That's not what they do, Sean. They're paid to act, not wank their way out of paper bags. If they were, if would be Mad Wank or Wankway or…'

'Wanklander!'

'Lethal Wank!!'

'No, no, no, I'm wetting myself.'

'Greywank, Legend of Tarzan, Lord of the Wanks! Oh fuck, my back!'

'Bey…Beyond…oh no, I've fucking wet myself…*Beyond Wankerdome*! Oh, I win, I am the **King of the Great Question Game**! I am the winner. Beyond Wankerdome.'

'I think Lethal Wank was better.'

'Not as good as Lethal Wank 2. It had Patsy Kensit in it. I'd shag her.'

'Shit. I'm depressed.'

'Me too, honey. Pass the Dairy Milk.'

Chapter 13 – Tinsel

It was nearly September, the summer of 1989 gone.

We look back at '89 now as a kind of watershed, a seminal point in world affairs, a time when Tianenmen and the riots in Paris flowed smoothly on from Polish Solidarity wowing the West and whispering seductively into the ears of Czechs and Rumanians and Berliners everywhere. But how were we to know? How could we have predicted that the Wall would come crashing down just two months later, why, I'd stood and had my photo taken in front of the damned thing only a few months before and there was no hint, nothing at all of any great revolution brewing. And just as the world sat complacent and all-knowing and yet in reality without a damned clue, so I thought that my life too would carry on in its stilted, mediocre way.

Just as East Berliners sat in their grey concrete blocks and prepared to queue for bread, so I lay on my bed and listened to Patti Smith and Green Day and The Poison Girls. *As it was so shall it always be. Forever and ever, Amen.* But the end was coming, the end was fast approaching but just like those East Berliners, I just couldn't smell the shit on the wind.

Marcus did not ring after I cancelled our romantic weekend away, his fury was made all the more apparent by his icy silence. And you didn't get second chances with blokes like that. Or so I thought at the time.

People were kind as I recovered, some more so than others. Claire insisted on rolling me three joints and baking hash brownies to help me through the pain. I turned them down politely like the stubborn fool I was. Many the time my back has gone since and I have prayed and prayed for Claire's chocolate angels. Pete kept me well supplied with gossip and chat and tapes of his favourite bands, none of whom had seen their eighteenth birthday save those who were pushing fifty. Sean Gummidge lay on my bed and moaned about his life being even worse than mine as we played stupid games. Cal just sat there, quiet and comforting, we watched TV in companionable silence. Even Gavin came once. He stood over me, looking down as I lay powerless.

'Can you really not move?'

'Lay a finger on me and see.'

'Like I'd touch you with a stick. I could take Ness though and you couldn't catch me.'

'No. But the knife under my pillow would find your back before you reached the door.'

And it was true. I did have a kitchen knife under my pillow and it was for Gavin, just in case. I was living the alternative dream; rent free, bill free, lock free, meat free and I slept with a knife under my pillow.

My chance had gone. My only chance to get out and away. The grey tentacles of 94 Elm Park tightened a little bit more around my rib cage, lovingly, gently, caressing me in their promise of easy living. I had fucked up and my punishment was to **stay here forever**. I would outlive them all. Cal would leave to go be a doctor or a diver or a chiropodist. Pete would stay until it finally dawned on him that squatter life was shit and he could do better. Jamie would eventually succumb and move to Jeffreys Road, Al would disappear through his own navel and Gavin would be summoned back to run Torment Workshops in Hell. Claire and I would live together, getting old and increasingly insane as we took so many drugs we were forced to inject our armpits, our eyeballs and our inner ears to get high. I would pass thirty, then thirty five, I would have UNEMPLOYABLE stamped on my UB40 and would shack up with Pete Astronaut. Finally, I would fall in love with Napoleon, 94 Elm Park would fall into the giant hole of subsidence we were currently balancing upon and we would both be found dead one day, arms wrapped lovingly around each other's throats for warmth, underneath a pile of old newspapers in Stoke Newington High Street. It was so exactly what I deserved that I was almost relishing the satisfaction of being right all along.

The road back up towards the sun perhaps began with Tinsel.

I had walked slowly and carefully to Brockwell Park with Ness one afternoon. The summer heat had gone, there was a welcome breeze playing around my hair. After the great chasm of despair which always comes when my back breaks down into spasm, eventually comes the slowburning warmth of pleasure that the pain is truly subsiding. I missed Marcus but it was an abstract, unreal kind of regret because I was missing a person made up in my head, not the real person I had met only five times. The Marcus for whom I mourned was the Marcus I had shared my body with, the Marcus I had left my home and friends to be with, the

Marcus I had married and born children to. He was fading away now and I was left with a painful gap in his place.

It was still warm enough to sit on the grass by the pond area although the ice cream vans had gone. Ness was nibbling at an empty juice carton, rolling over with a happy groan as she hinted for me to rub her belly. Shadows moving across the park were long and low as the sun began to give up the sky, one shadow came closer and closer until it spread over my own foot.

'Hi.'

The sun was behind her so I had to squint but there was no mistaking that utterly sublime body swathed in layers of shapeless black.

'Hey, Tinsel! How are you?'

Tinsel was a mystery to us all, a shadow-figure who drifted in and out of London life, in and out of conversations and relationships, in and out of people's emotions like a damned ghost. The one thing everyone agreed on was that she was the most beautiful woman any of us had met in real life. Even ordinary people, horrified by her dark purple panda-smudged eyes, her black lipstick and Goth-white skin, could see how lovely she was underneath the mutilation. She had that sort of elfin vulnerability that Isabelle Adjani hinted at in *Subway*, she had eyes as huge as Bambi's, great sweeping eyebrows like swifts in flight, full chiselled lips and almost Icelandic cheekbones. If Peter Jackson had met Tinsel, Liv Tyler wouldn't even have got a screen test.

Tinsel broke hearts with a casual apathy. She wasn't a cruel person, she just wasn't...*engaged* in any of her many relationships. I had known great burly punk rockers with

Statue of Liberty hair and tattooed necks break down and cry when told, quietly and calmly, that she really wasn't interested anymore, that she was bored. And women suffered too. I don't think Tinsel was actually bisexual, I don't think she was actually a sexual being at all, she participated in sex because it vaguely interested her, because it gave her partners an experience she could then view from the safe distance of second hand. I had seen Tinsel naked when I first met her at Greenham Common in 1983 and she was truly incredibly sublimely lovely. She had reached out her slim white hand to me as she danced around the fire and I had declined, not through disinclination but simply through sheer terror. And here she was in Brockwell Park, just as lovely, just as ethereal, just as full and just as empty.

'I like your dog.' She knelt down and smoothed Ness's head, slow, practised waves as if she were seducing. I could see Tinsel properly now, her jet black hair was crimped and backcombed away from her ashen face and she wore a Hindu bindi between her eyes.

'You've met Ness before, at Meanwhile Gardens last year.'

'I don't remember.'

I'm not sure whether it was Ness she didn't remember, Meanwhile Gardens or the whole of last year. Probably the whole of last year and the twenty or so before that. I used to assume that Tinsel was on drugs, that she was permanently stoned or high but now I'm sure she wasn't. I think Tinsel was the sort of person who could drink a bottle of vodka and not get drunk, who could inject morphine and watch it scurry around her veins with vague interest and then get bored and order her system to flush it out.

'That's the last time I saw you, Tins. The Free Nelson Mandela Concert.'

'Oh.'

'How are you? Where've you been?'

She gracefully slipped to the ground and sat crosslegged, the manoeuvre a poem of grace and effortless ballet. Oh, what I'd have given to have what Tinsel had! She was a magnet, a great Black Hole pulling everything towards it and yet like that Black Hole, a force of physics that had no awareness of what it did or empathy for those pulled helplessly in. We weren't supposed to judge people on their physical looks, of course we weren't. That would be playing along with the patriarchal, Neanderthal **System** which had enslaved women for ten thousand years and from which we had successfully broken free. And yet it was a sad fact of life that alternative men didn't actually go out with fat alternative women, or buck-teethed alternative women, or bog-eyed alternative women. And it was a sad fact of life that beauties like Ben and Jamie got a hell of a lot more female devotion than big guys like Sean or nice-looking guys like Pete. We had moved along the path away from stereotypical image judgements in that we knew that they were wrong but we hadn't quite moved along the path far enough to let this knowledge actually change our mating habits.

Tinsel was thinking. 'Where have I been? Wales, I think. Teepee Valley. It was nice, it was really pretty. Lots of little white windmills.'

'Cool. I'd like to go there. Did you go with friends?'

This clearly needed thought too. 'I think so. Someone I met at Henge last solstice. I think he was a druid.'

'Uh huh? I bet he told you that you were the reincarnation of a Celtic priestess.'

'He did actually. He was just trying to screw me of course. Most men I meet are trying to screw me.'

'Well, that's because you're beautiful, Tinsel. Beautiful and disinterested, an irresistible combination. I'm not very good at being either.'

'I could make you beautiful.' Tinsel was back in seductive mode, her hand now on my leg. I knew Tinsel well enough now to know you simply couldn't offend her and gently pushed the hand away.

'Where are you going, Tins? Anywhere nice?'

'Not really. My mother's fortieth birthday party. Can you come?'

This was not what I'd been expecting but then Tinsel always had had the ability to abandon lines of thought in mid sway and drop something entirely new into the conversation.

'Oh. Now? You're going now?'

'Yes. Come on, there's a bus on Herne Hill.'

I didn't have anything else to do and Tinsel was pretty good at being effortlessly persuasive simply by being there.

'Are your parents OK with dogs?'

She was already walking towards the path and I don't think I got an answer but then any answer would not necessarily have reflected the truth anyway. The truth as

Tinsel perceived it and the truth as reality had fashioned it were often two different things.

So, we walked companionably enough, out of the Park and up Herne Hill to a bus stop which would take us south. We were, apparently, going to Forest Hill which was where Tinsel had grown up.

'It's not very nice.' She informed me casually, 'Lots of 1930s semi detached prisons and old ladies twitching their net curtains as you walk by.'

'Your parents must be nice though.'

'Why?'

'Well, because otherwise you wouldn't bother going home for your mum's birthday.'

'Oh.' This was a new thought, 'I suppose so. They don't like me very much though. I am a Disappointment.'

'Me too, Tins, me too.'

The bus came, we lifted Ness on, we sat upstairs and ignored the jeers from the lads at the back. Lads at the back of buses had been jeering at me since I was fourteen but it didn't really get much easier. It was just more bearable when you weren't alone.

Tinsel's house was indeed a sensible 1930s semi with a neat garden complete with waist high privet hedge and well positioned shrubs and flowers. I knew nothing about plants then but I could appreciate a property that was cared for as opposed to one that was neglected and this house was obviously the object of quiet, middle class pride.

A man in his mid-forties answered the door. Beginning to grey, a nice blue shirt and matching tie, a casual

Marks and Spencer's pullover; he could have been my dad. A momentary flash of panic came and went as he saw us, a stab of *Oh shit, she came! What the Hell is she going to do now?* But then it was gone and there was only love and relief.

'Teresa, how nice…'

'Tinsel.'

He swallowed and tried again. 'Tinsel. I'm so pleased you came, darling, your mother will be thrilled. Your Aunty Pat is here and Robert, you haven't seen him since he was little. And the Parkinsons from next door and Eileen Granger from Mum's work, do you remember her?'

'No. I don't remember any of them.'

'Oh. Well, come in, come in.'

He smiled at me in what was clearly relief. And when I consider who Tinsel could have brought home with her (and might well have brought home with her in the past) then I suppose he was right to look relieved. I hadn't had the energy to re-plait my hair yet and hadn't bothered putting any makeup on for what I thought was just a walk around the park so I probably looked quite normal. Scruffy but normal.

'I'm sorry,' He extended an outstretched hand as Tinsel moved past him into the hallway, 'I'm Bob, Bob Harrison, I'm Tinsel's father.'

'Nice to meet you, I'm Siân, Siân Jeffreys.'

I knew how to behave with other people's parents. Suddenly I knew how to shake another human being's hand, suddenly I remembered my own surname.

'Lovely, lovely, well, we're all in the conservatory. Follow Teresa through.'

I nearly asked if I should take off my boots. He was in slippers and the carpet, although horribly swirly and garish, was very clean and thick. I had never quite worked out the taking off the shoes when you enter someone's house thing. Some parents don't seem to worry about it, others assume you've been brought up in a barn if you don't immediately unshoe yourself before even saying hallo. He was ushering me through and talking about a glass of wine so I didn't bother. I suppose, with a daughter like Tinsel there were other things to worry about than boots on the shagpile.

	A group of a dozen or so middle aged men and women were fussing around Tinsel who was standing unmoving and unmoved in the midst of them all. I knew them all. Not them as individuals of course but their types. Hard working people, one or two teachers probably, maybe a solicitor, a couple of housewives, others who had gone back to work part time now that the children were teenagers. They would live in houses just like this, the solicitor in a detached house in a slightly better road. They would have dinner parties and encourage their reluctant offspring to socialise with each other and very occasionally they would drink too much, realise the utter hopelessness of their lives and sleep with each other's husbands.

	And when their children turned out like me and like Tinsel and like Jamie and like Sean, they would genuinely try to understand. They would tolerate the hair dye and the piercings and the awful houses, they would try not to worry when the phone didn't ring as often as it should, they would try not to worry when it did ring, usually in the middle of the night. They would suffer the swearing, the obnoxious dismissal of all that their hard work had achieved; the comfortable houses, the food on the table, the help with the homework. They would tolerate being called crypto-fascists and bourgeois hypocrites and stooges of **The System**, they would gamely try to enter conversations about vivisection and pacifism and then retreat bravely when contemptuously shouted down by a fourteen year old who knew better. I knew these people, they were Sean's parents and Jamie's parents and Cali's parents and they were my parents. They did their best and when it was all thrown back in their faces, they put the kettle on and waited for better days.

      Tinsel's mother was clearly overwhelmed that Tinsel had come. A small woman with neatly cut blond streaked hair and sensible shoes, she was nearly in tears as she tentatively hugged her daughter. I realised what everyone else there had no doubt realised years ago, that these two nice respectable middle class parents were absolutely terrified of their daughter. Terrified of what she might do, of what she might say, of who she might bring home, of how they might inadvertently upset her. They were terrified of her but also terrified for her. For the DIY wiring that might kill her as she switched on the light, for the smackhead junkie boyfriend who might share his needles, for the long walk home up the dark lane, for the protest marches, the police cells and the criminal record. This mother hugged her daughter as if she were china, hardly daring to touch and yet you could see in her eyes that if she'd been allowed, she would have squeezed so tight and never let go.

Pleasantries were exchanged. I was introduced to a whole set of people I would never meet again and yet who were painfully pleased to see that Tinsel hadn't brought Frankenstein's Monster. When asked what I did, I knew I had it in the bag.

A PhD student?! This was manna from heaven, there were smiles all round. This was a world they knew about, this was a world they had all desperately hoped Tinsel might fly away to one day.

'She lives in my dealer's squat.' Tinsel was helping herself to sandwiches. No one else had started the food yet and wild horses couldn't have made me break such a middle class diktat but Tinsel didn't care. The atmosphere, so briefly joyful, deflated once more.

'Oh. Oh I see.' Tinsel's mother looked at me despairingly, 'Is it nice dear?'

I gave a plucky little smile. 'It's not bad. We have electricity and water, that's more than millions in the Third World.'

They liked this, they really liked this. Not only was I a university student with hopefully a future, I also had a heart. They too cared about the starving of the Third World and had the Oxfam standing orders to prove it. I felt I had to allay their fears a little more.

'Claire only deals in…'

'She gets me my heroin.' Tinsel dropped an egg sandwich on the floor where a yappy little Scottie came racing to snap it up. There was an excruciating silence, painful and long. Tinsel wasn't on heroin, her arms were too white and smooth and beautiful. And Claire certainly didn't deal it so I knew Tinsel was lying. But her parents didn't and stood ashen, engulfed by private misery made worse by the poignant witness of their friends.

'Well. Anyway, enough of all this chit chat,' Tinsel's father retreated into the only escape he knew, meaningless noise disguised as words. The little crowd leapt in to help him out and all began talking at once; the weather, the football, the next general election, anything but the imminently early death of a daughter from heroin.

Ness was being bugged by the little Scottie but like me, knew how to behave. Ness was one of those dream dogs that you could take anywhere; she never jumped up, she never growled, she never dribbled, she never sneaked up onto the table to nick the Christmas turkey. The Scottie was trying to push his runty little nose under her tail but she sat impassive, as dedicated to me as any bearskinned guard outside the Palace.

'Time for presents!' announced the man of the house and there was a flurry of giggles and thanks and oohs and aahs as various china cats and gold clocks and kitchen pinnies were unwrapped. Tinsel's parents had clearly not expected her to bring anything, past disappointments had prepared them better this time. But Tinsel was not to be predicted.

'Mum,' It was a paper bag with string handles and golden embossed sides, a Fortnum and Mason's gift bag. Her mother looked stunned, could hardly bear to reach out and take it lest it disappeared into thin air or bit her. There was an expectant hush, one full of fear that this would prove to be all the more dreadful because of the sweetness of the hoping.

'Teresa...'

'Tinsel.'

'Tinsel darling, thank you! What a lovely bag.' She gingerly reached in and took out a blue jewellery box with silver piping. The atmosphere now was tight, there was not enough oxygen in the tiny B&Q conservatory for all this anticipation. I hoped against hope that Tinsel had not put some hippy peace symbol or feminist fist in the box, but it seemed to me that the woman was so overwhelmed with the box itself that what was in it hardly mattered.

'Oh,' An exhalation like a gentle orgasm. 'Oh, Teresa, it's…it's the most beautiful thing I've ever seen.'

We all crowded round. It was a broach, silver with diamante and in the shape of a dove. Nestling against the blue velvet of the cushion and with the Fortnum and Mason's crest picked out in silver on the inner lid. I didn't personally care much for broaches, they were for old ladies, but Tinsel's mother was almost fainting with relief and delight. Her dad looked over proudly.

'Well done Tinsel, love. I couldn't have chosen better myself. It's the nicest piece of jewellery your mum's ever been given. I'm going to have to buck my ideas up!'

There was a general titter of laughter and comments and requests to see the broach out of its box. The solicitor wandered over towards the sandwiches and I wondered if it was time for me to grab a cake or two. Then Tinsel, having flown up on her fairy wings to such a great height, came crashing back down to destroy them all with her bombshell.

'It took a lot to get that out. It wasn't easy.'

'What do you mean, love?' Her mother was still floating on the clouds of self-delusion but I caught the twinge of pain and panic around her father's eyes to know that he felt the *whoosh* of the bombshell falling. He slowly put his hand on his wife's shoulder, as if to hold her steady.

'It's really hard to nick things from Fortnum's. They have security everywhere. I had to go in three times before I managed it.'

The chatter had stopped. Some were wearing expression of wearied *here we go again.* The solicitor was angry and dropped his sandwich back onto the plate in exasperation but none of them dared to speak. Tinsel's mother raised clear, brave eyes.

'You…*stole* this? But…but what about the box and the bag?'

'I spent ages after closing looking in the bins at the back of the shop. Rich people throw so much stuff away. They really shouldn't be allowed to get away with it.'

'Teresa. That's enough.' Her father was angry now, the need to protect his wife overriding the love for his only child. 'We don't need to hear any more.'

'But it's important to take things from the rich. I took more effort to get that broach than any millionaire simply walking in and writing a cheque. Didn't I?'

This was undeniably true. It was also undeniably not what the birthday party needed to hear right now. Tinsel's mother was close to tears.

'I can't believe…I can't believe that you would steal my birthday present. Anything… anything would have done, darling, flowers picked from my own front garden, that would have been enough.'

'Don't you like the broach?'

'It was the most beautiful, wonderful thing I had ever seen.'

'So why are you crying?'

Her father stepped forward. 'Tinsel, I think you'd better go. I'll make sure the broach gets back to the shop, your mother can't possibly wear it now.'

Tinsel's great big Bambi eyes got wider. 'But that's totally stupid. They won't care, they probably haven't even missed it. Rich shops need to be stolen from, otherwise they forget about the poor, they think the whole world is like them.'

Suddenly, I thought of Marcus and his father's jewellery shops and how he'd attacked the security guard whose inefficiency had allowed a robbery to happen. Did Marcus and his father think of the poor and their desperation every time they were ripped off? No, they thought of their own hard work going into someone else's pockets and for once I felt a little sympathy for the likes of Mr Hartnett and his kind. Tinsel's father was gently ushering her out.

'You'd better go now, before you upset your mum even more. I know you can't help it, Tinsel love, I know it's the drugs that make you do these things to us and I know you love us really but I just….I just can't deal with you today. Here, take this...' He pushed a couple of ten pound notes into her hand. As he opened the front door, he gave me a wan smile of despair and entreaty mixed. But what could I do? Tinsel wasn't even on drugs, that much was clear enough to me and if her parents weren't so desperate to fool themselves that such an external monster could be conveniently blamed, then they would see it too.

We got the bus back northwards to Brixton. Tinsel seemed unaffected or perhaps vaguely cross might have been as far as it went.

'I told you my parents were odd.' She hadn't actually told me any such thing but I muttered something anyway.

'They expect me to ruin things for them so I do. And then they get upset when I give them what they're expecting.'

'You didn't have to give your mum a stolen broach though, that was well out of order, Tinsel. Or you could have at least pretended that you'd saved up and bought it.'

She looked at me perplexed. 'But I did save up and buy it. It cost me nearly two hundred quid.'

'What?'

'You can't steal jewellery from Fortnum and Mason's, even I know that.'

'Right.' And we sat in silence until it was two stops before mine and I couldn't bear it any longer, made an excuse and led Ness off. I never saw Tinsel again or heard anything of her but I do honestly hope she managed to sort herself out. I sometimes wonder if she had a touch of Asperger's or autism; there simply wasn't the awareness of such problems back in the eighties, she would just have been dismissed as weird or on drugs. Yes, I like to think that Tinsel got herself some therapy and worked out how to like people and be liked back. But I think in my heart of hearts that Tinsel simply went on being Tinsel. Horribly honest and yet lying 'til the end of the world with those great Bambi eyes and those gorgeous pouting lips. I won't ever forget her absolute loveliness but then I won't ever forget her mother's face as the little silver broach fell to ashes either.

The sad little afternoon at Tinsel's home stuck in my mind and gave me a mantra to repeat whenever things got tough. *I am not as bad as Tinsel. I am not as bad as Tinsel.* No matter how stroppy or self-righteous or obnoxious I had been towards my parents, I could never ever have done what she did that September afternoon. I annoyed my friends and family, I upset them sometimes through selfishness and immaturity. I was self-obsessed and frequently brash and even more frequently illogical and stupid but I did at least know how to behave when I had to. I knew what it was to be nice. I knew how to smile and say thank you for horrible presents I'd never wear or use or even look at again. I knew how to reassure my friends that they weren't ugly, they weren't boring, that their lives weren't wasted. I knew how to love people and not just with that irrational, all-encompassing love I had felt for Ben but the quiet, trusting, often overlooked love that shows itself in laughter and confidences and hugs. I wasn't always very good at relationships but at least I knew what a relationship was. *I was not as bad as Tinsel.*

Two nights later, Elm Park had a house supper. I can't remember exactly why, it might have been Al or Jamie's birthday, but Jamie cooked (which meant lots of pastry and dhal) and Sean had come over (which meant girly pop on the stereo) and eight of us had all huddled around the tiny kitchen table which usually sat two before someone suggested digging out the old wallpaper table that was dumped in the cellar. So we had ourselves a feast. Even Gavin was there, as far away from me as he could get and clearly warned by someone to be on his best behaviour because he didn't speak. It was a nice evening, an unremarkable meal shared by people who shared a house and who in most cases were friends. If I had known then that this was to be my last meal at Elm Park, then no doubt I would have taken more notice of everything said, everything laughed at, everything promised, everything derided as *bollocks mate! Absolute bollocks, mate!* But I didn't. And so I can only remember bits and pieces.

People were starting to move on.

Jamie had an announcement.

'I'm gonna leave Blyth. I'm finally gonna do it, man, I'm going to set up my own band, my own songs, my own gigs. I'm gonna go for it.'

This was greeted with cheers and congratulations and *'about time too, mate*'s. Cali also had an announcement which she'd already confided in me.

'I'm giving up the diamonds. I'm going back to college and I'm going to be…a lawyer!'

This was treated with much merriment and more congratulations although how many of us there really thought she'd make it is open to question. But what did we know? It's a long hard slog from the depths of hell to the sunlit lands above but if anyone would make it, it would be Cali. Pete then added his two pennies worth.

'I...I, folks, am finally going to give up my job!'

There were groans at this (Pete's income fed most of us on a weekly basis) but Pete shook his mad mop of curls. 'Not just yet, folks, not just yet. But I've come up with an idea. A plan to set up my own business.'

This sounded like one of the Young Enterprise cons but we let him speak, he was so enthusiastic it was hard not to be carried along with it.

'You know those old Haynes car manuals you used to get, with the skeleton of the car on the front?'

The lads seemed to know, I remembered something vaguely familiar from my childhood. Pete got even more excited.

'Well I just *love* those pictures, man! They're so cool! And I was wondering whether anyone owned the copyright to print them on t-shirts.'

This took a bit of digesting.

'Pictures from car manuals? On t-shirts?' We were all slightly perplexed but Pete could enthuse for England.

'Really good quality t-shirts, no crappy fall apart after ten minutes ones. Just think how blokes get about their cars, they love them more than their girlfriends sometimes! They spend all day polishing them, they sit and look at the magazines. I reckon someone with an original Ford Escort or a Landrover or a Beetle would love to have a t-shirt with it on.'

I could just hear Gavin mumbling something rude so I jumped straight into the other side's boat.

'Brilliant idea. **Pete's T-shirts**!'

Pete laughed. 'I'll have to find a better name than that.'

I like to think, all these years later, that it was me who suggested the final name. It may have been, it may well have been. Whatever the truth of it, someone called out in the melée; 'What about CHUNK? CHUNK's a good name for a label.'

Pete considered this, head on one side. 'But what about the band? Wouldn't it be confusing having a band and a t-shirt label with the same name?'

None of us quite had the heart to tell him that his t-shirt label had a damned sight more chance of still being around in two years time than his band but he got the message.

'*You bastards*! Are we really no good then?'

'No,' I said tweeking his cheek, 'it's just that your t-shirts will be even better. And you won't have to put up with that idiot Straight Edge guitarist of yours tripping over his own trainer tongues on stage.'

'To CHUNK!' The toast was raised, the toast was drunk, the tofu flans were demolished, the Big Veg and Baked Potatoes duly annihilated. People were moving on, people were making plans and I felt sad. Sad that my only contribution to the general air of motivation was that at least *I wasn't as bad as Tinsel*. And then the phone rang and it was Sam. And then the phone rang again and it was Marcus.

Marcus had given Sam two hours to gather up all his belongings and move out. No warning, no argument, just go. I met Sam down at the Spud-u-Like down by Brixton Tube and he looked terrible. Over two baked potatoes we sat awkwardly, me listening, he trying to make sense of it.

'He was like a bloody robot, no talking to him, no discussing it. Just 'It hasn't worked out, I don't trust you any more. Pack your stuff up.' I've known that man for fifteen years and I get two hours notice.'

There wasn't really anything I could say.

'You know, I asked him why he couldn't trust me anymore and he said I was a liar. A liar. I couldn't think what the hell he was talking about, the only lie I've ever told him is how I knew you and there was no way he could have found out about that and then I thought…'

He looked at me and I hurriedly shook my head.

'Not me, not a word.'

'I know. But then I thought….when he took you to see the Mishima film, did you pretend you knew it?'

'Nope, I didn't see much point. I told him I'd never heard of the bloke. He didn't seem that bothered.'

Sam took a gulp of coffee which must have hurt as it was almost melting the tawdry little plastic cup it simmered in. 'Well, that's it then. I knew he took you to Mishima for a reason. If you had known me at Bristol, you'd have heard of Yukio Mishima. I told you, I was a pain-in-the-arse bore about him. There is no way you could have met me more than once and not heard of Mishima. Marcus was testing you, testing us.'

This was odd. But the truth of it was that Marcus had been vindicated. We *had* both lied to him, a small lie sure, but still a lie and he'd a right to be pissed off. I said as much.

'And, Sam, it clearly isn't that big a deal because he arranged to see me after that night. We had a Mexican and then he met me at a gig and we went for a walk in Clapham...it's not that big a deal.'

'He's giving up his job too.'

'What?' This was news. Marcus had been very brief on the phone the night before, he certainly had not hinted at anything like this.

'Yup. It's been coming awhile. He's been getting ready for the next move, laying the ground.'

'For what?'

'Politics. Marcus has always wanted to go into politics. But he needs serious money to do it properly. And now I guess he has enough.'

'Wow.' I didn't know whether this was good or bad. All politicians were lying, cheating propagandists for the illusory party machine of course but there was Ken Livingston who was a living god in London and Tony Benn who most of us had a bit of time for. Marcus would need a lot of coming round to in any way resemble Tony Benn but I was up for the challenge.

Sam finished his coffee, steam burning his swollen lips. 'So. I'm staying at a friend's. Marcus has nearly sold the flat anyway. Everything's up in the air. Are you seeing him again?'

'No,' I lied. 'No plans to.'

'Oh. Oh well. I just thought I'd see if you knew what was up with him. He's scaring the shit out of me at the moment but he is my oldest friend...'

'I can't help you, Sam. Sorry.' But I was lying. I knew exactly what was wrong with Marcus, he'd hinted as much on the phone. *Things have come to a bit of a head, haven't they? We really need to sort this out, I need to know about the future. I'm making some big changes in my life. I need to know where you fit in.*

I knew what he was saying. It was time to jettison the old and venture ahead with the new. He was saying good bye to the suits and the cons and the fair weather City friends with their empty promises and empty eyes. It was time to pack in the Barbie doll Sophies and Helenas and Clarissas, it was time to embrace the real world, time to accept the quiet voice which had been saying 'No, I don't actually want to do this shit any more. Stop The City, I want to get off.'

Sam scribbled down a number on a napkin.

'If you do hear from him…I just want to sort things out. For his sake as much as…well, anyway.'

I didn't expect to ever see him again. He was probably a really nice bloke and clearly as unhappy in his world as Marcus but as long as he clung on to us like unwanted baggage we could never be free of the past. He would always been a reminder and we didn't need him, we really didn't need him. I scrunched the serviette up and put it in my purse, never thinking for one moment that I would ever use it.

Chapter 14 – Ness

Meet me tomorrow and we'll sort things out. I've thought things over, the last three weeks or so, and I think we can work this out. If we both compromise a little, we can come to an arrangement that makes us both happy.

Rotherhithe. Rotherhithe at nine. And no hint as to why. The grottiest part of East London, the hardest to get to. I'd only ever bothered using the line because there was a decent venue at New Cross Gate, right at the end. All the way to Whitechapel on the Hammersmith Line, walk miles to the East London Line, past Shadwell where no one lived and no one went, past Wapping where Murdoch's printers had scurried beneath police shields and taunts of *scab!*, no such thing as Canada Docks or Surrey Quays in 1989, the next stop was the fleapit of the world that was Rotherhithe.

Lock-ups, abandoned buildings, crumbling empires of another age. Rotherhithe was only good for two things; one, there was a decent recording studio called Elephant and two, there was a decent pub called the Prospect of Whitby with beams and wooden floors and a terrace overlooking the Thames. Snuff had recorded their first single at Elephant back in the spring and that was the last time I'd ventured into this part of town. People spoke a lot about its regeneration, about extending the Jubilee Line but no one could actually imagine it happening.

Marcus was already at the entrance when Ness and I arrived, a little late and out of breath. I hadn't seen him since Clapham Common and he didn't look too well; thinner maybe, certainly less composed, less full of himself. He was wearing tracksuit bottoms and a sweatshirt. I hadn't realised before what a ….*structured* body he had. Everything ordered into proportion, muscles pushed just to the right shape and texture, chest and shoulders broad but not foolishly so. He was like an animal in a land with not quite enough food; lean and on his toes.

He seemed pleased enough to see me, a rueful *Well, here we are again* kind of smile. We didn't turn right down the grey filthy street that led to the Prospect but ahead down an alleyway and then along a disused path between old Victorian factories long earmarked for demolition. We made small talk or at least we tried. It was as if we had, between us, sown so many mines in the No Man's Land that kept us apart that sometimes silence was the only way not to detonate a social disaster.

'Been out jogging? You look fit.' Those were the days when you could actually say fit and mean well-exercised and not mean **Bloody Hell**, *I fancy you!* He shrugged.

'I might go later. I'll see.'

'Right.'

We turned down another narrow road, this one full of vans and the detritus of building projects gone awry. Ness didn't like it here, she was the sort of dog who liked grass beneath her pads. Here, she was having to dodge the broken Coke bottles, the sodden newspapers turned yellow and green. I was never much good at silences.

'Marcus. I really am sorry about the weekend away. It wasn't my fault. Family shit.'

'That's alright. Whatever might have happened there, we can still sort out tonight anyway.'

This seemed unlikely. Unless there was a five star hotel nestling somewhere hidden and completely unknown in the neglect of the East London docklands, I couldn't quite see us resurrecting a romantic weekend in the New Forest. This narrow road appeared to be a dead end. Ahead was one of those seven or eight storey Victorian factory buildings in dull redbrick, with rows and rows of narrow windows, all smashed in. Every wall was covered in graffiti and there was litter everywhere. To our right was a building site, a massive expanse of steel pillars pointing up from half finished concrete floors. It was getting dark, so dark I couldn't see how far away the space stretched.

'Where the hell are we?'

'This way,' Marcus took my hand and led me over a barrier of wooden beams piled up as a makeshift gate. Clearly there was nothing here worth nicking because security precautions were minimal. The steel pillars rose up about twenty feet above our heads towards the evening sky, the air was still filled with dust from the day's work.

'What is this place?'

Marcus looked around as if to get his bearings and then stopped. He had dropped my hand which felt clammy from his. 'It's a new development. A Japanese client of mine has bought the whole area up and he's turning the old factories into luxury apartments.'

Suddenly I knew why we were here. This desolate piece of land, this chaos of cement mix and square shaped holes, the fingers of a great monolithic construction surrounding me like the stones of 'Henge…. Luxury apartments. Spacious and full of light, set apart from the rest of London over to the west, an island of privilege upon the eastern river where the elite could come and relax. I realised then that Marcus was going to ask me to share his life, share his life in some way at least. If he was going to reinvent himself as a London MP, he needed to know the grievances, the problems, the lives of the underprivileged and dispossessed. He needed me. He actually needed me. And perhaps some day soon, we might even be able to live like a couple, a couple who went off to work in the morning and kissed each other goodbye and then came home to collapse on the sofa and share the complaints about the day. Normal. One day soon he would give me Normal.

My head felt a little dizzy, a little full. We were standing in what would be a massive room. It had newly breeze-blocked walls and a concrete floor still covered with spilt mix and powder. A huge square hole in the wall to my right would one day be a window looking out over….I walked across, Ness at my heels. Probably a courtyard. There was an excavated pit in the middle, square sides dark and deep. The surrounding area was a mess of mixers and blocks and girders but if you had a little imagination (and I had a lot more than a little imagination) you could just see the palm trees and the Moroccan tiles and even hear the gentle fall of water from some Moorish fountain.

Marcus hadn't joined me and was fiddling with the drawstring of his tracksuit top, the other hand in a tracksuit pocket. I noticed then a label half sticking out at the back of the neck, the silly idiot had forgotten to cut it off, the tracksuit must be brand new. It seemed to me that he was becoming a little more human every time we met. There was cement dust in his hair and a smudge on his chin. I realised how easy it was going to be to fall in love with him.

'So?' I said brightly, turning away from the window. 'These are going to be pretty impressive. Shame about the Tube line.'

It had only been meant as a throwaway but the recent improvements to his personality and appearance had not included a better sense of humour.

'What's the matter with the bloody Tube line? Who wants to catch the Tube anyway? And once they build the Jubilee Line extension, this flat's going to be worth a fortune.'

I didn't want to hear any more about the Jubilee Line extension. 'I know, I was joking. They're great.' I paused, called up the heavens for guidance and then thought *Sod it!* and jumped straight it. 'So is one of these yours then? Have you bought one?'

He looked slightly caught out and I felt like kissing him again, just as I had at the Greyhound that night. The memory of what had happened just moments after that kiss stirred but I forced it back down again. That was gone, that was past, this was the future we were skirting around now.

Marcus loosened his sweatshirt neck. 'I'm thinking about it. The Jap developer will give me a good deal. They won't be ready for at least six months but...'

'It's good to be prepared. To have everything in place. To know where you are and where you're going.'

'Yes. That's exactly what I need to know. Where I stand. We've been dodging around this for weeks now…but it's time to sort it out. '

I swallowed. This was it then. And if I could avoid making a mess of just one thing in my whole sorry life, then please God let it be the next five minutes.

'I agree, Marcus. We need to be straight with each other. About what we want from the future. I know you've left your job, I know you're making some big changes to your life. And I just want you to know that I'm going to be there, every step of the way.'

This was supposed to sound reassuringly positive but came out a little harsh. Marcus was very pale.

'How did you know about my job? You've been talking to Sam?'

'Yes, last night. He said you wanted to go into politics. I think it's a brilliant idea. We can get so much done together.'

'So it's not just about money then?'

'Money? No, of course not. How could you think that?' But I suppose he'd had a great many gold diggers over the years, a great many pretty women talking sweet talk but with their eyes on his wallet. He should have realised by now that I wasn't like them.

'So. You want more than money from me?'

'Of course!' I walked a little closer so that we were just an arm's length apart. Ness was at my heels on her lead but I was hardly aware of her, she was so still. Marcus looked all over the place, as if I had rugby tackled him from behind. Perhaps I had been too quick to offer such commitment, we hardly knew each other after all. Perhaps, he was wary of any kind of relationship with anyone, perhaps he had been hurt as I had been. We would have to take this very carefully. Suddenly it dawned on me how much my life was going to change and for a brief moment reality bit down hard.

*Jamie and Sean would **never** visit me here.*

Cal would come, she was at home anywhere, but Jamie would bring mud in on his boots and then sit right on the edge of the sofa with his arms crossed over his chest which was always a surefire sign that he was uncomfortable and wanted to leave. Sean wouldn't even come. He'd only seen Marcus for a moment outside the Greyhound but he'd known in that instant that the ocean between them could never be crossed. And what about going to gigs? Marcus wouldn't want to stand around watching bands every night, Marcus would want to go to see Sade and Heaven 17…but what was so great about the bands I went to see anyway? With Marcus, I could actually go to the theatre and the cinema and out for meals, for weekends away. We could drive to secluded hotels and swim at midnight and have croissants in bed. This hotel would allow dogs of course….

All this had taken two seconds and then I was brought back to the present.

'Do these flats allow dogs?' I wasn't thinking straight. We'd been talking about money, me reassuring him that I didn't care about any of it but Ness was more important. Marcus was getting irritated.

'What?'

'Do they allow dogs? Your flat doesn't, does it?'

'What the fuck has that got to do with anything?'

I wasn't sure how to respond to that. I could hardly tell him I'd guessed we were going to live here together, here in this wonderful flat, not before he'd actually asked me. But surely Ness being here was part of the deal, surely she had everything to do with anything? Then I finally grew up and accepted the truth. *He didn't want her*. He hadn't even considered her. Just as he hadn't bothered to find a hotel which allowed dogs, so he was going to buy a flat with a no pets policy and expect me to just accept it. I was going to lose Sean and Jamie and Pete and gigs and now I was going to lose Ness too….

For a moment I wavered. For one horrible moment I actually considered sending her home to Surrey to live with my mum (who did after all adore her). I actually considered visiting her at weekends (or more often if I wasn't working), becoming a part time owner, some distant figure to the most precious thing in my world….

No. No, I would **not** abandon her. Flat or no flat we would work it out, she was my baby and Marcus would just have to come round. And when I look back at that dreadful evening my one crumb of comfort is that I didn't abandon her in my head, I didn't.

'I've had enough of this.' Marcus's voice sounded high, unnatural, as though it was being stretched. 'Why the hell are we talking about your dog? Why don't we talk about what really matters? Why don't you just come clean and tell me what you want.'

'What's the matter?' I moved even closer but he held his hand to his head as if warding off a blow. Then he pointed a shaking forefinger at me as if lecturing a naughty child. Ness stirred unhappily against my legs.

'I...just....I just want to know what you're going to do....I need to know if you're going to tell anyone about this.'

Even someone as blinkered and self-centred as me could have sensed that the conversation was not now about us living together and changing the world. Neither, I dimly began to realise, had it ever been.

'Tell anyone about what?'

His face flushed, red over the pale. His finger was still outstretched and pointing. Ness made a low noise in the back of her throat. I hadn't heard her do that in years.

'You know damned well what! There you go again, playing your stupid games with me. I'm sick and tired of you playing your damned stupid games with me.'

'I... really don't know...Marcus?' I was out of my depth, suddenly a stranger in a strange place. 'Marcus, calm down and tell me exactly what's....'

'Are you going to the police?'

'What?'

'Are you going to tell the police what you saw?'

It made sense at last, relief washed over me, cold and fresh, I actually laughed out loud.

'*The police*? Marcus, what you did that night was really out of order but...you wouldn't do that normally, would you? That wasn't the real you, you wouldn't be so worried about it now if you were really a violent sort of person.'

But even as I spoke, I remembered his expression in the streetlight as he laid into Napoleon. The second kick from anger, the third and fourth from pleasure, the fifth from something cold and calculating buried not so very deep within. I tried to remember something Sam had said about Marcus and his temper, Marcus and animals…

He had calmed down a little, the finger was no longer pointing at me but fiddling with the drawstring again.

'No. You're right. I wouldn't do that sort of shit again, that was a one-off. It was pretty stupid but I was desperate.'

'Desperate?' A half-crazed Hackney crusty scratches his Porsche and he feels desperate?

Marcus went on. 'My father had never cut off my allowance before. I had nothing. I needed money to set myself up. The tight bastard had it coming to him.'

I felt as though a significant piece of the conversation had been deleted from my version of it.

'Your father cut off your allowance? But you have loads of money. And why should you take that out on Napoleon anyway? It wasn't his fault.'

Marcus looked at me as though I were either insane or deliberately trying to wind him up and he couldn't decide which.

'What the *bloody hell* are you talking about? Who the fuck is Napoleon? What the fuck has this got to do with Hartnett's?'

'Hartnett's?' The name rang some distant bell, of course it was Marcus's surname, but there were so many competing clouds swirling around in my head….It began to dawn on me that we were talking at cross purposes and then the grim realisation hit me like a brick that we had been talking at cross purposes all the time. From the very first moment we met.

'Marcus, can we go to the Prospect and have a drink? Sort it out over a pint? Ness is really bored here. The Prospect lets dogs in, they've got a nice terrace...'

'Sod Ness. If you hadn't seen that bloody photograph we wouldn't be in this mess now. And yes, Sam finally came clean about you snooping around my flat, just before I threw him out.'

'I wasn't doing any harm, I was just…'

'I don't care. Now, who the fuck is Napoleon? What does he know about the job at Harnett's?'

Marcus was actually sweating. I realised then that I had never really seen him anything but composed, not even when laying in to Napoleon, with each blow he'd been measured and deliberate. Now though, now he had ugly patches under his arms.

I tried to send waves of calm across the space between us. Perhaps if I spoke slowly…

'Napoleon is the bloke you kicked outside the Fulham Greyhound.'

He still didn't remember. It was so unimportant to him, even as Napoleon was rolling up like an animal in the mud of the gutter, Marcus had been moving on and forgetting him.

'What the hell has that freak got to do with all this?'
'With all what?'
'With you seeing me in the security van that morning?'

I was scared now. Not of him exactly, no, but I was scared that we were losing touch of each other in some crazy misunderstanding, that if we didn't reach out and touch some common ground soon, we would never be able to move back in.

'Marcus, let's go somewhere else and…'

'You. Sit *down*!' And he shoved me in the chest so hard I flew backwards and landed *crack!* on my backside. My back screamed with old wounds waking up as Ness jumped up, growling at him and then turned back to me whimpering.

Pain. The muscles so newly repaired threatened to go into spasm, I could feel the cracks rippling up and down. It was going to go, it was going to go into spasm again. *Hold! Hold!* With every ounce of mental energy I willed my back not to collapse. He had hit me. Marcus had hit me.

I had slapped Ben once. After I found out about him and Emma I had walked three miles to his house at five o'clock in the morning, got him out of bed and slapped him. There were still people in London who wouldn't even look at me because of my unspeakable, inexcusable, my *unconscionable* display of violence which had so shamed us all. But no one had ever hit me. No one had ever laid a finger on me.

Marcus and I had crossed some kind of Rubicon that night and I couldn't see, as I sat in shock, how we could ever really cross back over again.

He towered over me.

'Stop playing your games. Stop playing your fucking games. Pretending you're as thick as shit, then letting me know you know everything and you're just stringing me along ready to dump me in it.'

'I wasn't stringing you along. I would never dump you...'

'Then what? Why pretend you didn't recognise me? Why pretend? What do you really want? I thought I could handle paying you off with cash but if you think you can follow me round blackmailing me... Why do you keep talking about coming to arrangements and then never telling me what you want? You don't live in Clapham, you never met Sam at Bristol. You didn't even know him before you poked your way into my flat. You're a bloody liar, you both are.'

I tried to sit up but I was shaking too much to risk putting any weight on my arms.

'Marcus, it was all so stupid. We didn't want you to think you were being manipulated, that's all. I didn't want you to know I'd been in your flat and seen the photo. What on earth would I want to blackmail you about?'

There was a silence. I could see him mentally trying to weigh me up. Was I still playing some game or had he got it all wrong? Was I double bluffing? Triple bluffing? For one awful moment, I didn't know myself. Somewhere in the back of my mind, it slowly dawned on me that Marcus had some nasty little secret he thought I'd uncovered and I could actually be in some trouble here. Instinctively I reached out for Ness's collar. Marcus swallowed, looking even paler.

'You don't remember the security van at East Ham three years ago? Me getting into it?'

'No.'

Silence. But he was too loaded up to believe.

'Bullshit! You smiled and said hallo! You bloody recognised me from UCL, you knew who I was, I spoke to you at Sebastian's party. That morning in East Ham, you saw me. You said hallo as you passed.'

'I say hallo to lots of people. I don't remember ever meeting you before Harvey's in July. I don't remember any security van and I don't have a clue what you're talking about. Can I go now?'

With a start, I realised that I should not have said that, not 'Can I go now?'. Suddenly, things had changed, suddenly I had acknowledged and perhaps made real some prisoner / captor situation. I had asked him if I could go and had in doing so, affirmed his power to say no.

He knew it too. And I knew then, like a cold river of water running down my back that he hadn't brought me here to talk about sharing a flat or planning election campaigns together. He had brought me here to do a deal and if not, to get rid of me.

'Marcus. I won't say anything to anyone. I don't remember ever meeting you before this summer. I hated being a student, I was scared to death of the lot of you and I don't remember anyone from UCL at all. You know I won't say anything, there's no one to tell.'

'Sam. You and Sam talk.' His thoughts played themselves out. 'He knows. He's always known it was me. He has a funny look on his face every time my old man mentions the fuck up at the Holborn store. Bloody sod. They were insured up to the hilt, they made a packet when we emptied the place. Half of the bloody rocks still dripping off my grandmother's neck were on that insurance claim.'

'You robbed your father's shop? The jewellers?'

'He cut off my bloody allowance, I told you.' He looked at me and finally understood.

'You really didn't know?'

'No. I really didn't know.'

'Oh. Oh. So why do you think I had a bloody photograph of your rancid mutt on my mirror? I went back to East Ham the next day, I was going to run you over with my car or something stupid but I lost my nerve. So I tried to photograph you so I'd know you for another time but my hands were shaking so much I only got your stupid, stupid dog. Why are you laughing, you stupid bitch?'

'I thought what you said at Harvey's was true, that you…you had a thing about me. That you wanted to see me again. I thought I meant something to you…'

The words echoed around the half-built room sounding more and more ridiculous as they circled.

'You stupid bitch. You stupid, stupid bitch.'

There was a new tone in his voice then, something I couldn't identify but I suddenly remembered Sam telling me about a young Marcus pulling the legs off spiders and then I remembered an article I'd read about serial killers always starting off when they were children by hurting animals....I knew then for sure that we wouldn't get out of this.

For the second time in four weeks I felt one of Plato's Absolutes, the Absolute Form of Fear. Not being frightened, not being scared. Fear. A cold wash of *something* from outside of myself, something invading my sense of being, racing through my veins like an Arctic express and freezing me over.

'How could I ever fancy *you*?' This was clearly more incredulous to Marcus than bringing me to a desolate building site to...to what? I knew then that I was destined for one of the great black holes which littered the place, holes soon to be filled in with crusher and concrete mix. Perhaps the very one I'd looked at and thought of Moorish fountains. He came a little closer, hand in pocket.

'I was going to pay you off. I was going to be reasonable. But oh no, do you really think that I'm having you hanging on to my fucking ankles as I rise up the greasy pole? I'm going all the way, you stupid cow, me and people like me are going to run this frigging country someday, run it. Thatcher's got a year or two left and then they'll fall apart, the whole damned party, leaving it wide open for young blood like me. Me. Do you honestly think that I'm going to put up with a hippy freak blackmailer telling me what to do, breathing down my neck?'

'But I wasn't trying to...'

'But you could now. Couldn't you? It would be all too easy now, wouldn't it, bitch?'

There was no denying this, even if I'd had breath to try. And as I fought tears and panic, he got out the shiny red penknife from his tracksuit bottoms.

'I should have got rid of you at Brockenhurst three weeks ago, nice rainfilled quarry a hundred feet deep. But they won't ever find you here either. Not for two hundred years.'

'I told Sam I was meeting you here.'

'Liar. I spoke to him this morning.'

'I told my friends at Brixton.'

'Liar. And who'd bother looking for a homeless little tramp anyway? A hundred girls like you go missing every week. Who cares? Who goes looking for them? No one. Who'd go looking for you? No one.'

I knew then that he was wrong. That a dozen people would never stop looking for me, that I had real family and real friends and if I didn't do something in the next five seconds I would never see them again and they would never know why. They would never know what had happened. And suddenly I thought of poor Diana Lamplugh. And then I thought of my mother and the two became one. And so I screamed. I opened my mouth, I took the deepest breath I had ever found and I screamed and screamed and screamed.

Things happened.

Marcus cursed and stumbled forward, his knife blade coming down towards my throat. Ness jumped up, I felt the pull of her body on the lead, I felt the thud as she reared up and into him, the deep warning barks turning to…something else, something I didn't want to hear but which wouldn't stop.

We were on the filthy floor, half entwined, her hot, furry body heavy against mine. My only sense functioning was hearing. I could hear her whining quiet and forlorn, her breathing deeper like a pant and then more shallow, footsteps running away into silence, a man sobbing in shock and then nothing. And then came the warm wetness upon my fingers, my hands, my arms. I let her cover me in her warmth, I held on tight so that she would know she was not alone. And I promised her that I would not let her go.

Epilogue

It's beautiful here.

When we first came, I used to test all my senses one by one as if I needed their assurance that it was real. Sometimes the first thing I hear when waking up is the birds in the garden. We have so many and I'm still too ignorant to name any but the most commonplace but I know we have jays and blue tits and three wood pigeons that the children think are doves and have named Lily, James and Harry. Sometimes I can't hear anything at all, not even the traffic from the main road a mile away, sometimes I can hear sheep and lambs from the field next to the house, sometimes I hear dogs barking and always seagulls, always we can hear the demanding call of the gulls.

The smells are all pervasive too. It's not roses and honeysuckle as the novelists would have you believe although I did smell real honeysuckle for the first time ever, growing up the wall of a farm a few roads away and it really did smell like honeysuckle which seems a strange thing to be surprised at, I know. Mostly of course, we smell manure from the fields or molasses from the Glaxo factory a mile or so towards the coast but even these I do not find offensive or invasive. These people were here before we were and I am only grateful that they have welcomed us in. Most of all, I smell sheer freshness which is hard to describe and equally as hard to forget. It is a wave of air coming down from the mountains and in from the coast and it seems to race with a *whoosh* in through our bedroom window on the first day of every spring.

We feel the wind upon our skin here all the time, even in summer. It is colder than we are both used to but we don't mind. Sam says it keeps us alive, keeps us alert and ready, I don't ask him what for. Autumn winds come racing across the field to batter our little cottage and we huddle in front of the fire and imagine we are Cathy and Heathcliff. Our eldest tells us ghost stories which frighten her so much that she has to have the light on all night. There is a calm spot here though, right at the bottom of the garden beneath the mound of the railway embankment with the shed on one side and the damson trees on the other. It is always quiet here – the trains are only one an hour – and rather overgrown but I know she wouldn't mind because the wild perennials have massive yellow flowers and seem to me to be a celebration of something. She lies here now, in the calm and the riot of yellow and something in me knows she's at peace.

Everything here is easy on the eye. The houses have flowers in tubs and Virginia Creeper climbing up cracked and peeling walls. There is green everywhere and the far off purple and grey of shadowed mountains. The dogs do not need leads, they race around barking along the little lanes and if the occasional car does come, it is always the car that slows down and then the drivers smile indulgently at the big dripping tongues and dumb amber eyes that leap up to greet them as they pass carefully by. They are golden dogs, not soft black and brindle, and their ears fall uselessly down, they do not prick up at the hint of trouble. They are good dogs, they are fun and sweet but they are not clever, they do not know my moods, they cannot judge how I am and what I need. They lollop around with bendy backs and untamed tails, they dribble uncontrollably at food and they playfight all over our herbaceous borders, breaking seedlings and pots alike. They are good dogs but they do not ever sit calm and patient, waiting, just waiting as she did. They are happy and full of health and energy but they are stupid where she was sharp and clumsy where she was sublime. They are good dogs but they are not her.

 It is beautiful here.
 We both work hard and sleep exhausted with the baby in between. Sam comes home with dirt beneath his fingernails and bits of tree bark in his hair and he is happy. Occasionally I see him tense and the lines of London appear again on his face but we quickly search for the remote control and the treacherous black box in the corner flickers and dies and he is gone until the next time. It happens less often now because we have chosen not to hear. We do not watch the news, we have sacrificed the radio, we check carefully which programmes to select and we rarely buy a newspaper. I do not think about Marcus now. Sometimes I feel a shiver up my spine, sometimes when walking the dogs alone along the deserted lanes I feel an impulse to quicken my steps and hurry home but that is all. That is all I will allow him.

It wasn't always so easy.

In the hour or so we lay on the filth and dust of the concrete floor, the sky darkened until it was almost pitch. The warm wetness became something cold and sticky, she became heavy against my chest, I grew tired of waiting for the sign to follow her on. The smells and the indignity that come with death held no horrors for me as I rubbed her ears, her head, her back to keep her warm, to keep her with me. She needed to be home, she needed to be in bed. If I could get her home to Sean, to Jamie, to Pete, to Cal – they loved my Ness and she loved them.

I had lifted her up so many times before, she was always so patient, so careless of my clumsiness and rough hands. One more time I asked her for her patience. Once to my knees, once again to my chest, she seemed heavier now than she had ever done but she was as good and as still as she had ever been.

I don't remember walking with her, I don't remember how I imagined I would get her home to the people who loved her. At the end of a road there was a phone box. A phonebox glowing silver and glass in the amber streetlight so I rang the only person I could, the only person who would be able to help, the only person who needed warning that he too was in deep trouble, very deep trouble.

We made a mess of the taxi he came in but he shoved enough money into the driver's hands to shut him up. I don't know where we went, some cheap hotel where they don't ask questions and don't expect you to tell them your name.

And I lay with her on the grubby little bed for a long, long time.

I wouldn't have given her up but he was insistent and I could sense Fear hovering over him. I allowed him to make the arrangements and so she was gone. A dull copper urn in her place. And then we left too.

For a long while we dared not look ahead. A series of bedsits and cheap motels and family spare rooms saw us looking over our shoulders and jumping at every sound. Our families thought us strange and in love, so close would we sit, so nervous would we wait whilst the other was out shopping or doing some such simple thing. It wasn't love then, it was an understanding that no one else could pretend to feel what we did, that there was a shadow haunting us and pushing us ever on. I thought I saw him once, in a car in Wallington whilst we were staying with my mother. I ran home, not afraid for Sam, not afraid for myself but convinced in my madness that he had come for her, that he would slowly take away the things that I loved and leave me with nothing. I did not love Sam back then but it grew from the bonds we wrapped around ourselves, from the ties of survival, from the desperate need not to be quite wholly alone.

One day he said to me that it could not go on. That we couldn't live our lives moving on but never looking ahead at where we were moving to, that we needed a goal or we were no better than animals escaping the hunt. We needed to know where we were running to and we needed to want to run there.

That night we got out a map of Britain and a big marker pen.

I want the sea, he had said, *I want to hear seagulls and taste salt on the wind.*

I want mountains, I had said, *I want forests and rivers and winding roads filled with border collies.*

We took the pen and crossed off south of the Midlands, the entire south-east. With one black line we cut ourselves off from our families and all our friends but a year of running had done that anyway. We were truly alone. House prices moved our fingers north, then west and north again. There. There were mountains and lakes, there to the south and east was the salty bay spreading out towards the sea. It felt right. We looked down upon the map and tried to visualise the colours and smells, tried to make it come to life.

The next day we bought a local map, an Ordnance Survey. Right amongst the mountains was too far from the sea but there, further south, was a town, a little market town just a mile from the bay and surrounded by countryside. I poured over this map, feeling a great wave of *rightness* flood me. Then I saw it.

'My God, Sam, look.'

He followed my finger and gave a quiet laugh. 'How odd. Let me see closer. Yes, it is, you're right. Can't be more than a hamlet, ten houses or so.'

'That's it. That's where I want us to go.'

'Sure? It won't be this year, we have to sort out money and jobs and a house won't just suddenly appear on the market exactly where you want it to be…'

'Yes it will. I know it will. Look at it!'

We both looked down again.

Next Ness. A tiny hamlet, just half a mile from the bay, a something and nothing place, somewhere you couldn't find on the map if you searched with a magnifying glass.

'That's where we're going,' I said again, feeling hope for the first time since she'd died. 'And can we take her with us?'

He hugged me like a brother at Christmas. 'We can take her. You can lay her down at last.'

And so I brought her home. I brought her to a place she'd have loved and I laid her down and finally, finally I let her go.

ISBN 1412026814

Printed in Great Britain
by Amazon